Clean Money

Clean Money

PICKING WINNERS IN THE GREEN-TECH BOOM

John Rubino

WILEY

John Wiley & Sons, Inc.

Published by John Wiley & Sons, Inc., Hoboken, New Jersey.
Published simultaneously in Canada.

For general information on our other products and services or for technical support, please contact our Customer Care Department within the United States at (800) 762-2974, outside the United States at (317) 572-3993 or fax (317) 572-4002.

Wiley also publishes its books in a variety of electronic formats. Some content that appears in print may not be available in electronic books. For more information about Wiley products, visit our web site at www.wiley.com.

Library of Congress Cataloging-in-Publication Data:

Rubino, John A.
    Clean money : picking winners in the green tech boom / John Rubino.
        p.   cm.
    Includes index.
    ISBN 978-0-470-28356-1 (cloth)
        1. Clean energy industries—Economic aspects.   2. Green technology—Economic aspects.   3. Investments—Environmental aspects.   I. Title.
    HD9502.5.C542R83   2009
    332.6—dc22
                                                        2008022837

Printed in the United States of America
10 9 8 7 6 5 4 3 2 1

*For Jamie and Alex, whose kids will grow up
in a rich, clean world.*

If the second half of the last century was about the world rewiring its nervous system, the first half of this century is going to be about the world reworking its musculature, how it makes things, moves things around. The paradox is that all of our energy systems were designed with the assumption of cheap and endless energy. So now all those systems have to be redesigned with the reality of expensive and limited energy. We see this tsunami of innovation that's gonna change it all.

—Michael Potts, CEO, Rocky Mountain Institute

Contents

Acknowledgments

This book has benefited from the insights of many clean-tech insiders. Especially knowledgeable and/or patient were Robert Bogden, Clark Wieman, Travis Bradford, Peter Schiff, Michael Potts, Jan van Dokkum, David Shoenwald, Oliver Peoples, Andrew Ertel, Reinhard Seiser, Chris Manning, and Andrew Wilkinson. Thanks also to my development editor, Kelly O'Connor, for bringing order to a chaotic first draft. And as always, thanks to my agent, Faith Hamlin, for her understanding of the marketplace and ability to open doors.

Introduction

Welcome to the next great bull market. It might take a while to really get going, for reasons this book will explain, but eventually it's going to be bigger and longer-lived than the tech-stock and housing booms combined. I'm referring, of course, to "clean tech" (also known as green tech and envirotech), a broad range of technologies and business practices designed to fix many of the things humanity has broken. Various clean technologies aim to eliminate pollution, replace fossil fuels, slow down and eventually stop global warming, and keep the food and water flowing. Most will fail to live up to their now soaring hype, but some will succeed beyond even their current fans' wildest dreams.

As this realization begins to dawn, everyone wants a piece of the action: Companies are going green, both for public relations and business reasons. Governments are passing environmental mandates and tax breaks as fast as legislators can dream them up. And the financial world is pouring capital into all manner of green projects and start-up companies.

Clean Money will explain:

- Why clean tech will be the investment opportunity of our lifetimes
- Why the hottest green sectors are also the most complex and risky
- How to approach this market wisely by identifying both investment opportunities and risks
- How to build a clean-tech portfolio that fits your temperament and circumstances.

Clean Money Terms

First, a few notes on the structure and content of this book. Because several concepts and technical terms pop up repeatedly in any discussion of clean tech, it will be helpful to get familiar with them at the outset.

Nanotech

Spend an hour researching solar power or next-generation batteries or pretty much any other clean technology, and you'll find numerous references to nanotechnology. These will mostly be along the lines of "Using a patented nanotech process XYZ Corp has created a [insert green device name here] that is 50 percent more efficient and significantly less expensive than conventional versions . . ." This explains little but sounds quite impressive. You'll also see lots of words with "nano" prefixes, as in "nanoparticles" and "nanofabrication." Here's what they're referring to.

Nanotech is the manipulation of particles, fibers, films, and coatings (along with less easily categorized things like buckyballs, carbon nanotubes, and "amorphous diamond nanostructures") that are between 1 and 100 nanometers in size. A nanometer is one-billionth of a meter, so 100 nanometers is smaller than the average bacterium. Being this tiny gives nanomaterials some unique capabilities. They can penetrate where bigger particles can't or combine into structures that have greater strength or conductivity or less weight. Substances made from them can be woven into fabrics or painted onto surfaces. Once you start working with that kind of flexibility, the possibilities become endless.

Right now, nanofabrication (i.e., making nanomaterials and turning them into useful products) is expensive and hard to scale up commercially. But it's getting easier and more powerful at an accelerating rate as new tools and processes are developed. In 2007, researchers announced some dramatic results that are both interesting in and of themselves and important as signs of things to come. For example, recently developed nanotech materials and processes appear to increase the speed at which batteries can be charged, while other nanoparticles capture more of the light spectrum, increasing solar cell efficiency and making cells lighter, more flexible, and cheaper. And far more radical departures are coming. A nanotech called thermionics appears to convert heat directly into electricity; silicon nanowires (which are, as the name implies, really thin silicon wires) reportedly produce a tenfold improvement in energy storage capacity over today's batteries; and harmless viruses can now be coaxed to fabricate nanomaterials. And that's just 2007. By 2012, we'll be deep in the realm of science fiction.

Energy Terms

Because renewable energy is such a big part of the clean-tech story—and because there are a lot of different energy sources out there—certain terms recur frequently:

- **Watt** is a measure of the strength of an electric current flowing from a power source.
- **Watt hour** is the amount of energy in 1 watt of electricity flowing for an hour.
- **Kilowatt (kW)** is 1,000 watts.
- **Kilowatt-hour (kWh)** is the energy of one kilowatt flowing for an hour. This is the unit by which utilities charge for electricity, analogous to a gallon of gas at the pump. A typical home central air conditioning system, for instance, draws about 3.5 kilowatts, so in an hour it uses 3.5 kWh. A 100-watt lightbulb uses 0.1 kW, so it takes 10 hours to use one kWh. If a utility charges $0.10 per kWh, then it costs a dime to leave the light on for 10 hours. Electricity's price varies widely, from upward of $0.20 per kWh in Japan to $0.05 in some parts of the United States. The factors that determine price include how the power is generated (coal is cheap, solar is expensive, and nuclear in-between), the condition of the grid and the cost of its maintenance, and government tax and rebate policies.
- **Megawatt (MW)** is 1 million watts, or 1,000 kilowatts. Most power plants operate in the megawatt range, as measured by their peak generating capacity. A 50-megawatt plant is capable of delivering that amount of power continuously when running flat out. One megawatt is enough power for 250 to 300 typical American homes (and maybe 500 European homes), so a 50-megawatt plant will power 13,000 or so U.S. homes.
- **Gigawatt (GW)** is a billion watts, or a thousand megawatts, enough to power a quarter-million homes. This is the scale on which the today's largest power plants operate.

- **Cost per watt** is how much a watt of generating capacity costs to build, and it's one of the most common yardsticks for comparing various energy sources. As you'll see in coming chapters, a coal-fired power plant might cost $3 per watt, while solar has fallen from $100 a watt in the 1970s to around $5 per watt today. Some energy sources are also quoted in cost per installed watt, which is the fabrication cost of, say, a solar panel, plus the cost of installation.
- **Load factor (or capacity factor)** is the percentage of time that a power plant is actually producing electricity. The higher the better. A coal plant might have a load factor of 75 percent, meaning that it's up and running that portion of the time and down the rest for maintenance and repairs. A wind turbine, meanwhile—because wind only blows for part of the day—might have a capacity factor of only 30 percent to 40 percent. To arrive at a value for a given power source, analysts look at the cost per watt, the load factor, and the cost of the fuel, among other things.
- **Baseline power** is electricity that comes from a source with a very high load factor which can thus be counted on almost continuously. Plants that use inexpensive fuels like coal and uranium are the main current sources.
- **Peak power** comes from plants that run only at times of high electricity demand, like a hot summer afternoon. Because such plants only run for part of certain days, their capital cost is spread over relatively little production, making this the most expensive kind of electricity.
- A **turbine** is a rotary engine that extracts energy from a flowing gas or liquid. The name comes from turbo, the Latin word for vortex, and the simplest turbines consist of a shaft with blades attached. Moving gas or fluid causes the blades to spin, which imparts energy to an electric motor. Lots of different green energy sources involve fluids or steam-running turbines to generate electricity.

What Is and Is Not Green?

Many technologies are sold as solutions to one environmental problem or another. Not all of them really do what their fans claim, and some do as much harm as good. So for the purposes of this book, "green" tech is defined as those that do far more good than harm. Here are three that don't qualify:

1. **Nuclear.** Nuclear power doesn't produce greenhouse gases, and to the extent that France and Japan have shifted to this power source, the air is a bit cleaner. It's also true that next-generation nuclear plants are far less likely to melt down than their predecessors. But nuclear energy has two downsides. First, it produces radioactive waste that currently can't be eliminated and so must be stored in places that are made radioactive for decades. Second, nuclear power produces materials that can be used to make nuclear weapons and dirty bombs, both of which are capable of rendering Lower Manhattan or central London uninhabitable. It's hard enough to keep track of today's radioactive waste. In a world with hundreds more nuclear plants, it would be impossible to keep it all away from people who would use it to do harm.

2. **Clean Coal.** In theory (but not yet in practice), it's possible to treat coal in ways that make it less polluting—or to capture the pollution at the source, rendering the resulting electricity nonpolluting. And because it's a domestic resource, the money we spend on it stays here rather than flowing to OPEC dictators. Fair enough. But no one is proposing changes in how we *get* coal, which right now involves (1) blowing the tops off of Appalachian mountains, which destroys sometimes unique ecosystems and pollutes everything for miles around, and (2) digging vast underground mines in which miners either spend their lives breathing coal dust or die in cave-ins.

3. **Traditional Hydropower.** The damming of rivers produces some of the world's cleanest, cheapest power. But its future potential is limited because we've already dammed the most suitable rivers. And it carries other costs, including the destruction of fish populations that used to travel from river to sea and the drowning of unique valley ecosystems to make reservoirs.

A Few Other Things

The following might require a bit of explanation:

Chapter 2. I've included a chapter that recounts a few notable ecological disasters of the past. They're small potatoes compared to the havoc that today's global economy is capable of wreaking, but the similarities to much of what's happening today are still eerie. This chapter can be skipped without sacrificing an understanding of the clean-tech investment thesis. But to paraphrase Mark Twain, while history doesn't repeat, it does rhyme, and seeing ecological degradation as a recurring theme will help when the accusations and proposed solutions really start flying.

Object Lessons. There are several general rules that, based on the history of other bull markets and my own sometimes painful experience, clean-tech investors should understand. Since these rules are best illustrated with real-world examples, I've turned them into "object lessons" and placed them in appropriate chapters. Their purpose is to help you avoid the mistakes (of both action and inaction) that often keep investors from fully enjoying bull markets.

Weights and Measures. Because this is the U.S. edition, it presents measurements of distance, weight, and temperature in miles, pounds, and degrees Fahrenheit rather than the globally more common metric system. Foreign-language editions will be rewritten accordingly.

Foreign Stocks. Because clean tech is a global market, some of the leading companies are headquartered in Europe and Asia, and their shares are frequently not listed on U.S. exchanges. The stock lists in this book present these companies with their home exchange ticker symbols. Don't let this throw you—Chapter 22 explains how to buy such stocks at favorable prices both in the United States and abroad.

Time. You'll notice that phrases like "as of early 2008" appear frequently here. That's because things are changing so quickly in clean tech that whatever this book says about specific technologies, companies, or market situations may be out of date by the time you read it. So understand that what you see here is a snapshot taken of a fast-moving game, not an eternal truth. What *is* eternal, or at least long-lived, is the amount of brainpower and energy that will be devoted to cleaning up the world—and to making you a great deal of money, if you play the game well.

Extraordinary Upside Potential

Clean Money is an introduction to the world of clean tech and its investment possibilities, aimed at readers who know their way around the market but may not be clear on how, for instance, solar panels or wind turbines work or how to profit from them. The explanations are in plain English (apologies to the technologists out there for the occasional lack of precision). And the chapters covering individual technologies follow a more or less standard-ized script, explaining how a given technology works, discussing the state of its market and its growth prospects, and listing the main publicly traded companies in each field. The final section of this book presents a series of investment strategies that can serve as guides or templates for building your own portfolio of clean tech stocks while, crucially, avoiding the pitfalls that always accompany markets with extraordinary upside potential.

PART

I

OVERVIEW

CHAPTER 1

Clean Tech

THIS TIME IT'S FOR REAL

It was nice while it lasted. More than nice. The age of cheap energy, free water, and abundant food was the smoothest stretch of highway that humanity has ever traveled. But now that road has developed some very big potholes. Oil, at the time of this writing in mid-2008, is more than $140 a barrel. Fresh water has become scarce or poisonous in many places. Food prices are soaring at double-digit rates. Sea levels are rising while deserts are spreading. Commercial fish stocks are collapsing. International tensions are growing over the remaining cheap oil, and civil wars are being fought over water. And industrial chemicals are saturating our kids' bodies. Whew!

The consequences of the past century's mistakes range from inconvenient to disastrous. But focusing solely on the bad news ignores the other side of the coin: Problems create opportunities, and big, complex problems create vast opportunities. Solving any of the looming environmental crises is worth literally trillions of dollars, so extraordinary amounts of capital are flowing into "clean" technologies, with completely predictable results: New energy sources, benign techniques for managing waste streams, even new ways of fishing and farming are being developed that have the potential to put us on a path to sustainable abundance—or at least to avert disaster. The rise of clean tech is, in other words, an investment theme with long, long legs.

Third Time's the Charm

Readers of a certain age may find this talk of a green boom familiar. That's because we've been here before—twice. The first time was in the late 1970s, when oil shocks and gas lines led Jimmy Carter's administration to boost funding for things like coal gasification and shale oil. But before the private sector had a chance to jump on board, oil prices receded, government funding evaporated, and alternative energy was largely forgotten. The next clean-tech mini-boom came at the tail end of the 1990s tech bubble, when hot money sloshed over into solar and fuel cell stocks, sending some of them through the roof. But that was just the irrational exuberance of the dot.coms rubbing off on other flashy stories. When the bubble burst, clean-tech stocks plunged along with Pets.com and Nortel Networks, and investors left in search of greener pastures (so many clean-tech puns, so little time).

The current revival of interest began a few years ago, as rising oil prices and ominous climate data put energy efficiency back on investors' radar screens. But this time it's for real, for the following reasons:

- **Peak Oil.** The oil shocks of the 1970s were primarily political and structural: Saudi Arabia halted oil exports in response to the Arab-Israeli conflict, and the United States failed to secure adequate new supplies. But there was plenty of cheap oil in the ground, and when the political turmoil subsided, the flow resumed and prices fell. Today, as you'll read in Chapter 3, there is emphatically *not* plenty of cheap crude. The world's great oil fields are in decline, and replacements are scarce. As a result, global oil production has plateaued (hence the proliferation of books with "peak oil" in their titles) while the growing number of cars on Chinese and Indian roads is sending demand inexorably higher. Oil prices, as a result, are likely to rise for years to come.

- **Surging Electricity Demand.** Remember those quaint 1990s predictions that the Internet would cut energy use by letting people telecommute and shop and play without leaving home? As it turned out, this forecast ignored the fact that our new electronic toys are energy hogs. A flat-panel television, for instance, might pull a third of the power that an average home uses at any given time. U.S. electricity demand is now projected to rise by 18 percent in the coming decade.

- **Clean-Tech Progress.** In the 1970s—and even the late 1990s—most clean technologies were nice-sounding pipe dreams, far too expensive and inefficient to compete with cheap, simple incumbents like coal and internal combustion engines. But thanks to steady progress on cost and efficiency, many clean technologies are or will soon be economically viable. So a utility, business, or homeowner can adopt them with the hope of actually saving money.
- **Climate Change Consensus.** The realization that the world is indeed warming, with potentially disastrous consequences, is now driving virtually every major country—including the previously skeptical United States—to pass laws and sign treaties aimed at limiting the damage. The result is a mosaic of subsidies and mandates designed to speed the transition from dirty and unsustainable to clean and renewable.

Capital Loves a Winner

Add it all up—a burning, multifaceted need for clean tech, new technologies that really work, and enthusiastic support from every major government—and you've got the financial world's dream market. According to the National Venture Capital Association, venture capitalists poured $2.6 billion into clean tech in 2007, up about 400 percent from 2005 levels. Silicon Valley legends have shifted seamlessly from info tech to clean tech, with names like Vinod Khosla, Elon Musk, John Doerr, and Paul Allen now cropping up constantly in deal announcements. And companies of all types have discovered that green technologies are both good business and good PR. Google, for example, has promised to pour hundreds of millions of dollars into alternative energy research in an attempt to become a leader in that field, and Wal-Mart is putting solar panels on the roofs of hundreds of supercenters. Meanwhile, virtually every major investment bank and mutual fund is building a presence in clean tech. Goldman Sachs, for instance, has stakes in a wide range of wind and solar power firms and Citigroup recently promised $50 billion for green investments and financings in the coming decade. As an analyst at one of the new green research boutiques told me recently, "Interest is significant to tremendous. Some clients have funds with dedicated investment categories for clean tech and other funds have an interest in high-growth technology, but there isn't a major account that I visit that doesn't understand the political, societal, economic, scientific, and business argument of clean tech. Everyone is aware of it."

In an influential February 2008 *Harper's Magazine* cover story, venture capitalist Eric Janszen makes a couple of other points that are crucial to the clean-tech argument. First, the global economy has evolved (or devolved) to the point that continued growth requires the inflation of one bubble after another. Second, for a sector to really boom, both extraordinary growth prospects and enthusiastic support of government are required. His conclusion is that alternative energy—the major subset of clean tech—is next in line:

> There are a number of plausible candidates for the next bubble, but only a few meet all the criteria. Health care must expand to meet the needs of the aging baby boomers, but there is as yet no enabling government legislation to make way for a health-care bubble; the same holds true of the pharmaceutical industry, which could hyperinflate only if the Food and Drug Administration was gutted of its power. A second technology boom—under the rubric "Web 2.0"—is based on improvements to existing technology rather than any new discovery. The capital intensive biotechnology industry will not inflate, as it requires too much specialized intelligence. There is one industry that fits the bill: alternative energy.

Why Are You Reading This?

If clean tech is so inevitable, why bother reading another word? Why not just access your brokerage account and move your life savings into a random list of solar, wind, and biofuel stocks? Because, to put it bluntly, hot markets are dangerous markets. When the reasons for investing in a given sector are this compelling, con artists and delusionals come out of the woodwork. In the coming decade, we'll be inundated with breathless accounts of new clean technologies that are sure to save the planet and make early investors rich beyond imagining. And the financial community—which, in a perfect world, would act as gatekeeper to protect investors from the untried and unwise—will become the main facilitator of the boom. Venture capitalists will feed these sure things to investment bankers, who will sell them to stock brokers, who will sell them to us.

Think back to the dot.com era for a sense of green tech's future. During the second half of the 1990s, virtually any company with even the vaguest relationship to e-commerce got venture funding and then was taken public by unscrupulous investment bankers, and then sold to credulous investors seduced by the promise of easy money. As it turned out, the Internet has worked as advertised, changing the worlds of entertainment, shopping, and communication almost beyond recognition. But the vast majority of people who loaded up on late-1990s tech stocks had lost most of their money by the end of 2001. Clean tech differs from the dot.coms in ways that will be explained in later chapters. But human nature is what it is. When something seems to have unlimited potential, it becomes, by definition, hard to measure and therefore hard to value. Tools for distinguishing fantasy from reality are crucial, and that's what this book attempts to provide.

The other reason to approach clean tech with caution is that, unlike information technology, it actually encompasses many different markets and technologies, each with its own strengths and challenges. Wind and solar power, for instance, have vastly different technical attributes and constraints: wind speed and consistency versus hours of daylight, turbine durability versus solar cell efficiency, and scalability versus flexibility. Fuel cells are chemistry, biofuels biology, batteries both physics and chemistry—and soon also biology. Some of these technologies work today, some will work in a few years, and some will never work. And frequently, the viable clean technologies are competitors; if one succeeds, it may be at the expense of another. So understanding one means understanding all.

Then there's the army of "pick and shovel" makers, including the firms that make solar cell production equipment, the miners that produce raw materials like platinum and palladium, the info-tech companies that help utilities manage their grids, and the banks and venture capitalists that finance start-up firms and create and trade carbon credits. The "green building" field alone includes makers of everything from light management systems to low-carbon building blocks to high-efficiency appliances. And because lifestyle choices figure prominently in most visions of a green future, the makers of buses, light rail, and bicycles also count as clean-tech players.

Last but not least, clean tech is global. Because of history, geography, and more far-sighted leadership, Europe, Asia, and, to an extent, Latin America have grabbed the lead in this race. Brazil, for instance, has already converted its transportation system to run on ethanol derived from locally grown sugarcane, and now has little to fear from peak oil. China is pouring resources into clean technologies that (it hopes) will prevent it from choking on its own exhaust. Japan's chip makers have become the world's biggest solar panel producers. And Europe, besides offering an array of generous incentives for renewable energy, began tightening environmental rules years ago, forcing local companies to reduce their carbon footprints and remove pollutants like lead solder from electronics. Today, as a result, many of the biggest players in wind and solar power are European or Asian. Given the amount of money and energy now flowing into American labs and start-up companies, the United States will no doubt catch up. But clean-tech money management will remain a global affair, with fund managers and private investors in any given country investing in green companies from many others.

Improving Your Odds

A growing number of web sites and books offer investors a sense of clean tech's potential. But few explain *how* to safely choose among all the possibilities in this complex, fast-moving bull market. *Clean Money* is designed to fill that void by presenting a wide range of strategies based on common sense, the history of previous booms, and the ideas of some of the money managers who are now grappling with the same issues. There is no one-size-fits-all answer, but for each investor, there are strategies that both feel right and increase the odds of ending up a rich person in a clean world.

CHAPTER 2

We Came, We Saw,
We Trashed the Place

The environmental problems that fill today's headlines seem thoroughly modern. Melting glaciers, oil shocks, endocrine disruptors, and nuclear waste are issues of this time, implying that the past has little to teach us about either cause or cure. But that's only partially true. Sure, we've never run out of oil before, and the scale on which the global economy is capable of malfunctioning is certainly unprecedented. But the idea that environmental degradation or even ecological collapse is new is, alas, false. Civilizations have been making similar mistakes and suffering the consequences since the dawn of history. Jared Diamond, a geography professor at the University of California–Los Angeles (UCLA), was able to fill a 560-page book, titled simply *Collapse*, with tales of how past societies cut down all of their trees or eroded their topsoil or poisoned their drinking water and paid a high price—sometimes the ultimate price—for their negligence. The names and details are different (sometimes amusingly so), but the attitudes, behaviors, and general cluelessness could have been lifted from today's *Wall Street Journal*.

We weren't there, of course, and historians are still debating the details of past societies' implosions. But the tools of archeology have come a long way in recent decades. Satellite imaging now gives clear outlines of buildings and other structures covered by jungle or desert. Isotope analysis of ancient skeletons can tell us what our ancestors ate and how their diets changed over time. And samples of soil, ancient garbage dumps, and animal nests yield a fair idea of what kinds of flora and fauna were common. From all this, the case can be made that some once-thriving societies simply trashed their environments in ways that made their economic and social systems untenable. They did so without understanding the consequences of their mistakes and were overwhelmed by the results. Here, then, are some of history's more notable ecological disasters.

The Anasazi

The southwestern United States is not a place where one would expect to find a complex preindustrial society. It's dry in normal times and prone to long droughts, with poor soil and forests that, when they exist at all, grow very slowly. Yet for a thousand years before Europeans arrived, people now called the Anasazi (Navajo for "ancient ones") lived here in settled villages, and eventually in cities. Far more of them lived off this land in places like New Mexico's Chaco Canyon than are able to do so today, and the remains of their stone houses, dams, and irrigation systems are a ghostly reminder of what was once a network of thriving towns.

This story is relatively easy to reconstruct, thanks to two pieces of evidence. First, because the Anasazi used wood to construct their buildings, tree rings can be read as a chronicle of rainfall. A year with good rain produces a wide ring, while a drought produces a narrower ring. Second, pack rats are common in the Southwest, and their nests have been preserved in the dry air, giving archaeologists a clear picture of the vegetation that grew nearby. So it's possible to know both the weather and the vegetation patterns within years rather than decades, as is normally the case with sites where researchers have to rely on carbon-dating. This evidence indicates that early on, small groups of people would build a settlement and stay there for a few decades, until the trees were gone or the soil used up, and then move on to a new site, a lifestyle that was possible while numbers were small and new territory available. As populations increased in the fifth and sixth centuries AD, locals who once lived by hunting and fishing settled down and began farming crops like corn. They soon discovered that Chaco Canyon was an ideal place (relatively speaking) to build a town. The canyon caught rain runoff from a large upland area, producing sufficient groundwater and rich soil. There was also plenty of wild game and edible plants, surrounded by forests of pinyon and juniper trees.

The first settlers lived in underground pithouses, but in 700 AD, they figured out how to build with stone and timber. The first structures were single story, but over the next three centuries they began building higher, eventually putting up five-story structures with roof supports of 16-foot-long, 700-pound logs. These were the largest buildings erected in North America until the Chicago skyscrapers of the 1880s. To exploit what was even then a barely adequate water supply, they dug arroyos, or channels, to guide the runoff into canals and reservoirs. For a while it worked. By 1000, Chaco Canyon was home to around 1,200 people, the capital city of a mini-empire that encompassed smaller towns for miles around.

But as the expansion continued, limits began to appear. By 1100 AD, the pinyon and juniper trees were gone, and the Anasazi began importing ponderosa pine, spruce, and fir trees from as far as 50 miles away—by hand, since there were no horses. In other words, the cost of lumber, in terms of calories per board foot, soared. Next came the inevitable water crisis. Storm runoff gradually deepened the arroyos, until the water level dropped below that of the fields. Since pumps wouldn't be invented for another 600 years, irrigation became impossible, and crop yields began to fall. Then nature, which seldom wastes an opportunity to point out human mistakes, decided to weigh in with a series of long droughts. The clincher was a dry stretch that began in 1130 and lasted long enough to deplete the stores of corn that the Anasazi had put aside. Without rain, it was impossible to grow enough food to support the population. The building boom ended; the last roof beam anywhere in Chaco Canyon was put up in 1170. People starved (evidence of cannibalism is controversial but accepted by many) and/or drifted away to join other communities. By the 1300s, Anasazi civilization had all but died out in Chaco Canyon. Today, more than 700 years later, there are still no pinyon or juniper trees, and the only year-round residents are National Park Service rangers.

Easter Island

Other than perhaps Antarctica, you don't get more remote than the Polynesian islands that dot the South Pacific Ocean. Sometimes a thousand miles distant from the next bit of land, they're worlds— tiny little worlds—unto themselves. Yet most of these islands were inhabited when European sailing ships chanced upon them in the eighteenth century. It seems that over thousands of years, people in canoes (very brave or very lost) made the journey from other islands, sticking around, having babies, and creating new, self-contained societies. There are advantages to such isolation. Being a thousand miles from the nearest possible enemy, for instance, makes invasion unlikely. But it also makes trade difficult, and closed systems tend to be fragile. There's not a whole lot of anything to begin with, and when you use up a given resource, importing a replacement is out of the question.

Not surprisingly, the fates of the Polynesian societies varied. Some remained stable for centuries, others died off for unexplained reasons, and some collapsed but kept a few inhabitants around to greet the first sailing ships. The most interesting case is Easter Island, which is, coincidentally, the most remote bit of habitable land in the world. Two thousand miles of the Pacific separate it from its nearest neighbor, which means the rest of humanity may as well not have existed for the island's inhabitants. When the first Dutch sailors dropped anchor off Easter Island in 1722, they found a sparsely pop-ulated land largely devoid of trees or birds. And they found hundreds of giant stone statues weighing up to 80 tons. This, remember, was before cranes and bulldozers, and in a place where horses and oxen had never existed. Yet the statues were everywhere. Their story, and the fate of the culture that created them, is still a subject of debate. But here's one interpretation, based on recent analysis of plant and animal remains:

When 100 or so Polynesians first landed on Easter Island around 300 AD, they found the prototypical tropical paradise covered with huge palm trees. There were parrots, owls, and herons on the land, and seabirds, 30 species by one count, on the rocks offshore. Between the fish, birds, coconuts, and the new rich farmland, there was plenty of food, and the population rose to around 10,000. Early on, it must have been the kind of place to which most sane people would relo-cate in a heartbeat. Then, around 1000 AD, someone got the idea that carving a huge stone statue and placing it facing the sea would please the gods or provide a nice home for an ancestor's spirit or show the neighbors who was richest. Whatever their original purpose, the stat-ues, called *maoi*, became a trend, and the trend became a mania. Stone was quarried inland and statues carved with hand tools. Then the statues were moved, apparently using the trunks of the giant palm trees as rollers, to shoreline positions atop massive stone platforms that had also been cut and moved. At the peak of the bull market in statues, there were 288 of them in a nearly unbroken line, half a mile apart, circling the island. The average statue was 14 feet tall and weighed 14 tons. The biggest was 33 feet tall and weighed more than 80 tons.

But then the trees ran out, and everything fell apart. With no more canoes (which were carved from tree trunks), the fish catch cratered. Without tree roots to protect against erosion, the rains washed away valuable topsoil and agriculture suffered. Sediment samples show that up to half of the native plants became extinct. The suddenly hungry islanders ate the birds they could catch, driving them to extinction. Then they went to work on the rats. And then they apparently began to starve—or at least they stopped having babies. The population crashed, and when Europeans arrived, there were perhaps 2,000 local subsistence farmers.

The truly spooky thing about this story is that another 600 maoi statues, in various stages of completion, were scattered around the island, either in quarries or along ancient roads between the quarries and the coastal areas where the statues were most often erected. Apparently no one was monitoring the palm tree supply; the crash had caught the islanders totally off guard, right in the middle of their statue mania. One of the partially finished statues, by the way, was 65 feet long and would have weighed an estimated 270 tons. Like a billion-dollar dot.com IPO in 2000, it was never going to work even in good times.

The Mayans

Even more astounding to European eyes than the stone statues of Easter Island were the Mayan ruins of the Yucatan Peninsula, which straddles present-day Mexico, Guatemala, Honduras, and Belize. Huge pyramids, 10 or more stories high with 100 or more steps leading to the top, were clearly the temples of a rich, advanced empire— or at least a network of small but prosperous kingdoms. Yet in 1525, when the first conquistadores were cutting a swath of destruction across the peninsula, they found only scattered farming villages, and in many places few of those. No kingdoms were apparent. It was only later, when explorers and archeologists began finding ruins all over the region, that the realization began to dawn that something very big had happened here.

Based on bits of pottery and other artifacts, it is generally believed that the Yucatan was inhabited as early as 1400 BC and that its inhabitants had developed a written language by around 400 BC. The so-called classic period of Mayan history began around 250 AD, when kings started to build temples. And the story of its eventual collapse begins with an understanding of the local climate and land. Rains in the Yucatan Peninsula are unpredictable, the dry season can be long, and droughts are frequent. Much of the ground is porous, so rainwater sinks and runs off, leaving little moisture in the thin layer of topsoil and few lakes. The terrain is hilly, with relatively little fertile bottom land and lots of harder-to-work hillsides. So the early inhabitants devised technological fixes. They dug deep wells or built villages around naturally occurring sinkholes called *cenotes* that filled with water. Others plastered the bottoms of depressions to create reservoirs, which collected rain and stored it for use in the dry season. The reservoirs at the Mayan city of Tikal, for example, held enough water to meet the needs of about 10,000 people for 18 months.

Farmers grew mostly corn, which, based on isotope analyses of uncovered skeletons, made up a really boring 70 percent of the average Mayan's diet. At first they practiced slash-and-burn agriculture, clearing a bit of forest and burning the scraps to temporarily fertilize the soil. When a given patch was exhausted they moved on, leaving the old land fallow for a decade or more. As you can imagine, this works well when the population is small and the forest vast, but not so well when the number of mouths is soaring. So as cities large enough to justify huge temples formed, farmers began shortening the fallow periods and clearing more land. This worked for a while, and the overall population soared to about 5 million in the eighth century AD. Real estate bubbles tend to coincide with cyclical peaks, and the Mayans followed the script, building not just monuments to glorify their kings but also palaces for their nobles, all achieved presumably by working the peasants harder then ever.

This was not a very flexible society. It had neither pack animals that would allow the importation of food from distant farms nor large meat sources like cows and pigs to supplement the corn-heavy diet. Meanwhile, the local climate was humid, which tended to rot corn stored more than a year, limiting the Mayans' ability to hang on through long droughts. As the food demands of a rising population surpassed farmers' ability to produce it in the valleys, they began moving up the hillsides, practicing the same agricultural techniques as below. Archeological research shows a steady increase in the number of home sites on the hills after 500 AD, while pollen samples show the disappearance of pine forests as the hills were systematically cleared. But slash and burn doesn't work well on hillsides. The newly denuded ground tends to wash away during heavy rains, and sure enough, analyses of building foundations on valley floors reveal increasing amounts of sediments washed down from above.

This caused a whole series of problems. No more trees meant both a firewood shortage and less rain, since pine forests were crucial to the water cycle. And so the Mayan kingdoms began to run out of both food and energy, just as dry seasons lengthened and droughts became more frequent. Peasants began moving back down the hills and clustering in the valleys, where there was insufficient land, food, and water. It is thought that the kingdoms began warring with each other in an attempt to acquire resources. But there was little to be had. Skeletal analysis shows that malnutrition and disease became steadily more common, and much more so among commoners than elites. The last big monument was built in 909 AD, and within two centuries, the forests had reclaimed the valleys.

The Roman Empire

Even in today's "unipolar" world, it's hard to imagine how dominant Rome was in its day. It ruled an empire of 60 million people, back when that was a major chunk of humanity. Its capital city was home to a million people, a concentration that was not to be matched in Europe until a thousand years later in London. Rome controlled pretty much everything worth controlling in Europe, and it did so for centuries. To the people of that time, it must have seemed eternal.

Key to Rome's success was its melding of military and civilian technologies. Its legions had state-of-the-art weapons and strategies, but they also traveled on well-paved roads that let them deploy faster than their enemies. And they ate well as a result of advanced agricultural techniques that freed huge numbers of soldiers and urbanites from the need to work the land, enabling them to go out en masse and impose their will on their neighbors—and their neighbors' neighbors. As a continent-spanning empire, Rome's story is as complex as that of any modern country, with political intrigue, ongoing demographic change, and near constant war. But for our purposes, the crucial point is the nexus of economy and environment.

Deforestation. Wood, back then, was both a key building material and an energy source. And early on there was plenty, since Europe was mostly forest. Trees were cut to house increasing populations throughout the Roman Empire, as well as for heating, mining, smelting, and ceramics. The forests surrounding the cities and mining areas went first. Then Rome's creative engineers devised complex supply lines that brought wood from more distant forests. When this became too expensive, the industrial operations moved to more optimal places and proceeded to cut down those forests. Cities, however, couldn't pick up and move. So the early Roman settlements, which had grown because of their proximity to water, land, and forest, found themselves importing life's necessities from ever-further away.

Soil Degradation. The development of the iron plow and domesticated animals increased the amount of land that a single (frequently slave) farmer could work, so food production kept up with population growth for centuries. Public policy encouraged this process: A 111 BC Roman law allowed anyone who occupied public land of up to 20 acres to keep it, provided they brought it into cultivation. But feeding tens of millions of nonfarmers required a lot of land, which, in turn, required clearing a lot of forests, in a process similar to that of mining and smelting: Work an area until it was played out, and then move on.

Frequently, after miners had cut down the trees and farmers had degraded the soil, herders moved in with cows, pigs, sheep, and goats. The sheep ate the grass, the pigs dug up acorns and chestnuts, and the goats ate the young trees that somehow got past the pigs. The resulting bare hillsides were vulnerable to erosion, and soils soon washed away down to the bare rock.

Expanding Empire. As local forest and farmlands were used up, capturing new resources became one of the drivers of imperial expansion. This required the conscription of more soldiers, many of whom would otherwise have been farming. And since traveling armies had to eat, they tended to decimate whatever land they traversed. If that wasn't enough, the Roman legions began to deforest the areas they were trying to conquer in order to prevent locals from conducting raids from the underbrush. And last but not least, a powerful navy—made up of wooden war ships—became necessary to protect supply lines for grains and other things that now had to be imported from distant lands. Rome had inadvertently set up a series feedback loops in which expanding the empire to acquire more resources used up those very resources at an accelerating rate. Put another way, it had reached a point of no return: Its population was too big to go back to the old limits, but the only perceived solutions led to even greater instability.

Meanwhile, there were hidden pollutants in the Roman ecosystem that may (this is controversial) have posed the gravest threat of all. Not knowing that lead can cause everything from learning disabilities to gout to full-on insanity, the Romans used lead acetate, or sugar of lead, to sweeten old wine. They drank from lead cups and brought water into aristocrats' homes via lead pipes. Take an increasingly inbred aristocracy and feed it toxic levels of lead, and it's no surprise that the result is Caligula, Nero, and Claudius, among the many other borderline personalities who had a hand in Roman governance and military strategy as the empire decayed and, in the fifth century AD, finally fell apart.

Could This Happen Today?

A reasonable reaction to this chapter might be, "Amusing stories, but those were primitive, preindustrial societies. We're way too sophisticated and flexible to allow the environment to be more than a speed bump. And there's no chance we'll actually *collapse* because of anything we're doing today. Our leaders are on top of it, and they'll fix whatever needs fixing." Well, maybe. But as you'll see in the coming chapters, the mistakes being made today are strikingly similar to those just described, with a couple of twists: Whereas previous societies had to grapple with just one or two environmental challenges (and frequently still lost), we've got five or six legitimate threats that are all coming to a head at once. And today's ecological imbalances are being driven by technologies and supply chains that operate globally and therefore have the power to affect everyone all at once rather than just a single country. When food, water, or energy ran out for past societies, most of the people just moved. Today, there's nowhere to move to. With that in mind, let's consider the environmental threats and investment opportunities of today's world.

PART

II

CLEAN ENERGY

CHAPTER 3

Fossil Fuels Fiasco

When you think about it, the idea of an energy shortage is ludicrous. The earth is bathed in free energy in the form of sunlight. The wind—more free energy—blows continuously in many places. Tides go in and out. Rivers flow. Plants absorb and store sunlight, just waiting for us to turn it into electricity and heat. And yet here we are, with oil and gas prices soaring and wars big and small being fought over access to rapidly shrinking oil fields. And the climate seems to be changing in potentially very bad ways, possibly as a result of our burning oil and coal. What happened?

In a nutshell, the earth is a bit too generous. Not only does it offer its inhabitants a steady current income of new energy, but over the past few hundred million years, it has accumulated an energy trust fund in the form of oil, gas, and coal. These fuels are cheap, highly concentrated, and at first appeared to be unlimited, which made drawing down the planet's bank account the easiest choice for a race just entering its technological adolescence. And so in the space of a single century, 2 billion frugal consumers of sunlight, candle wax, and firewood became 6 billion car-driving, home-heating practitioners of factory-scale agriculture and global war. Then, like most trust fund babies, we discovered the error of our ways. Fossil fuels turned out to be either finite or unacceptably dangerous, and therefore incompatible with a global economy that depends on cheap, abundant energy. The resulting problems are of several distinct types, so let's take them one at a time.

Peak Oil: Soaring Prices

Oil is formed through a series of chance events, each of which is essential to the process. A body of water develops a circulation pattern that traps and preserves plant and animal matter containing phosphates and nitrates in an oxygen-deprived layer of sediment. This carbon-rich layer is gradually covered with other layers until it's 7,500 to 15,000 feet deep and above 175 degrees Fahrenheit. Heat and pressure cause complex molecules to break down into simpler forms. Molecules with 5 to 20 carbon atoms become liquid crude oil, while those with fewer than 5 carbon atoms are gases at room temperature and pressure, that is, natural gas.

Because oil is lighter than water, once created, it tends to drift upward. More than 90 percent makes it all the way and seeps through porous rock to the surface, where bacteria and the elements break it down. The other 10 or so percent bumps up against nonporous "cap" rocks and is trapped. And there it waits, diffused in sandstone or limestone, to be liberated by an act of nature or a drilling rig.

Lately, we've been liberating it with a vengeance. After the first big find—generally credited to Texan Edwin Drake in 1859—explorers discovered fields ranging from tiny to "supergiant" all over the world, with clusters in Texas, the Middle East, and a few other places. Early on, there was so much oil and so few uses for it that the United States limited the amount of oil its wells were allowed to produce. Even after the automobile age began in earnest, it was commonly believed that oil existed in virtually unlimited quantities. The supply shocks of the 1970s were shrugged off as political and logistical rather than fundamental, and as recently as the mid-1990s, a barrel of West Texas crude could be had for $20.

To understand how glut became shortage, let's begin with how oil is extracted. Early in the life of a large oil field, when the oil is close to the surface and under intense pressure, it is possible to simply drill down into a reservoir and allow the oil to flow up. But as a field ages, pressure decreases and oil flow declines. Drillers respond by pumping water into the rocks around the deposit. The water flows through the rock and raises the pressure on the oil sufficiently to allow it to keep flowing upward. Today's drillers also employ advanced drills that branch off at angles underground like multipronged straws in order to access more of a deposit.

This combination of water injection and sophisticated drilling technology allows more—though still not all—of the oil in a given field to be extracted, lengthening the productive life of existing reserves. But no technology can extract oil that's not there, and sooner or later every great oil field, region, and country sees its production decline.

Hubbert's Peak

The theory that is cited most often to explain (or at least to illustrate) the challenges facing the oil industry originated with an American geophysicist named Marion King Hubbert. After observing a career's worth of oil wells, Hubbert sketched out some calculations that depicted the life cycle of a typical oil field. The idea, in a nutshell, is that the amount of oil in a given field is finite, and its productive life follows a bell-shaped curve, with output increasing rapidly at first, then peaking, and then declining at about the same rate that it increased. The oil industry's reaction was a big yawn, since Hubbert's calculations looked rather arbitrary. Any given field might contain a lot more oil than originally thought, said the skeptics. And what if some new technology lets drillers suck the last drop from fields that currently yield just a fraction of their oil?

But as the years went by, Hubbert's calculations turned out to fit the data startlingly well. In 1956, he predicted that production of oil from conventional sources would peak in the continental United States between 1965 and 1970. It peaked in 1970 and has since declined by about 3 percent a year—despite the application of state-of-the-art drilling and exploration techniques. The United States is the most heavily explored piece of land on earth, and American oil companies are the best in the world at squeezing the last drop from their wells. Yet the United States now produces just 5 million barrels a day, about half of its 1970 peak (see Figure 3.1).

The story is the same for most of the world's other great oil fields. Production in Europe's North Sea basin peaked in the early 1990s and has since declined at an annual rate of around 10 percent. Alaska's Prudhoe Bay peaked in 1998 at about 2 million barrels a day and now produces less than half that amount. The output of Mexico's giant Cantarell Field is plunging by nearly 20 percent per year. Hubbert, it appears, got it right.

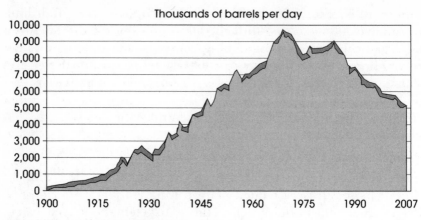

Figure 3.1   U.S. Crude Oil Production
Source: U.S. Energy Information Administration

But the key to the peak oil thesis is Saudi Arabia. Under the vast Arabian Peninsula sit the world's most impressive oil fields, the Abqaiq and Berri, and the granddaddy of them all, Ghawar. For over half a century, these fields have been pumping out cheap, high-quality ("light sweet," in oil field parlance) crude in immense quantities. And Saudi Arabia would like the world to keep believing its resources to be limitless, periodically announcing that it has the ability to ramp up production from the current 9 million or so barrels a day to twice that or more. Even today, most energy experts seem to buy this line despite the Saudis' refusal to allow independent verification of their operations or reserves. Enter Matthew Simmons, a Houston-based oil investment banker who decided to test the Saudis' unlimited oil claims by painstakingly reviewing the obscure technical papers written by engineers working for Saudi Aramco, the state oil company. His findings, which he presents in exhaustive detail in his unlikely best seller *Twilight in the Desert*, are stark, but not surprising when you think about it: Saudi Arabia's great oil fields are aging according to the typical Hubbert's peak script. Early on, the oil flowed without much effort, production soared, and then—exacerbated by overproduction for political reasons during the Cold War—the fields began to need the usual help. The Saudis pumped water into the surrounding rocks and deployed sophisticated horizontal drills. The result, according to

Simmons, is that oil production has held up, but the proportion of water extracted along with the oil is growing steadily. This is a sign that the main Saudi fields are entering the steep downslope to oblivion, and are destined to go the way of the North Sea and Prudhoe Bay. Meanwhile, despite intensive exploration by the world's top geologists armed with the latest instruments, no new fields of consequence have been found under the desert sands.

If even Saudi Arabia is subject to the law of oilfield depletion, what does that imply for global oil supplies? Hubbert weighed in on this, too, predicting back in 1956 that global production would peak in "about half a century" and then begin a terminal decline. Not bad, considering the time frame. Fifty years later, global oil production is about 85 million barrels a day, and its rate of growth is slowing dramatically. And the major global oil companies are generally failing to discover enough oil to replace what they pump. If Simmons is right about the imminent decline of the Saudi supergiant fields, peak oil might indeed be upon us.

One crucial qualification to the peak oil discussion is the definition of oil. Hubbert and Simmons define oil as relatively high-quality crude that can easily be run through today's refineries to produce gasoline. This kind of oil does seem to be in limited supply. But there's plenty of low-grade oil available from things like tar sands and oil shale—much of it in North America—that can be turned into useable oil for a price. In other words, we've found the easy oil, and we are now working through progressively harder-to-get-and-use layers. One way to measure this process is to calculate the energy required to bring a barrel of oil to market: When oil production first began in the mid-nineteenth century, the largest oil fields recovered 50 barrels of oil for every barrel-equivalent of energy used in extraction, transportation, and refining, a statistic called *energy return on energy investment*. Currently, between one and five barrels of oil are recovered for each barrel-equivalent of energy used in the recovery process. For the really nasty oil shale and tar sands, the ratio is less than one, which means oil prices will have to keep rising—or technology will have to improve dramatically—to make them viable. Hubbert summed it up nicely in his congressional testimony in 1974:

> What is most strikingly shown by these complete-cycle curves is the brevity of the period during which petroleum can serve as a

major source of energy . . . For the world, the period required
to produce the middle 80 percent of the estimated 2100 billion
barrels will be about 64 years from 1968 to 2032. Hence, a child
born in the mid-1930s, if he lives a normal life expectancy, will
see the United States consume most of its oil during his lifetime. Similarly, a child born within the last 5 years will see the
world consume most of its oil during his lifetime.

Less Oil from OPEC

For the global economy, the overall supply of oil is less important
than the amount available for export from producing countries—
and that amount is already declining. By and large, countries like
Saudi Arabia and United Arab Emirates recognize that their oil is
a temporary blessing, and they are trying, wisely, to diversify and
modernize their economies. Modernization, of course, means cars,
lights, computers, refineries, factories, and all the other energy-
gobbling artifacts of twenty-first-century life. Which, in turn, means
that these countries will need more of their oil and have less to
export to customers like the United States and China. Saudi Arabia,
to take the most important example, is building new seaports, power
stations, refineries, rail lines, and whole new cities, at a projected
cost of more than $500 billion over the next decade. Its strategy is
to use cheap local oil as the feedstock for a series of downstream
industries like refining and chemicals. The jobs thus created will be
filled by Saudis, who will then buy cars and air conditioners and all
the rest, which will lead them to use more domestically produced
oil. Assuming that Saudi oil production plateaus in this decade,
that country's own rising demand will cut its exports, perhaps dramatically. But at least it will continue to export some oil; other current exporters will become net importers. Indonesia, for instance,
was once an exporter but now imports oil. Mexico will cross that
threshold in a few years, and Iran, assuming that the United States
refrains from invading it, will become an importer a few years
after that.

Hungry Dragon, Thirsty Tiger

While the supply of available oil is peaking, demand for it is soaring, thanks to the emergence of China and India as industrial

economies. China alone has 1.3 billion people, and its middle class now exceeds the entire U.S. population. In another generation, India will be more populous than China, and it is industrializing almost as quickly. The impact of 3 billion people suddenly becoming car owners is hard to overstate. In the coming decade, the number of cars on the road worldwide will increase from around 700 million to over 1 billion, and total world oil demand will rise inexorably, from today's 85 million barrels a day to upward of 110 million. Combine rising demand and flat or even declining oil production, and you get, well, what we have today: much higher oil prices. On January 2, 2008, oil traded above $100 a barrel for the first time. On June 27, it hit $140 (see Figure 3.2).

Expensive oil is a problem for most industrialized countries, but it is a potential disaster for the United States, which is designed around the assumption of cheap energy. In a breathtaking misallocation of resources, we've been pushing suburbs further and further away from cities, building bigger, harder-to-heat houses, and buying heavier and less fuel-efficient cars. And now millions of suburbanites find themselves in a financial predicament in which their electricity and gas bills are soaring while their wages stagnate. The image of McMansion ghost towns, once the wishful thinking of a tiny anticapitalist fringe, is suddenly a little too close for comfort.

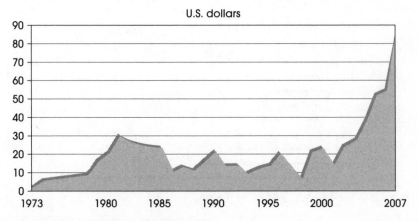

Figure 3.2 Price of a Barrel of Oil
Source: U.S. Energy Information Administration

Geopolitical Complications

Now let's assume that the global economy is able to muddle through with expensive oil. Would the result be peace and prosperity? Probably not, because oil is distributed unevenly, and the countries with the most oil are, at the moment, unfriendly to capitalist democratic ideals like private property and free speech. To use the framework that Henry Kissinger made popular in his 1980s best sellers, the world can be divided into status quo powers, which would by and large prefer that things continue along the current path, and revolutionary powers, which would like to tear up the script and replace it with something radically different. Today, the revolutionary powers have the oil. (See Figure 3.3.) And now that nuclear weapons can be built by any engineer with access to the Internet and a few hundred pounds of fissionable material, the revolutionary powers will likely use their growing wealth to build bombs and/or to finance the nuclear ambitions of others. In effect, the oil and gas economy is fueling the ramp-up to World War III. Let's illustrate the point with a look at four of the beneficiaries of high oil prices:

1. **Russia.** Owner of the world's largest natural gas reserves and the seventh-largest oil reserves, this once-great power has, since the fall of communism, been searching for a global role and a national philosophy to fit its character. It seems to have found both in the person of Vladimir Putin, a former KBG

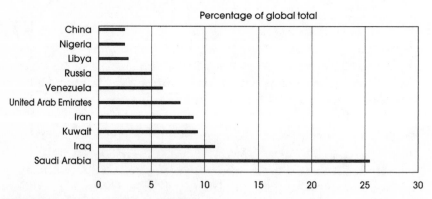

Figure 3.3 Conventional Oil Reserves
Source: CIA World Factbook

operative who rose to power democratically and then proceeded to eliminate the opposition both at home and abroad.
Oligarchs who had grown rich by consolidating formerly
state-run enterprises found themselves jailed for corruption.
Journalists who had criticized the government were shot down
on their way to work, while exiled dissidents were poisoned
with exotic radioactive isotopes. When his term in office
ended in 2007, Putin engineered the election of a protégé
who then named him prime minister, thus keeping him in
control, apparently for life. Beyond its borders, Putin's Russia
is behaving more and more like the Soviet Union of old,
threatening its neighbors with a cutoff of natural gas supplies
and helping Iran develop both nuclear weapons and missile
defense capabilities.

2. **Saudi Arabia.** This desert kingdom sits upon the earth's most
   impressive oil fields, and is ruled by a family descended from
   Muhammad ibn Saud, a desert warlord who long ago made
   a deal with a strict Muslim sect called the Wahhabis. Saud
   offered the Wahhabis government protection, in return for
   which the Wahhabis gave the royal family religious legiti-
   macy. This arrangement was little more than a curiosity in
   the days of nomads wandering the desert. But when its vast
   oil fields were discovered, the Saudi theocracy had to adapt
   to sudden wealth and the inevitable intrusion of modernity.
   Its solution calls for the Saudi government to finance radical
   Islamic schools both at home and abroad, in return for which
   Wahhabi leaders continue to support the monarchy. The
   result: A growing number of kids in the Middle East, Europe
   and, incredibly, the United States are indoctrinated from birth
   in the belief that women are slaves of their families, homosex-
   uals deserve death, and nonbelievers (infidels) can be killed
   with impunity. The 9/11 suicide bombers were Saudis.

3. **Iran.** A "democracy" that's actually ruled by a small group
   of mullahs (clerics) who pick the president and the judges,
   Iran's oil revenues exceeded $60 billion in 2007. Much of this
   cash is going to develop a "peaceful" nuclear power industry,
   with the help of Russia. Meanwhile, the mullahs' handpicked
   president, Mahmoud Ahmadinejad, doesn't mince words
   when it comes to his future plans for the West in general and
   Israel in particular, routinely promising to wipe Israel off the

map. In a few years, he'll have the ability to do just that. In June 2008, Israel was threatening a preemptive strike against Iran's nuclear facilities, so the situation may have changed dramatically by the time you read this.

4. **Venezuela.** Venezuela has the world's sixth-largest oil reserves, and historically it has been one of the most important suppliers of oil to the United States. With oil prices above $100 a barrel, the state-run oil company takes in over $60 billion a year. The country's current president, Hugo Chavez, first tried to gain power through an unsuccessful military coup, and then, like Adolf Hitler, went legit and ran for office. He eventually won, and again like Hitler, quickly set about replacing his country's democratic institutions with a one-party state. In late 2007, he lost a referendum that essentially would have made him president for life, but as this is written, he remains in power and continues to work for a socialist paradise. He has also expressed an interest in nuclear energy.

Just to be very clear about this section: Criticism of other countries should not be construed as approval of U.S. foreign or domestic policy, which, from some perspectives, is more destructive than that of any oil-exporting country. Our inability to limit our gas-guzzling is one of the main reasons so much money flows into OPEC's coffers. And our continuous meddling in the affairs of other countries fuels the anger that drives the revolutionary powers. The U.S. political economy, in other words, is the key part of yet another feedback loop in which, like the Roman Empire two millennia ago, our lifestyle choices cause us to consume resources from abroad and then use military force to ensure adequate supplies.

Climate Change

Now, let's make the wildly optimistic assumption that despite soaring oil prices and the rise of rich, nuclear-armed, oil-producing dictatorships, the global political economy continues to thrive in coming decades. Is the current system viable? The answer may still be no, because the climate appears to be changing. Admittedly, global warming is a controversial issue, and I won't presume to have any special insight into the science of climate change and humanity's role therein. But four things now appear to be true:

1. **The World Is Getting Warmer.** Climatologists have spent the past decade measuring air and ocean temperatures and drilling soil and ice samples in an attempt to determine whether the world is really warming up. The answer is a resounding yes. Recent studies by the Scripps Institution of Oceanography and the United Nations' Intergovernmental Panel on Climate Change, among others, have found that in the Northern Hemisphere, the average temperature during the past half century was the highest in at least the last 500 years. Fifteen of the past 20 years rank among the warmest years on record. Spring now arrives nearly two weeks earlier in many parts of North America and Europe compared to 30 years ago.

2. **The Warming Process Seems to Be Accelerating.** Recent warming seems have triggered a series of feedback loops. For example, as temperatures rise, the top layers of the polar ice packs melt, exposing darker, heat-absorbing ice and liquid water, thus speeding up the melting of ice at the margin. Newly liberated water then seeps down to the rock below many glaciers, lubricating their slide into the sea. Today, the rate of decline of the world's ice sheets is far ahead of the climate model predictions of just a few years ago. In early 2008, climatologists were updating their models to catch up with reality.

3. **Atmospheric Carbon Dioxide Is Up, Along with Global Temperatures.** The dominant climate change theory is that carbon dioxide, or CO_2, and other greenhouse gases like methane, nitrous oxide, sulfur hexafluoride, HFCs (hydrofluorocarbons), and PFCs (perfluorocarbons) trap atmospheric heat that might otherwise be radiated into space. So as sunlight warms the earth, more of the resulting heat sticks around, similar to a car parked in the sun. One study puts atmospheric CO_2 concentrations at levels last seen 650,000 years ago.

4. **Human Contributions to Atmospheric Carbon Dioxide Are Increasing.** Since 2000, CO_2 emissions worldwide—as measured by hundreds of sensors in dozens of countries—have accelerated, growing at three times the rate observed during the 1990s. Once again, China and India are key variables. As they get richer, they burn more fossil fuels—a lot more. The increase in China's energy demand between 2002 and 2005 was equivalent to Japan's current annual energy use. And there appears to be no end in sight. China and

the rest of the developing world need more power, and they need it now, so they're building coal-fired power plants—the simplest and best understood and therefore the quickest fix—as fast as possible. And their growing middle classes are clogging the roads with cars. More cars and more coal-burning power plants mean more carbon dioxide in the air. The International Energy Agency estimates that atmospheric CO_2 will jump by 57 percent between 2005 and 2030. China will, by the time this book hits the stores, have surpassed the United States as the world's top emitter of greenhouse gases.

In short, there is no chance whatsoever of actually lowering greenhouse gas emissions in the near term. Assuming that the causal link between atmospheric CO_2 and temperature is valid, the Earth is likely to continue to warm for the rest of this century. What does this mean? Well, warmer air and rising sea levels don't sound all that bad in the abstract. One could make the case that a warmer planet would support more life and generally be a nicer place to live—the Bahamas versus North Dakota, if you will. The hitch is that humanity is set up for today's environment. Cities holding hundreds of millions of people and trillions of dollars of property are sitting on various seacoasts. In the warmer world that the more extreme (and recently more accurate) climate models now envision, we might literally have to wave good-bye to Manhattan, Vancouver, Miami, and Amsterdam, among many other cities. Post-Katrina New Orleans cost U.S. taxpayers and insurance companies several hundred billion dollars, so an increasingly warm, wet world might bankrupt the global economy.

Now that you're suitably anxious, consider what you'd be willing to pay for something that solves the world's energy problems. Then multiply that figure by 6 billion, and you have a sense of the potential market for alternative energy sources that don't emit greenhouse gases or enrich dangerous regimes. Read on for the most promising technologies.

4

Solar Power

SEIZE THE DAY(LIGHT)

Solar power has been the Next Big Thing for as long as most people have been alive. Way back in the 1970s, the idea of using clean, abundant, *free* sunlight to break the grip of Big Oil first led homeowners to bolt solar panels onto their roofs and wait gleefully for their meters to start running backward, and they've been at it ever since. Unfortunately, almost without exception, those early solar arrays ended up serving only the social consciences of their owners. Sunshine may have been free, but solar power was anything but. Until very recently, solar panels were so inefficient that they cost more than they saved, which is why, despite all that free sunlight, they currently adorn only a relative handful of U.S. homes.

But during solar's long gestation period, researchers were making steady progress. Each year, the ability to turn sunlight into energy improved. And now, at last, solar is ready for prime time. How ready? Well, with a little help from improved energy storage technology, solar power will soon be able to literally replace the entire fossil fuel infrastructure in the world's sunnier climes. It is, in short, going to be huge beyond words.

Solar power comes in two versions:

1. **Photovoltaics**, which includes both the familiar rooftop solar panel and its more exotic thin-film descendants.
2. **Solar thermal**, one of those old-is-new-again ideas that suddenly looks like a viable alternative to coal-burning power plants.

Photovoltaics

Photovoltaic (PV) cells are made of semiconducting material—most commonly crystalline silicon of the same type used in computer chips—that produces electricity when struck by sunlight. Photovoltaic modules (i.e., solar panels) are composed of multiple PV cells. Two or more interconnected panels make an array. Solar arrays can be placed individually on home rooftops, connected by the thousands in desert solar farms, or any combination in between. The two keys to turning PV into a viable energy source are efficiency (the portion of the light striking a cell that's converted to electricity) and cost. Both are headed in the right direction.

> **Efficiency.** Over the years, the efficiency of commercially available solar cells has crept from 6 percent of the original 1954 Bell Labs prototype to between 14 percent and 21 percent today, depending on the design. That's not far from silicon's theoretical limit of 29 percent, though other materials, both alone and in combination with silicon, are producing results in the 40 percent range.
>
> **Cost.** Longer solar cell production runs generate economies of scale, making each panel less costly. As demand increases, solar panel makers have built new factories and refined their manufacturing processes, and costs have declined by 3 percent to 5 percent a year in the past decade. Looked at another way, the price of solar power has decreased 20 percent for every doubling of capacity. And with the industry now doubling its capacity every few years, the result is a nice, steady decline in manufacturing costs. The average cost of PV fell from nearly $100 per watt in 1975 to around $4 per watt in 2006. Since then, a shortage of silicon has increased the price of that crucial input and slowed the decline in manufacturing costs. But that's a temporary blip. With silicon supplies rising in response to higher prices, the cost of PV is generally expected to resume its decline in 2009, falling to an average of $2 per watt by 2012.

Wholesale Versus Retail

PV is used in both wholesale and retail power generation. The former involves large-scale arrays, where an electric utility places thousands of panels in a sunny place and ships the resulting electricity over high-capacity power lines to users. Worldwide, over a gigawatt of power was coming from such plants in early 2008, 80 percent of which were in Europe, where government policies are friendliest to renewable energy. But at the power-plant level, today's PV is far more expensive than conventional sources like coal. So while PV farms exist and new ones are being built, they only generate an adequate return for their owners when paired with massive subsidies and/or mandates requiring that utilities derive a portion of their power from renewable sources. Large-scale PV will not replace coal in the foreseeable future.

The real excitement is at the retail end of the market, where PV has a whole host of advantages. Unlike wind, coal, or natural gas, PV scales down. Three solar panels on a rooftop are just as efficient as a thousand in the desert. This kind of "distributed" power generation doesn't require any new real estate, since the buildings are already there. It doesn't require environmental impact assessments, since a roof is not an ecosystem. Distributed power makes the grid more robust, since it's much harder to disrupt a system that is fed by a million homes than one in which a single plant's power is transported over long-haul lines. Because daylight coincides with peak power demand, rooftop solar helps utilities avoid building new, expensive gas- and coal-fired plants. And—this is suddenly a big one—PV locks in a given electricity price for two or three decades, something no utility burning coal, gas, or oil can promise.

Because rooftop solar panels compete with the retail price (i.e., the cost that utilities charge their customers for electricity after shipping it long distances from large power plants) rather than the wholesale price of electricity, PV's cost disadvantage is modest in most markets. Meanwhile, utility power costs are rising along with fossil fuel prices, wages, and carbon taxes. These two trend lines—conventional power up, solar down—are intersecting in more and more places. In early 2008, when tax breaks and other incentives were included, solar was competitive in Japan, much of California, and several European countries, meaning that an installed solar system would pay for itself in 10 years or less. The next stage is "grid parity," where solar becomes cheap enough to compete head to head with the retail price of grid-delivered coal or natural gas–derived electricity. No new breakthroughs are needed; all it will take is another 5 or 10 years (depending on the market) of the same steady progress that's currently taking place. Even in cloudy Britain, solar should reach grid parity by 2020.

Thin Film, Fat Margins

Promising though they are, conventional solar panels have some serious drawbacks. Because their semiconductor layers are sandwiched between panes of glass in a thick frame, they're heavy and bulky. They're relatively expensive to make and install, and their weight and rigidity limit them mostly to rooftops. These limitations create an opening for PV materials that are lighter, thinner, and cheaper. And they're coming. Known as thin-film solar cells, they take advantage of new manufacturing techniques that can deposit extremely thin layers of photosensitive materials on glass, metal, or plastic substrates. And some are made of nonsilicon materials like cadmium telluride (CdTe) and copper indium gallium selenide (CIGS, pronounced "sigs") that appear to have potentially big advantages in cost and/or performance. Silicon inks, meanwhile, are being developed that appear to combine the strengths of silicon and thin film.

Today's thin films produce less electricity per unit area, with efficiency in the 12 percent to 15 percent range. But because they contain far less semiconducting material, they're cheaper to make and so much lighter and more flexible that they cut down on installation costs while opening up new real estate on walls and elsewhere. As the price of thin film drops relative to the wages of installers, its installation cost advantage over traditional solar panels will loom ever larger. From about 11 percent in 2007, thin film's market share is expected to soar going forward. As for which kind of thin film grabs the biggest share of this growth, that's where it gets interesting. Each producer has its own recipe, and right now they all sound revolutionary. Here's a brief look at three of the early leaders:

1. **First Solar** (headquartered in Arizona) turns cadmium telluride into a frameless laminate that it sells to utilities for large-scale installations. A proprietary production process enabled it to deliver PV in quantity for an industry-best $1.19 per watt in early 2008. Utilities are impressed, and they are buying whatever First Solar can make, which is quite a bit. In

the quarter that ended in December of 2007, its sales nearly quadrupled, year over year, to $200 million. And its stock price gave a taste of what's in store for the best solar cell makers when the next leg of the bull market gets going: From a low of $24 in late 2006, it soared in one gorgeous arc to $280 before being caught in the early-2008 market downdraft and falling back to $200.

2. **United Solar Ovonics** (Michigan) uses "plasma-enhanced chemical vapor deposition" to lay down half-micron-thick layers of amorphous silicon, which, unlike traditional crystalline silicon, produces electricity even in overcast conditions. The laminates come in 18-foot-long rolls. "They're extremely lightweight and are backed with adhesive and a release paper," says United Solar chairman Subhendu Guha. "You can ship it to site, remove the paper and bond it to the roof. We have a big advantage in cost of installation." United Solar doubled its production capacity in 2007, to 58 megawatts, and plans to double that again in 2008.

3. **Nanosolar** (Silicon Valley) had the industry buzzing in late 2007 with a CIGS "nano-ink" that costs far less than traditional solar cells while operating at efficiencies close to that of silicon. If Nanosolar's process lives up to its billing, the possibilities are endless: The ink can be sprayed onto foil, plastic, or glass or incorporated into cement and other building materials, conceivably turning the entire exterior of a house or office building into a solar generator. Venture capitalists have showered the company with enough cash to build one of the world's largest PV factories, capable of producing 430 megawatts of solar cells a year, and as of early 2008, its first year's production run was pre-sold to European installers.

As thin film encroaches on crystalline silicon's turf, the war of words is heating up. "The smartest investors are going short on silicon and long on thin film, especially CIGS," Nanosolar CEO Martin Roscheisen was reported to have said in late 2007. To this, T. J. Rodgers, CEO of Cypress Semiconductor, a major stockholder in the silicon panel maker SunPower, was reported to respond, "Silicon has a reliability record which is unmatched by any other material . . . They could rename the company NanoDollar, because that's all they are going to be left with after we get done kicking their butt."

Which form of PV will win? They'll all find a niche, says Travis Bradford, venture capitalist and author of *Solar Revolution*, the best primer on this industry. "I see the market breaking in two directions: Where cost is crucial, thin film will do well, and where space is crucial crystalline PV panels will continue to do very well." The various thin-film materials, meanwhile, "all hit the price points necessary to compete with crystalline silicon. Cadmium telluride has the first-mover advantage, CIGS has the theoretical best price and cost, and amorphous silicon has unlimited feedstock."

Concentrating Solar

At the high end of the cost-efficiency spectrum are PV materials like gallium arsenide and multilayer cells that are more expensive than crystalline silicon but produce more electricity from a given amount of light. These materials and designs haven't caught on because their cost more than offsets their efficiency. But researchers are working on a solution: By using mirrors to focus and amplify the amount of light hitting the PV material, "concentrating" PV systems are able to generate efficiencies that are high enough, just maybe, to more than cover the extra cost of the system. Soliant Energy, a California start-up staffed by former NASA scientists, uses "triple-junction" cells that capture a wider range of solar energy, making them 40 percent efficient. Acrylic lenses then concentrate incoming sunlight by a factor of 500 and direct it at the cells. The result: less PV material required for a given power output, and an overall lower cost. But concentrating solar still faces some technical hurdles. Using mirrors to concentrate light requires direct sunlight rather than the generalized light that normal solar cells utilize, which offsets some of the new materials' efficiency advantages. And both the PV materials and the mirrors are expensive, which raises the bar further. So although this technology might eventually be viable, it's further away than thin film.

State of the PV Market

PV's *future* looks pretty bright, obviously. But if it's just now reaching grid parity in a few places, why has it boomed for the past few years? In three words: Japan and Germany. By deciding not to wait and embracing solar before it was cost competitive, those countries have turbocharged the market. Japan's energy vulnerability—it imports all of its oil—led it, starting in the late 1980s, to aggressively diversify in two different directions. First, it built a lot of nuclear plants and now gets 35 percent of its electricity from this source. Second, and more interesting from a clean-tech point of view, it adopted solar. In a textbook multifront effort dubbed the Sunshine Program, the Japanese government funded research and development, educated consumers and utilities on the how and why of solar, and set up demonstration projects with homes and businesses. And it offered generous rebates to buyers of solar panels. It worked: PV installations soared, which led panel makers to build more factories, which, in turn, lowered costs by about 10 percent each year. By 2005, the program had become so successful that it was phased out.

Germany, though not exactly sunny, does have a powerful environmental lobby. So embracing solar became the green equivalent of cutting taxes, easy to do and a surefire vote getter. In 2000, Germany began offering a "feed-in tariff" that obligated electric utilities to buy the power generated by rooftop solar systems at triple the going retail rate. At this price, it actually paid for homeowners and businesses to go solar, and with the economic risk removed, Germans have installed more than 300,000 PV systems, triple what the original plan envisioned and more than all other countries combined between 2004 and 2006. In 2007, fully half the world's solar power was generated between the Baltic Sea and the Black Forest. And German PV companies, led by giants like Q-Cells, are global market leaders. See Figures 4.1 and 4.2 for a sense of today's PV market.

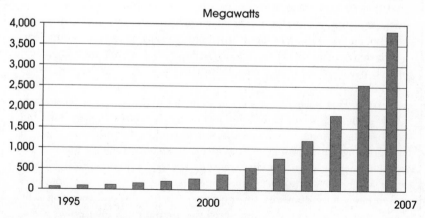

Figure 4.1 Global Photovoltaic Production
Source: WorldWatch Institute

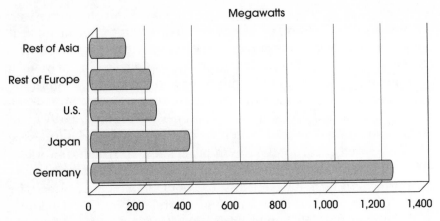

Figure 4.2   2007 Photovoltaic Installations
Source: Renewable Energy World

Object Lesson: When the Story Is Real . . .

One of the key pieces of advice this book offers is to "avoid the story stocks." That is, don't get sucked into an unproven technology or company just because it sounds revolutionary. In hot markets, everything sounds revolutionary and every company has unlimited potential. You'll see examples of such stocks and the dangers they pose to excitable investors in later chapters. But it's also important to understand that not all young companies with promising technologies fall into the story stock category. Some are for real, and though they come along only rarely, they're worth seeking out. The trick, of course, is distinguishing reality from hype, and the way to do this is to demand proof that (1) the technology is gaining acceptance in the marketplace, (2) real orders that produce real cash flow are in hand rather than merely promised, and (3) the company is capable of satisfying those orders profitably.

When First Solar went public in 2006, it had the look of a classic story stock: glamorous sector (solar), hot technology (exotic CdTe thin film), and the backing of some prominent investment banks (often a danger sign). It was growing but unprofitable, and as the pioneer in CdTe, it was way out on the bleeding edge. *And* its target market was utility-scale solar installations, where PV was not yet cost competitive. Investors wary of story stocks could easily have dismissed this one out of hand. But had they dug a little deeper, they would have discovered that even though solar power wasn't competitive with grid-delivered electricity, Germany was offering subsidies

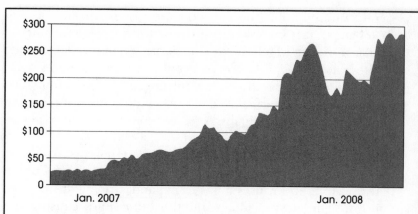

Figure 4.3   First Solar Stock Price (FSLR)

that made it viable. First Solar had signed contracts with major German utilities (rock-solid companies unlikely to renege) to supply all the solar panels it could produce. And its thin-film technology and production methods had been proven over the previous few years to produce PV at a cost per watt of $1.50—vastly lower than anything else on the market. In other words, this young company was the real deal, and as Figure 4.3 illustrates, its early investors had themselves a ten bagger.

Solar Thermal: Replacing Smoke with Mirrors

PV is a spectacular technology for distributed generation and, in coming years, will adorn rooftops and eventually walls and windows around the world. But its future in utility-scale power generation is less certain, for reasons already discussed. To replace coal and natural gas in utilities' portfolios, something else is needed. And that something might be solar thermal. Whereas PV converts sunlight directly into electricity, solar thermal converts sunlight to heat and then uses that heat to generate electricity. Its current versions are cheaper than PV, and some new designs appear to put it within range of coal. The main solar thermal designs include the following:

- **Parabolic trough**, which uses curved mirrors to reflect sunlight onto a hollow tube running along above the trough. "Thermal oil" passes through the tube and is heated by the concentrated sunlight. The oil then passes through a heat exchanger, turning water into steam, which runs a turbine.

- **Solar tower,** in which mirrors track the sun and reflect its rays onto water pipes at the top of a central tower. The water boils, generating steam that drives a turbine. The first commercial solar tower, with a capacity of 11 megawatts, was completed in 2005 near Seville in Spain. A second tower, capable of generating 20 megawatts, is scheduled for 2008.
- **Stirling engine,** which uses dish-shaped mirrors to direct solar energy at an "external combustion" engine in which heat at one end causes a gas to expand, driving an internal piston. The heat dissipates at the other end, causing the gas to contract, and sending the piston back for another go-round. This process converts thermal energy (i.e., concentrated sunlight) into mechanical power and thus electricity—apparently very efficiently. Tests at Sandia National Laboratories were promising enough to lead Southern California Edison and San Diego Gas & Electric to put in big orders for Stirling engines.

Solar Thermal's story is similar to PV's: a hot idea during the first energy crisis that turned out to be too expensive to compete with coal and natural gas and was largely abandoned in the 1990s. But a few diehard fans kept plugging away, refining their designs and proselytizing to anyone who would listen. And now a lot of people are listening. Because it's easier to generate heat than electricity from sunlight, modern solar thermal is already far cheaper than PV. Existing solar thermal plants generate power for about $0.15 per kilowatt-hour (kWh), tantalizingly close to the $0.10 that's widely seen as the magic number for head-to-head competition with coal and gas.

And as with PV, there's a solar thermal start-up that claims a radical breakthrough and has attracted big bucks from VCs: Silicon Valley-based Asura. Whereas the standard solar thermal design uses curved mirrors, Asura uses relatively cheap, mass-produced flat mirrors. And instead of heating oil, it runs water through high-strength tubes. The water turns directly into steam, which runs a turbine. Asura claims that it's already at $0.11 per kWh, and in early 2008, it secured $40 million to build a square-mile, 175-megawatt plant in California.

Storage: The Key to Killing Coal

Even at $0.10 per kWh, solar thermal has a very big flaw: The sun only shines half the time, which means the capital cost of a solar thermal array is spread over fewer hours of operation, making it both more expensive than plants that can operate 24/7 and unsuitable for base-load (continuous) power generation. To challenge coal, solar needs a way to store excess electricity in the daytime and feed it to the grid at night. And here again, solar thermal appears to have the edge on PV in large-scale generation because heat is easier to store than electricity. Whereas a PV array might require giant, as-yet-undeveloped batteries or flywheels or other esoteric devices to store its electricity, solar thermal engineers have come up with several simple but promising heat storage solutions. The furthest along uses most of a solar thermal plant's daytime heat to generate electricity and the rest to heat a mixture of sodium and potassium nitrate, known as molten salt, that liquefies when heated to between 550 degrees and 1,200 degrees and then retains its heat for 16 hours. When the sun goes down, the stored heat can be used to run a turbine to keep the power flowing. The current design is a closed loop that doesn't expose the solution to the air and so doesn't pollute, while degrading only gradually. This kind of system had yet to be proven in the field as of early 2008, but if the claims now being made for solar thermal and related storage technologies pan out, it might soon be competitive in the parts of the world where 16 hours without sun is a rarity.

Solar's Growth Prospects

Though both fall under the general heading of solar power, PV and solar thermal are very different technologies with generally separate destinies. So let's consider each in turn.

Photovoltaics

Italy and Spain have launched their own feed-in tariff programs, while California is offering cash incentives that subsidize new PV installations by up to $2.50 per watt. By the end of 2008, 20 nations and most U.S. states are expected to have solar incentives of some kind in place. And China, with its big trade surplus and desperate need for electricity, will both produce more solar panels domestically and import more from overseas. Demand, in short, will remain strong in the near term, mostly as a result of government incentives.

But PV profitability is another story. In 2007, demand was so strong that solar panel makers were able to hold the line on prices while their production costs fell, sending profit margins up. This combination of rising sales and widening margins has attracted an avalanche of capital, which the recipients are using to build new factories. When that capacity comes on line in 2008 and 2009, the result will be a temporary glut similar to what the semiconductor industry goes through periodically, says Travis Bradford. "[In semi-conductors], every eight or nine years you get a supply bottleneck. Then profits go up and people invest a lot of capital and prices adjust. In PV, we're probably between the 'invested a lot of capital' and 'prices adjust' phases. By late 2008 PV prices will be falling like a rock . . . There's a massive margin squeeze coming." It will take a couple of years, says Bradford, for supply and demand to come back into balance, during which time the profit margins of the solar panel makers may fall below 2007 levels.

Then things get really interesting. During the margin squeeze, costs will keep falling. By 2012, module prices will pierce $2 a watt ($3 to $4 installed), predicts Bradford. At that point, solar power will be economically viable without government subsidies, and it will embark on a long, long run in which rising demand drives new supply, which lowers prices, which spurs more demand, with no real end in sight. At last, a *positive* feedback loop!

For an idea of what kind of growth this implies, start with the fact that Germany, the world's most solarcentric economy, gets less than 1 percent of its electricity from PV. Outside Germany, solar barely registers. Its U.S. market share is 0.05 percent, which means it could expand 20 times from 2007 levels and still be at only 1 percent. Meanwhile, China and India by themselves will install more new solar generating capacity each year than the whole world used in, say, 2004. Demand for solar panels and related gear is projected to exceed $100 billion a year by 2015, at which point it will *still* be an emerging growth industry.

Solar Thermal

New power plants take a lot longer to build than rooftop solar arrays. So the numbers—in terms of both capital spending and total generating capacity added—will be lower for solar thermal than for PV. But they might still be very impressive. In late 2007, for instance, Europe was reportedly considering a $10 billion plan to build a string of 100 solar thermal power stations in North Africa and the Middle East that would generate electricity and transport it via undersea cable to Europe. If fully realized, the network would provide the European Union (EU) with a sixth of its electricity while lowering its carbon emissions. The Swiss Center for

Table 4.1 Solar Power Stocks

Company	Ticker/ Headquarters	PV Manufacturing Capacity (MW)	Market Value, 6/27/08 ($ millions)	PV Material
Canadian Solar	CSIQ/China	150	1,110	Silicon
China Sunergy	CSUN/China	100	359	Silicon
Energy Conversion Devices	ENER/U.S.	100	2,890	Silicon
Ersol	ES6G.F/Germany	260	1,592	Silicon
E-Ton	3452.TWO/Taiwan	280	709	Silicon
Evergreen Solar	ESLR/U.S.	225	1,180	Silicon
First Solar	FSLR/U.S.	275	21,230	Cadmium telluride
JA Solar	JASO/China	175	2,930	Silicon
Kyocera	KYO/Japan	300	17,960	Silicon
Mitsubishi Elect.	6503.T/Japan	200	25,543	Silicon
Nanosolar	NA	430	NA	CIGS
Q-Cells	QCEG/Germany	795	7,669	Silicon
Renewable Energy	REC.OL/Norway	225	12,998	Silicon
Sanyo Electric	6764.T/Tokyo	260	4,669	Silicon
Sharp	6753.T/Tokyo	950	19,050	Silicon
Solarfun	SOLF/China	360	873	Silicon
Solar Millennium	S2MG.DE/ Germany	NA	117	Solar thermal
SolarWorld	SWVG.F/Germany	500	5,025	Silicon
SunPower	SPWR/U.S.	400	6,160	Silicon
Suntech Power	STP/China	540	5,590	Silicon
Trina Solar	TSL/China	150	766	Silicon
Yingli	YGE/China	400	2,060	Silicon

Electronics and Microtechnology and the United Arab Emirates, meanwhile, are collaborating to design and build an artificial island covered with solar concentrators. The island would float offshore and generate electricity to make hydrogen, which would be shipped ashore as needed. More such projects are being proposed all the time, but you get the idea. Now that solar has arrived, it's got everyone thinking big.

All Solar Stocks Are Not Created Equal

For investors, solar presents some unique challenges. As you'll see in the chapters that follow, most other clean-tech sectors support a handful of major companies and a few promising newcomers. Such small populations limit an investor's choices but also make stock picking relatively straightforward. Not so with solar, where dozens of publicly traded PV companies process materials with varying supply and demand and performance characteristics in countries with varying labor and environmental regulations. So even with PV demand soaring, differences in execution will produce winners and losers in this space, and buying a random list of solar stocks is a recipe for mediocre returns. The solution? Old-fashioned security analysis in which you get familiar with the industry and track a list of companies according to criteria designed to separate winners from losers. In PV, the main (though not the only) criteria that analysts monitor are production capacity, production costs (cost per watt), raw material availability, profitability trends, and access to capital (see Table 4.1 for partial list of solar stocks).

CHAPTER 5

Wind

NO BREAKTHROUGHS NEEDED

The stretch of Interstate 84 that runs along the Columbia River from Idaho to Portland, Oregon, looks, on the map, like it should be a scenic, peaceful drive. But it's not, because the wind, funneled between the basalt bluffs of the Columbia River gorge, blows hard and continuously, moving your car (or, for a real thrill, your boxy minivan) a few feet to either side with each gust. Since the same thing is happening to the other nearby cars, the scenery tends to take a back seat to accident avoidance. And when you stop at a roadside rest to give your white knuckles a break, the wind either yanks the door out of your hand and slams it against the car next to you (personal experience talking) or shoves it back, mousetrap-like, onto your extended leg as you're trying to get out.

There's a town along I-84 called Hood River that once must have been a truly disturbing place to live, with the wind an ever-present poltergeist. But a few years ago, the residents—mostly fruit farmers—had an epiphany: The combination of a wide, slow-moving river and nonstop wind is something that extreme sports enthusiasts might pay to experience. So Hood River became a mecca for the tiny subset of the population that craves the "perfect wind" capable of propelling a kiteboard 40 feet into the air. They fill hotels and restaurants, and occasionally they settle down and buy houses. The locals, in short, have turned the wind into a valuable asset.

A breeze that can levitate a parasail can also turn a windmill. And the epiphany that led Hood River to embrace windsurfing has led hundreds of other breezy places around the world to embrace wind power. Turbines, their blades spinning night and day, are now a common sight off the coast of Europe and on the Texas plains and the Russian steppes. In the right place with the right equipment, wind is the cheapest form of alternative energy, and it is now, after solar, the world's fastest-growing renewable energy source.

How Wind Power Works

Wind is created when sunlight heats air, causing temperature and pressure differentials, which, in turn, cause air to flow one way or the other. For centuries, people have been capturing some of this energy with windmills—towers with blades turned by the wind to produce a force useful for grinding grain or pumping water. More recently, engineers have figured out how to connect really big blades to generators to produce electricity. A typical utility-scale turbine is 150 feet high with a rotor diameter (the span of the blades) of 120 feet, while a top-of-the-line model might be three times that size. The world's biggest turbine, the Enercon E-126, is 453 feet tall and has a rotor blade width of 413 feet. It produces more than 7 megawatts, enough electricity to power 2,100 U.S. homes. Not bad for a single windmill.

Some turbines operate at a constant speed and produce the most power when the wind blows steadily within a given range. Others are designed to operate with variable wind. Each design has a unique "power curve" that governs the relationship of its output to various wind speeds. Because the wind is intermittent even in the best spots, a typical wind turbine will have a load factor of only 30 to 40 percent, meaning that it will generate power for around one-third of a given day. But its fuel source is free, which offsets the downtime.

Because load factor is crucial to a turbine's profitability, matching the turbine and the site is the key to building a profitable wind farm. As a result, site selection has become a science, with industry experts—the wind equivalent of petroleum engineers—measuring historical wind patterns and analyzing topography for a sense of how much wind a turbine in a certain spot can expect. A good turbine site also requires soil stable enough to hold these massive structures and access for the earth-moving equipment, trucks, and cranes necessary to deliver and set them up. It should be close enough to the grid to make connection affordable. And it must be free of neighbors who object to giant towers spoiling their view. Juggling all of these considerations produces a long list of offsetting costs and benefits: Offshore sites are flat and frequently have steady, strong wind, but they're far from the grid and hard to set up and maintain. Isolated plains have cheap land and frequently good wind but are also far from the grid. Areas near population centers offer good grid access but expensive land and frequently touchy neighbors.

But where wind works, it works beautifully. Large turbines can be installed for about $2 per watt, or $2 million per megawatt, which enables a well-sited turbine to generate power for $0.04 to $0.06 per kWh, a price that is competitive with natural gas and coal. And that's before governments start penalizing the latter two for their carbon emissions. Then wind's cost advantage becomes very real and very big. Here are some of its other advantages:

- Wind turbines leave most of the area they cover open for other uses. Cattle and sheep, for instance, can happily graze on a wind farm.
- They're safe. Because the blades are far aboveground, they don't threaten people. Wind power organizations like to claim that their turbines have never injured a member of the general public.
- They're reliable. Early turbines broke down frequently, but today's models have an expected working life of 20 to 25 years and require very little maintenance.
- The price of wind never changes. Coal, oil, and natural gas prices surged in 2007, while the wind, as always, was free.

State of the Market

The financial profile of a wind turbine is a mirror image of a traditional fossil fuel plant. A coal plant, for instance, can be built for about 20 percent of its total lifetime cost, with most of the other 80 percent coming from the fuel it must buy to generate power. With a wind farm, the up-front cost is 80 percent of the lifetime operating budget, the fuel is free, and maintenance accounts for the other 20 percent. This huge up-front cost was a roadblock when fossil fuels were cheap and wind turbine reliability was questionable. But both of those issues have swung decisively in wind's favor lately, making banks and other investors more willing to finance wind farms. Now everyone with a steady breeze is looking into it. Global installed wind capacity rose twelvefold in the past decade, and it is now growing at about 25 percent per year—and would grow faster if turbine manufacturers could meet current demand. Wind now supplies 3 percent of Europe's power needs and fully 20 percent of Denmark's. Germany has 22 gigawatts of wind capacity installed, which provides 6 percent of its power, and the European Wind Energy Association hopes to supply 22 percent of Europe's electricity demand by 2030. China, of course, is installing turbines as fast as they can be delivered.

The United States installed 5 gigawatts of wind power capacity in 2007, boosting its total by 45 percent, to nearly 17 gigawatts. That's still just 1 percent of the country's total electricity generation, a figure that should rise dramatically in the coming decade, since the United States is actually richer in wind than it ever was in oil. All those flat, blustery prairies, deserts, and hardscrabble dairy farms suddenly find themselves with the equivalent of geysers. A University of Delaware study, meanwhile, concluded that the Middle Atlantic Bight, a region of the Atlantic Ocean that runs from Cape Cod, Massachusetts, to Cape Hatteras, North Carolina, could provide enough wind power for the entire U.S. East Coast.

Texas especially is turning into one big wind farm. In 2007, it was the first state to install a gigawatt of wind power in a single year, and now it has over 4 gigawatts of wind-generating capacity. Its Horse Hollow Wind Energy Center is the world's biggest wind farm, with 421 turbines spread across 47,000 acres generating 735 megawatts, and several of its other farms are in the global top 10. This being Texas, even bigger things are coming: Shell and TXU Corporation are planning a 3-gigawatt wind farm in the Texas panhandle, while oil icon T. Boone Pickens is planning a 4-gigawatt, $10 billion installation nearby. To ship all this power to customers, Texas utilities are building new transmission lines capable of carrying another 2.5 gigawatts.

In Europe, wind is getting nearly as warm a welcome as solar. Denmark's favorable wind power experience has led it to shoot for double its current capacity by 2025. Spanish wind capacity will exceed 15 gigawatts in 2008 and, under the current plan, will reach 29 gigawatts within a decade. The United Kingdom in early 2008 had five offshore wind farms up and running and another 10 in various stages of planning. The proposed London Array project in the Thames Estuary will, if built, generate more electricity than any other offshore plant in the world. And if all its current plans come to fruition, Britain will get over 15 percent of its electricity from wind a decade hence. See Figures 5.1 and 5.2 for a snapshot of current global wind power capacity.

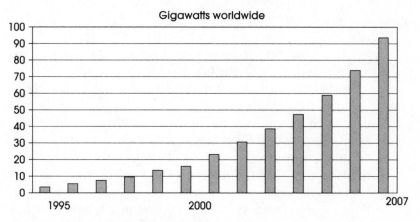

Figure 5.1 Cumulative Wind Power Capacity
Source: Global Wind Energy Council

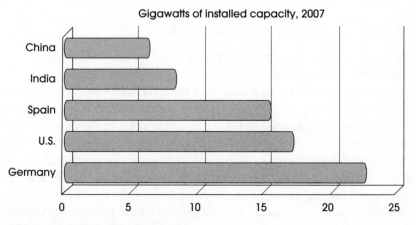

Figure 5.2 Wind Power Leaders
Source: Global Wind Energy Council

Fixing Wind's Flaws

Wind isn't a perfect power source, however. Unlike PV, which operates at basically the same efficiency on a Spanish rooftop as in a mile-square desert array, small wind turbines are less efficient than big ones, so they're not economical for distributed power generation. Turbines tend not to like ice, so wind power isn't a great choice for cold climates. Because you never know when the wind will blow, and therefore when wind farms will feed power to the grid, excessive dependence on wind can cause destabilizing fluctuations in the flow of power. Because of its intermittency, wind can't supply baseline (continuous) power.

Some partial solutions are on the horizon, though. Having multiple wind farms feeding the same grid lessens the intermittency problem, since the wind might be blowing in one place when it's quiet in another. Since hot, sunny days tend to be less windy but more favorable for solar, wind and solar farms feeding the same grid can smooth out power fluctuations. And electricity storage technology is improving. One interesting idea involves using surplus wind power to pump water from a low point to a high point. When the wind dies down, the water is allowed to flow back down through a turbine, generating electricity. Such a system would add maybe 25 percent to the cost of a wind farm but might be worth it if it converts intermittent power to baseline. Another possibility is to use cheap, excess wind energy to make hydrogen, which can then generate power as needed. (See Chapter 8 for other energy storage technologies and Chapter 10 for more on hydrogen.)

Wind Power's Growth Prospects

Right now, wind power is in such demand that it will grow as fast as new turbines can be made, which is about 25 percent annually. In early 2008, the waiting list for many components stretched for more than a year, and though turbine makers were building new plants, demand was keeping pace, making it unlikely that they'll be able to cut their wait times before 2010.

For investors, wind offers a range of choices. (See Table 5.1.) The turbine makers are mostly giants like General Electric, Germany's Siemens, and Denmark's Vestas. Vestas is the biggest pure play turbine maker, with 2007 sales of around $8 billion and projected growth of about 25 percent in 2008. Wind farm operators

Table 5.1   Wind Power Stocks

Company	Ticker/Exchange	Headquarters	Market Value, 6/27/08 ($ millions)
Clipper Windpower	CWPR.L/London	U.K.	1,375
C. Rokas SA	ARCr/Athens	Greece	465
EDF Energies Nouvelles	EEN.PA/Paris	France	3,857
Energiekontor AG	EKTG.F/Frankfurt	Germany	96
Gamesa Tecnologica	GAMbl/Madrid	Spain	11,580
General Electric	GE/NYSE	U.S.	261,000
Greentech Energy Systems	G3E.CO/Copenhagen	Denmark	781
Hansen Transmissions	HSNT/London	Belgium	3,673
Japan Wind Development	2766/Tokyo	Japan	470
Nordex AG	NDXGk/Frankfurt	Germany	2,667
Plambeck Neue Energien AG	PNEGnk/Frankfurt	Germany	191
Renewable Energy Generation	RWE/London	U.K.	221
Repower Systems AG	RPWGn.F/Frankfurt	Germany	2,512
Siemens	SI/NYSE	Germany	99,520
Suzlon Energy	SUZL/Bombay	India	8,046
Theolia	TEO.PA/Paris	France	1,016
Valmont Industries	VMI/NYSE	U.S.	2,680
Vestas Wind Systems	VWS.CO/Copenhagen	Denmark	24,650
Western Wind Energy	WND/TSX	Canada	91

range from the world's largest power companies, like Spanish utilities Iberdrola and Acciona and America's FPL, all the way down to single-farm entrepreneurs. And new entrants are pouring in as quickly as land can be leased and turbines delivered. Then there are the component makers that supply the industry with everything from carbon fiber for turbine blades, to specialized electronics, to information management services. Here again, new companies are forming and private firms are going public, so the supply of interesting, not-yet-widely followed wind power stocks will continue to grow for years (see Table 5.1).

Geothermal

THE HEAT BENEATH OUR FEET

Iceland is not a country that one would normally expect to be powered by its own heat. But it is. Though it's a lot closer to the North Pole than to the equator, it straddles the Mid-Atlantic Ridge, a mostly underwater mountain range that separates the North American and Eurasian tectonic plates. At such boundaries, cracks can form in the earth's crust, allowing magma that's normally hundreds of miles down to bubble up, causing geysers, hot springs, and the occasional volcano.

In the 1970s, Icelanders recognized that this heat was actually a useful form of energy and began using it to warm homes and generate electricity. "Geothermal" power (*geo* meaning earth, *thermal* meaning heat) now supplies a fourth of the country's electricity (the rest comes from hydropower). Most of its buildings are heated with geothermal water, and (envious New Yorkers take note) many Reykjavik sidewalks are heated in winter. Most of its outdoor swimming pools are filled with warm geothermal water, making them comfortable year-round. And since geothermal is almost completely nonpolluting, Reykjavik is now one of the world's cleanest cities.

Not only is geothermal electricity power clean, it's so inexpensive in Iceland that local companies now import bauxite from the Caribbean and refine it into aluminum, a highly energy-intensive process. This combination of cheap power and new industry has transformed Iceland from a poor country into a rich one with the confidence to push the energy envelope. In the coming decade, it plans to use geothermal electricity to make hydrogen to run fuel cells (see Chapter 10) for its cars and fishing boats, thus becoming the first country to be completely powered by renewable energy sources.

Wow. If only we all sat on tectonic boundaries, the energy crisis would end in a puff of volcanic steam. Well . . . as it turns out, a lot of places sit on such boundaries and could, with the right expertise, tap just as much geothermal power as Iceland. And new geothermal technologies now make it possible not only to exploit existing hot springs but also to access and use the earth's heat from pretty much anywhere. As for how much energy this could make available, estimates range from merely huge to completely off the charts. A recent study from the Massachusetts Institute of Technology (MIT) concluded that available geothermal power is several million times greater than current worldwide energy demand.

How Geothermal Works

Let's start with the somewhat disturbing theory that the earth is a big nuclear reactor. At its core, the decay of naturally occurring isotopes under immense pressure produces temperatures of around 7,000 degrees Fahrenheit. This heat radiates outward through a semimolten mantle, eventually diminishing enough to allow a solid crust to form. From our vantage point here on the surface, the further down you go, the hotter it gets. Start drilling on a cold winter day in Siberia, and by the time the drill bit travels a few miles, it's hot enough to boil water. This heat mostly stays down there where it belongs. But every once in a while, a crack forms in the crust, and rainwater seeps down until it meets superheated rock, at which point it vaporizes and rises through a different set of cracks to the surface. The result is a geyser like Yellowstone's Old Faithful or the type of hot spring around which resorts are built. But sometimes hot water doesn't make it all the way to the surface and gets trapped by a layer of impermeable rock, where it becomes a "geothermal reservoir." Drill into it and steam and/or hot water capable of running a turbine is released. Such reservoirs are being discovered all over the world, but like I said, they're most common in tectonically active places like Iceland and along the Pacific Rim's "Ring of Fire."

An Italian prince named Piero Ginori Conti is generally credited with building the first geothermal power plant in Italy in 1913. The first geothermal plant in the United States was built in 1962 at Geysers Field in northern California, which is still the world's largest producing geothermal field. The original technology is still in use, though the future belongs to some newer variants. Here's an overview of the main forms of geothermal power.

Dry Steam

The original version, this kind of plant captures steam at temperatures above 455 degrees Fahrenheit and routs it through a turbine. The process is simple and cheap, but it requires active steam vents, which are rare.

Flash Steam

Most geothermal reservoirs produce hot water rather than steam. "Flash steam" systems capture this water in a pressurized tank on the surface and vent steam (which forms at lower temperatures under pressure) to run a turbine. Lots of reservoirs produce water in an acceptable temperature range, so flash steam still has considerable growth potential. And though both dry and flash steam plants vent carbon dioxide, hydrogen sulfide, and nitric oxide from the underground water, it's generally in such small amounts that these plants are far cleaner than conventional coal or natural gas.

Binary Cycle

This is the technology that has everyone excited. Instead of requiring very hot water or steam, these plants use lower-temperature geothermal water to heat and vaporize a "working fluid" that has a lower boiling point, and use that vapor to power a turbine generator. The geothermal water is never exposed to the air and is injected back into the reservoir, so the plant generates no pollution. And because it can use lower-temperature water, it broadens the number of places where geothermal is a viable resource.

United Technologies' UTC Power division has a line of binary cycle geothermal generators that are cousins of industrial air conditioners—except that they run backward, using heat to produce electricity. They're even made on the same assembly lines as

Carrier (another United Technologies division) air conditioners. "We took a standard commercial product that's being used in high-rise buildings for cooling and reversed it. Instead of a compressor we use the same device with a turbine," says UTC Power president Jan van Dokkum. This turned out to be more complicated than it looked. "What was going to be a two-year project took four years," says van Dokkum. But the process yielded a number of patents, along with the ability to build bigger units that are more efficient than stringing together several smaller ones. And UTC now has several different working fluids suited to different temperature ranges. "We can go anywhere from 200 to 300 degrees," says van Dokkum.

The ability to generate power with lower-temperature water immediately opens up a lot of known but previously uneconomical reservoirs because, in the past, when operators drilled exploratory wells they simply capped and abandoned anything registering less than 250 degrees. So there are hundreds of wells out there that have already been found, just waiting for binary cycle plants. Utah-based Raser Technologies, for instance, is placing UTC units on a number of known low-temperature reservoirs. It's not yet clear how many new reservoirs are out there, because the U.S. Geological Survey has mapped only resources of 350 degrees and above. But van Dokkum estimates that it expands the present market by 60 percent to 80 percent. Meanwhile, many oil wells produce hot water, which drillers now consider a nuisance. Small-scale geothermal units able to turn this water into electricity will both lower utility peak-power requirements and improve the economics of oil drilling.

An example of what becomes possible with low-temperature geothermal is the Chena Hot Springs Resort, which is 60 miles northeast of Fairbanks, Alaska, and way off the grid. Consisting of a few tourist buildings, a greenhouse, and an "ice museum," the resort was originally powered by a noisy, expensive diesel generator but today is energy self-sufficient thanks to two 200-kilowatt UTC power plants that use the hot springs' 165-degree water to generate electricity. Chena is currently the world's lowest temperature commercial geothermal resource.

Geothermal Heat Pumps

Also known as "geoexchange," this variation on the geothermal theme exploits the fact that while air temperature varies with the season and time of day, 6 feet below ground, the earth is usually between 45 degrees and 75 degrees Fahrenheit. Sink some pipes into the ground below a building, circulate liquid through them, connect the pipes to a compressor, and it's possible to use the heat differential between ground and air to both heat and cool a building. Geothermal heat pumps use between 20 percent and 79 percent less electricity than conventional heat pumps. And because they're so simple, they need little maintenance and last a lot longer. The result: a climate control system that's cheap, durable, clean, and quiet. In various polls, the vast majority of people who had installed a geothermal heat pump say they would do so again. This technology is viable almost everywhere and qualifies for a variety of government incentives.

Enhanced Geothermal

Recall from Chapter 3 that in order to keep oil wells producing, petroleum engineers have learned to drill deep shafts and pump in water, which raises well pressure and makes the remaining oil more accessible. It turns out that something similar can produce a geothermal reservoir from scratch. Known as hot-dry-rock, or enhanced geothermal systems (EGS), this involves drilling down to where the rocks are hot, pumping in water, and capturing the steam that rises through another shaft or existing rock fractures. EGS still faces some technical hurdles, including how to create and maintain fractures to let the steam rise without being trapped by nonporous rock and how to inject the water under sufficient pressure. But engineers are making progress, and as drilling technology improves, more of the earth's heat will become available. To sum up, there's a lot of geothermal energy out there, and more is becoming available all the time.

Advantages of Geothermal

Here's a concise listing of geothermal's many benefits:

- It's very clean. Binary cycle plants produce virtually no pollution.
- It's available 24/7. Unlike wind and solar, which are intermittent, a geothermal plant can run continuously, generating baseline power, making it direct competition for coal.
- Because most of the action is underground, geothermal plants have small physical and environmental footprints. This makes them relatively easy to guide through the permitting

process. There are geothermal plants operating successfully in cornfields, tropical forests, and, as you just read, tourist resorts. They could theoretically be sited in the middle of cities, with no adverse pollution or other consequences. The ability to site a geothermal plant close to end users cuts transmission costs, further improving its economics.

- The technology is well understood and easy to mass produce, so a geothermal plant can be installed more quickly than, say, a wind farm, where turbines are on a waiting list.
- It's relatively inexpensive. At $3 to $4 per rated watt, geothermal is comparable to wind and coal and considerably cheaper than solar. And because it has a higher load factor (it runs continuously while solar is down when the sun sets), a geothermal power plant produces far more electricity than a similarly rated PV system.
- It's very low maintenance. With low-temperature binary plants, "There are no pressurized steam loops to worry about, so they can be unmanned," says UTC's van Dokkum.

State of the Market

Estimates of the amount of geothermal power now being generated worldwide range from 9 gigawatts to 12 gigawatts, depending on how geothermal is defined. The United States is the largest producer, with about 3 gigawatts, followed by the Philippines, Mexico, Indonesia, Italy, Japan, New Zealand, and of course, Iceland.

Geothermal's Growth Prospects

Geothermal, both for power generation and climate control, is one of those technologies that sounds almost too good to be true. Right now, the only fault worth mentioning is the theoretical possibility that enhanced geothermal—where operators inject water deep into the ground—might eventually affect the stability of the bedrock, perhaps causing earthquakes. But that's a long way off and not very likely in any event. In the near and intermediate term, geothermal looks like an energy source with a clearly defined future.

The U.S. mountain states and Pacific Coast have vast, mostly untapped geothermal potential, while the countries bordering the Rim of Fire have Iceland-scale resources. Indonesia, for instance, has hundreds of active and extinct volcanoes, giving it geothermal potential upward of 25 gigawatts. But geothermal's growth will probably be slower than that of solar or wind, for three reasons. First, finding new geothermal reservoirs is a bit like drilling for oil: It's expensive, unpredictable, and therefore risky. Second, geothermal plants require big up-front capital investments, limiting the number of potential projects. And third, the world's governments haven't been as forthcoming with subsidies for geothermal as they have for solar and wind. So most estimates now call for geothermal to grow at a single-digit rate in the coming decade. For investors, that's not necessarily a bad thing, since the resulting lower profile increases the odds of finding mispriced stocks. Table 6.1 illustrates the variety of companies in this space. The two biggest makers of geothermal equipment, UTC Power and Connecticut-based Ormat (which dominates the high-temperature side of the market), are both growing quickly. Ormat is the pure play, building, owning and operating geothermal power plants and selling the electricity to local utilities. United Technologies is a conglomerate, of which geothermal is just one small part. But as you'll see in coming chapters, it's also a leader in several other green fields. Independent power

Table 6.1   Geothermal Stocks

Company	Ticker/ Exchange	Headquarters	Market Value, 6/27/08 ($ millions)
Geodynamics	GDY/Australia	Australia	340
C. Rokas SA	ARCr/Athens	Greece	465
Geothermal Resources	GHT.AX/Australia	Australia	22
Nevada Geothermal Power	NGP.V/Toronto	Canada	112
Ormat Technologies	ORA/NYSE	U.S.	2,010
Petratherm	PTR.AX/Australia	Australia	39
Polaris Geothermal	GEO.TO/Toronto	Canada	88
U.S. Geothermal	HTM/AMEX	U.S.	183
Torrens Energy	TEY/Australian Exchange	Australia	15
Western GeoPower	WGP/Toronto	Canada	67
WaterFurnace Renewable Energy	WFI/Toronto	Canada	326

company Calpine is the largest operator of geothermal plants, with 19, but it generates most of its revenues from traditional gas-fired plants. And Canada's WaterFurnace is a leading maker of geothermal heat pumps.

There is also a growing population of exploration and development companies. Today's geothermal is a bit like gold mining, wide open for small operators willing to devote time and capital to discovering and bringing to market a viable resource. Many will succeed, since there's so much geothermal potential out there. Some will turn a single well-run property into a nice earnings stream. Others will roll up less well-capitalized "juniors" and build major producers, just as mining firms do today.

CHAPTER 7

Transportation

GREEN MACHINES

For a painfully clear idea of just how delusional Americans became during the era of cheap oil, take a drive on the nearest freeway at rush hour. You'll see thousands of big, heavy internal combustion vehicles driven by single occupants on long commutes to and from 3,000-square-foot suburban houses. We've designed a continent-spanning society around the assumption that energy would always be cheap and plentiful. As gas creeps toward $5 a gallon, the breathtaking scale of this misallocation of resources has begun to sink in, and the prognosis has become inescapable: One way or another, the gas-guzzler is history. This can happen through the death of suburbia, whereby today's megasubdivisions are deserted by workers moving closer to their jobs and McMansion prices fall below their cost of construction. Or it can be a less wrenching transition in which 15-mile-per-gallon SUVs are replaced by vehicles that go all day on little or no gas, cutting the cost of most commutes and allowing the 'burbs to survive in a familiar, if more modest, form. Which course the transition takes depends on whether the coming generation of superefficient cars and trucks lives up to their promise.

Traditional Hybrids

Back in 1999, Toyota caused a ripple in the tiny part of the car-buying world that cared about fuel economy by introducing an ungainly little stub of a car called the Prius. It had an interesting hook—a battery-powered electric motor that helped out a standard four-cylinder gas engine. The battery was charged when the driver used the brakes, enabling the electric motor to handle stop-and-go driving. The result was better mileage in the city than on the highway and over 40 miles per gallon overall. The Prius was the first mass-produced "hybrid," so called because it combined internal combustion and electric drivetrains in one system. And the timing couldn't have been better. As gas prices rose—and rose and rose—the Prius went from novelty to must-have second car. By 2007, Toyota was selling more than 300,000 of them a year (see Figure 7.1), and every major carmaker was after a piece of the hybrid action. By 2009, car buyers who previously had just a handful of hybrid options will have dozens, ranging from high-mileage econoboxes to full-size SUVs. According to auto consultancy J. D. Power, annual hybrid sales will exceed 1.1 million vehicles in 2014.

There's just one problem: Hybrids don't actually save their owners money. Having two drivetrains instead of one is inescapably expensive, both in terms of the extra gear required and the complexity of making and managing the system. A typical hybrid costs several thousand dollars more than its conventional counterpart and doesn't save nearly enough gas to offset its higher price. And that's before you consider the $5,000 or so to replace the battery pack when it wears out, a prospect that owners of nonhybrids don't have to face. Carmakers are bringing out hybrids because they sell, but—a general rule of thumb for all green investing—if it doesn't

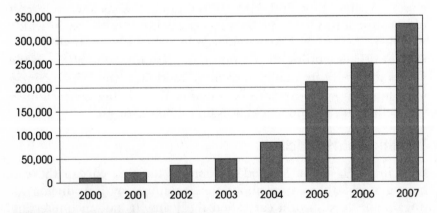

Figure 7.1   Hybrid Vehicle Sales
Source: Electric Drive Transportation Association

make financial sense, no amount of feel-good environmental hype will make it a long-term hit. The conventional hybrid, in short, is merely a transition technology that paves the way for something that really saves money.

Plug-In Hybrids

As soon as the Prius was introduced, enterprising tinkerers started retrofitting it with bigger batteries and onboard AC-to-DC chargers to plug into a household socket. The idea was that starting each day with a fully charged battery would allow the car to go further in electric mode, boosting gas mileage into a range that makes economic sense. Toyota, for reasons of its own, discouraged this practice, threatening to void the warranty on any Prius converted to a plug-in. This, plus the fact that such tinkering is beyond the average person's capability, kept plug-in conversions from becoming a form of mass civil disobedience. But the fact that some people would go to such lengths—and the resulting boost in mileage—wasn't lost on auto executives. Now they're shifting en masse to this configuration, and though plug-in hybrids won't hit the market in serious numbers until 2010, they are potential game changers. Here's a more detailed look.

A plug-in hybrid starts with the standard hybrid configuration of dual internal combustion and electric drivetrains but reverses the emphasis. Whereas a hybrid employs a relatively small battery to handle stop-and-start driving and turns to the internal combustion engine for higher speeds and longer runs, the plug-in hybrid uses bigger batteries and a more powerful electric motor to handle more of the driving, turning to gas only when more power is needed or the batteries are depleted. In some versions, the gas engine serves only to recharge the battery, which provides all the motive power. The first generation of plug-ins will go about 40 miles on a charge. For someone who drives less than that each day, their gas mileage would be effectively infinite.

As for plug-ins' overall mileage, it depends on so many factors that an average is virtually impossible to calculate. Someone who takes long trips would get far less favorable mileage than an around-town driver. This variability presents carmakers and regulators with a bit of a challenge, since they have to calculate and report some kind of mileage number. The Environmental Protection Agency (EPA) has been working on this problem for over a year, and as of early 2008, it had yet to come up with a suitable formula. But whatever the mileage, battery-powered driving looks like a bargain. Electricity rates vary from place to place, but several studies have put the cost of recharging a typical hybrid battery at the equivalent of $0.75 per gallon of gasoline.

Will plug-ins work as advertised? Probably. Most of the required know-how already exists. Efficient electric motors and drivetrains are common, as are small, cheap gas engines. The only thing missing is a battery with sufficient power and reliability, which is why plug-ins aren't ubiquitous in 2008 and why their launch dates keep slipping. But better batteries are coming (see Chapter 8), and the automakers are planning accordingly. Toyota is now road-testing a plug-in hybrid, which it plans to mass produce in 2010. General Motors (GM) is publicizing its Chevy Volt and Saturn Flextreme concept cars, which combine a plug-in hybrid configuration with a "flex" engine that is capable of using several different fuels. Virtually every other major carmaker is aiming for the same launch window with variations on the plug-in theme.

Electric Cars

The advent of plug-in hybrids leads to an obvious question: If a mostly electric car is possible, why not dispense with internal combustion altogether and go completely electric? Wouldn't such a car—with only one relatively simple drivetrain and a single motor—be both cheaper and cleaner? The short answer is "yes, but." *Yes,* a world of mostly electric cars powered by solar- and wind-generated electricity would be a much better place, for a variety of obvious reasons. *But* based on the difficulties carmakers are having with their plug-in hybrid introductions, a viable all-electric car seems to be at least several years away. But, you wouldn't know it from all the activity in this space. In late 2007, I interviewed Michael Potts, CEO of the Rocky Mountain Institute, a Colorado-based green think tank, for a magazine article. Toward the end, I asked him if there was anything that had him especially excited, and he responded,

> Right now this is the first time since the 1930s that there are real plausible new car companies going out and raising money, because the technologies available to transportation are just so groundbreaking. A lot of investors are speculating that the old-line companies are just too stuck in their ways. Right now

there are six or seven electric car start-ups that are getting funding. All have interesting niches and very innovative technologies, in an industry that's been dominated for years by huge multinationals. Some big money is backing them, and there will be a couple of IPOs within eighteen months.

Now that's cool. Start-ups bringing out slick new electric cars that challenge the conventional wisdom of internal combustion, mile-long assembly lines, and dealership networks. No doubt most, if not all, of these guys will lose out to Toyota and BMW, but the fact that they're getting funded implies that some smart money sees a very big opening here, both in terms of business model and technology. So maybe they won't all fail, and among the DeLoreans and Tuckers is a future Porsche. Here are a few of the more interesting start-ups, as of early 2008:

Tesla Motors. The grizzled veteran of this bunch, Tesla Motors was founded in 2003 and, by late 2007, had raised $105 million from mainstream venture capital firms and tech entrepreneurs like PayPal co-founder Elon Musk (who became the company's chairman) and former eBay president Jeff Skoll. Instead of following the Japanese car-maker example of starting at the low end of the market and working its way up, Tesla is emulating the early introduction of cell phones and microwave ovens by building an expensive piece of must-own hardware aimed at people with big bucks and a taste for new toys. Its $109,000 Tesla Roadster is a very fast, very slick, two-seater. With a carbon fiber body and a top speed of 130 miles per hour, it's a sports car first; the fact that it's electric is icing on the cake. As such, it has star power. George Clooney and Matt Damon reportedly put down deposits in 2007, and a lot of other big names will no doubt follow if the car lives up to expectations.

Addressing the Achilles' heel of today's electric cars— heavy batteries that nevertheless deliver inadequate power and range—Tesla bundled 6,831 lithium-ion cells, each about the size of a AA battery, into a 950-pound pack that it claims delivers a range of 200 miles and takes only four hours to recharge.(Again, the next chapter covers battery tech.)The initial response was so positive that Tesla announced plans to start selling the battery packs to other carmakers. But, not surprisingly, the trip from concept to commercial launch has been rocky. In August 2006, the Roadster flunked a 30-mile-per-hour side-impact crash test, necessitating design changes. In September 2007, Tesla cancelled plans to sell its battery pack and pushed back its production schedule into 2008. In December 2007, it announced that because suppliers had failed to deliver the "dual-speed" transmission that would give the Roadster the promised 0-to-60 in four seconds acceleration, the early version won't be that fast. Fixing the transmission will cost another $40 million. Still, look for considerable buzz to accompany the launch of the upgraded Roadster when and if the real transmission is ready in 2009.

Phoenix Motorcars. California-based Phoenix Motorcars is acting as general contractor for a line of electric cars, beginning with a small SUV. It starts with a "glider," or complete vehicle minus the powertrain and fuel system, from a Korean carmaker. Then it buys power plants and battery packs from outside suppliers and contracts with an engineering shop to turn the parts into a working vehicle. The result is an attractive little SUV/pickup with moderate acceleration, a top speed of 100 miles per hour, and a range of 130 miles. One interesting twist is the battery pack, from Reno, Nevada, start-up Altairnano, which can charge in 10 minutes with a high-power commercial rapid charger. This is irrelevant for homeowners but intriguing to large companies that operate vehicle fleets and can afford the specialized hookups. One cab company is said to have ordered 20, while California utility Pacific Gas & Electric has ordered 200. Here again, the delivery schedule has been bumped back from late 2007 to 2009 because of delays in getting the cars through California's air-quality certification process.

Think Electric. Back in 1999, Ford bought a Norwegian electric car start-up called Pivco, renamed it Think Nordic, and pumped $150 million into it in an attempt to build a viable electric car. Like all previous electric vehicles, this one failed. Enter Jan Olaf Willums, a venture capitalist in search of new frontiers who, for $15 million, bought Think's assets, including the design for its next car, called the City. Under

Willums, Think Electric's car and its business model are both radical departures. Instead of building cars and stocking showrooms, Think will build cars to order. Instead of operating a single huge assembly line, it will place a number of small factories near target markets, where technicians will build Citys from prefab parts. Every City will be Internet and Wi-Fi enabled, allowing drivers to access the Internet—and to communicate back and forth with the car itself. A City will e-mail its owner, for instance, when its battery is running low. Because the battery is the most expensive part of an electric car, Think will sell the car but lease the battery. Take the battery out of the equation, and the car might go for as little as $17,000, with a "mobility fee" of $100 to $200 per month that might also include services such as insurance and wireless Internet access. Production of Citys began in Norway in late 2007, and testing was under way in early 2008. A first-year production run of 7,000 was planned.

Zero Motorcycles. California-based Zero is bringing out a line of battery-powered motorcycles that it says are high performance and price competitive. The first model, Zero X, is a $7,500 dirt bike that goes 40 miles on a charge. Next will come bigger street bikes. Because they're electric, Zeros are quiet, which is a big plus from a lot of different angles. As one reviewer noted, the same technology applied to snowmobiles would eliminate the controversy of those vehicles in national parks. But silence has one amusing drawback: Early test riders tended to get off and walk away without turning the engine off. In response, Zero added a safety bracelet that attaches to the bike and cuts off the engine when removed. According to the company, the first run of Zero X bikes sold out in early 2008.

ZENN Motor. Toronto, Canada-based ZENN (which stands for "zero emissions, no noise") has been selling its $15,000 ZENN coupes in the United States since 2006 and has a network of dealers already set up. To call this a "car" might be stretching it, though. With a top speed of 26 miles per hour, it's strictly for tooling around the neighborhood. But for some that's apparently enough, and in any event, ZENN intends to power future models with advanced "ultracapacitor" batteries (see Chapter 8) that will give them a bit more pop.

Project Better Place. Now envision a world populated by electric cars gliding silently around town, running low on juice and looking for a plug, much the same way that today's drivers seek out gas stations. There's a market here, but not necessarily for plugs, since recharging a battery takes an unacceptably long time. What if instead of charging them, tomorrow's "filling" stations simply replace a car's batteries? You pull in, they pop the hood, swap your old batteries for newly charged batteries, and send you on your way. That's the idea behind Project Better Place, a California start-up founded by former SAP Software executive Shai Agassi. Treating the battery like gasoline or oil makes the car cheaper—since batteries are a big part of the initial sticker price—and solves the slow charge problem. By early 2008, Agassi had raised $230 million and was planning a gradual rollout.

Vehicle-to-Grid Electricity

Here's where the plug-in hybrid/electric car story transcends its category. Picture a fleet of these cars being charged overnight with off-peak power and then driven into town by commuters who will spend the day at the office. Thousands of batteries, full of energy downloaded from the grid during the night, represent a huge potential source of peak power. Plug them back into the grid, and they can feed some of that energy back at a time—the middle of the day—when it's most needed. Called "vehicle-to-grid," or V2G, such a system might save money all around. The local utility avoids having to build expensive new peak generating capacity, while the car owner gets paid peak power rates for juice he or she bought during the night for less. The downside is that the extra work might shorten battery life, but several possible solutions are being proposed, including creating a secondary market for batteries that are no longer efficient enough for automotive use but still have a bit of life, and/or having the electric utility actually own the battery and charge customers for its use on their monthly electric bill. When a battery falls below a given performance level, the utility would swap it for a new one and add the old one to solar or wind power storage systems.

Object Lesson: Toyota and GM

Bird in Hand versus Pie in Sky

In the early 1990s, gas was cheap and Americans weren't much interested in fuel economy. Toyota and GM, not surprisingly, responded to this complacency in very different ways. Toyota began moving up the food chain, using its engineering talents to morph Camry into Lexus and strike directly at the heart of the luxury car market. But at the same time, true to its incremental-improvement, small-car culture, it sought to raise its vehicles' fuel economy in the near term, eventually pioneering the hybrid concept. GM, meanwhile, surveyed a world of low gas prices and rising American incomes and concluded that fuel economy wouldn't matter for at least another couple of decades, if ever. So it followed its Big Iron instincts and brought out a line of ever-larger gas-guzzlers that culminated in the T-Rex of the oil age, the Hummer. To prepare for the far-off day when fuel efficiency might matter, GM created a high-profile, rhetorically rich program to leapfrog the whole internal combustion engine paradigm by developing fuel cell vehicles. Chapter 10 explains that technology, but for now, it's sufficient to say that fuel cells might indeed change the world someday. And to many observers, GM's highly public push in that direction made it look like the more advanced company. But today fuel cells are still far from viability, and GM's effort is still longer on press releases than products. Whereas Toyota went for something achievable, if imperfect—the hybrid—in order to be covered should gas once again become expensive, GM used fuel cells as an excuse to avoid the hard work of raising fuel efficiency in the present. Now Toyota is selling all the Priuses it can build, while GM dealerships are

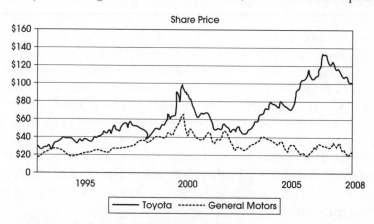

Figure 7.2   Toyota versus General Motors

(*Continued*)

(*Continued*)

quiet places full of large, increasingly dusty SUVs. Figure 7.2 illustrates the stock market's opinion of the two companies' strategies. The moral: Anyone can announce a plan to develop a flashy new green technology. But something less flashy that works in the here and now is a far safer investment. So beware of companies that appear to be using green initiatives as a means to avoid tackling their current problems.

Clean Diesel

I wasn't expecting to include diesel in a discussion of future green engine technologies, since my only experience with it is a neighbor's pickup truck that's so noisy it spooks my dogs. So it was a surprise to find out that a new generation of "clean diesel" engines might be a possible competitor for plug-in hybrids and that carmakers are racing to bring out new models. So here goes: Both diesel and gasoline engines convert the chemical energy of fuel into mechanical energy. But they do so in slightly different ways. A gasoline engine takes in a mixture of gasoline and air, compresses it, and ignites the mixture with a spark plug. The energy released pushes a piston, which eventually turns the wheels. A diesel engine takes in air, compresses it—which raises its temperature—and then injects fuel into the cylinder. When the fuel contacts the hot air, it ignites. Diesel fuel is a bit heavier and contains more energy than the same amount of gasoline. And diesel engines' higher "compression ratio" results in more force being exerted on the piston when the fuel ignites, which gives it more motive power per unit of fuel, which is another way of saying better mileage. And because diesel engines have to be built more solidly to withstand the extra pressure, they tend to last longer. Their better mileage made them briefly popular in the United States after the 1970s oil crises. But they were noisy (as my dogs can attest) and emitted sulfur and nitrogen compounds from their tailpipes. And they weren't very fast. So when oil prices dropped, demand for diesel tapered off. In Europe, where gasoline is taxed more heavily than diesel, they've remained popular, and more than half of the vehicles sold on the Continent are diesel powered.

Now diesel is preparing for another run at the U.S. market, thanks to several developments: The EPA tightened the rules governing diesel in 2006, causing oil refiners to start producing ultra-low-sulfur diesel, frequently referred to as "clean diesel." Combined with exhaust-scrubbing systems that catch most other pollutants and better noise control, the result is an engine that runs cleanly and quietly, with hybrid-level mileage. Small diesels like Volkswagen's Polo Bluemotion seat four adults and get over 60 miles per gallon. At the high end of the market, BMW's Series 3 diesel sedan is fast and comfortable, while getting better than 35 miles per gallon. Virtually every other carmaker has clean diesel models in the pipeline that fall somewhere in between these two. The prognosis: If plug-ins take longer than expected or don't live up to expectations, and if "biodiesel" fuels made from nonfood crops pan out (see Chapter 9), clean diesel might have a window of opportunity.

State of the Market

As of this writing in early 2008, there isn't much of a market. Plug-in hybrids and electric cars are on the drawing board rather than in the showroom, and clean diesel models are just now being introduced. But by 2010, it will be possible to compare and contrast real products and a variety of business models.

Green Vehicles' Growth Prospects

In a word, huge. Demand for efficient, clean vehicles and related gear and infrastructure is almost incalculable (certainly north of $1 trillion in the coming decade). So to the winners in this race will go massive spoils. As for how to invest in the coming transition to cleaner vehicles, the choices are limited at the moment. The major automakers are stuck with an obsolete legacy technology—internal combustion—and won't be primarily plug-in hybrid makers for a decade or more. The electric car start-ups aren't public and, in any event, are too risky for non-venture capitalists. So file green machines away for 2010.

CHAPTER 8

Energy Storage

THE KEY TO A CLEAN-TECH TAKEOVER

Solar and wind produce electricity only when it's sunny or windy, and they will only displace coal if a cost-effective way of storing their excess power is developed. Plug-in hybrids and electric vehicles, meanwhile, will replace internal combustion engines only if they can get suburban commuters to work and back on a single, quick charge. The upshot: For clean tech to take over the world, cheap, powerful energy storage solutions are essential. And they're coming. After decades of ignoring this field, researchers and venture capitalists are pouring in, and interesting news is pouring out. Without doubt, the next generation of batteries and other storage technologies will be a lot better than the current one. But which will end up winning is very much an open question. So let's start by dividing the field into two categories: mobile and stationary.

Mobile Storage

It's easy to power something that just sits there. You plug it in and turn it on, without much regard for the size or weight of the energy source. But if the device you're powering moves around, like a cell phone, laptop, or car, it has to carry its energy along for the ride. Size and weight matter, and all else being equal, the best mobile energy storage technology is the one with the highest energy density (i.e., the ability to pack the most power into the smallest, lightest form). This concept explains the dominance of the internal combustion engine: Gasoline is an extraordinarily efficient way to store energy, with a vastly higher ratio of energy to mass than any existing battery. GM's famous EV-1 electric car needed 1,200 pounds of lead acid batteries just to travel 100 miles on a charge, while a 20-gallon tank of gas weighs only about 150 pounds and can take a 20-mile-per-gallon car 400 miles. But in the coming decade, gasoline's dominance will be challenged by several new energy storage devices. These are among the most promising.

Next-Generation Batteries

Generally speaking, a battery is an enclosed store of chemicals that react under controlled conditions to produce an electrical charge. In some batteries, like the common alkaline versions used in toys and flashlights, the chemical process goes one way, and once it's done, the battery is exhausted. With other kinds of batteries, the chemical reactions are reversible, and a current flowing through them converts the chemicals back to a state where they can again release a charge.

Today's batteries come in several forms and use a lot of exotic components with odd acronyms. Beginning at the common end of the spectrum, the *lead acid* batteries now used to start the typical car are made up of plates (or electrodes) of lead and lead oxide, with an electrolyte solution of water and sulfuric acid in between. Putting those chemicals in contact with those metals produces an electric potential that can be drawn down as needed. And it's reversible: As the engine sends a current back to the battery, it regains its ability to start the car. Lead acid batteries are cheap, well understood, and generally safe. But they're too crude to save us: They hold too little energy per unit of weight, take too long to charge, and need to be maintained and replaced regularly. It's just about over, in other words, for traditional lead acid batteries.

Alkaline batteries sandwich an alkaline electrolyte between electrodes of zinc and manganese oxide. They're cheap but not especially powerful and can't be recharged. But they're adequate for toys and flashlights, which until recently accounted for the bulk of the mobile device market. With no reason to pack more power into a smaller space, little research was directed at small, powerful batteries. Then along came the laptop and cell phone, and suddenly the consumer products industry developed a burning, multibillion-dollar need for light, powerful, long-lasting batteries that can be recharged hundreds of times. The result: a wave of progress that might just culminate in the something powerful enough to allow green tech to really take off.

The first new battery model was *nickel-cadmium,* or NiCd, with potassium hydroxide as the electrolyte and electrodes of nickel hydroxide and cadmium. NiCds are rechargeable, which makes them acceptable for digital cameras. But they lack the energy density to run a hybrid vehicle. Next came *nickel-metal hydride,* or NiMH, which is similar to NiCd but replaces cadmium with a hydrogen-absorbing alloy. A NiMH battery has two or three times the capacity of a comparable NiCd, which makes it adequate for the secondary role played by a traditional hybrid vehicle's battery. But it still lacks the energy density necessary to run a plug-in hybrid or an all-electric car.

This brings us to a battery technology called *lithium-ion* (Li-ion), with electrodes of lightweight lithium and carbon. Currently the battery of choice for laptops and cell phones, its power-to-weight ratio is better than NiCd and five times that of a conventional lead acid battery. It holds a charge longer and can be recharged more often. As you'll recall from the previous chapter, next-generation plug-in hybrids and electric vehicle makers hope to use such batteries in various configurations. But the lithium-ion batteries on the market in early 2007 were far from perfect. For one thing, they tended to burst into flames, which is a problem for laptops but more than a problem at 70 miles per hour on the highway with the kids strapped into the back seat. They also took a lot longer to recharge than a gas tank takes to refill. And they still lacked the power to give an electric car a range comparable to today's internal combustion models. The safety issues in particular caused most major automakers to push their heavily hyped plug-in hybrid introductions back from 2008 to 2010 or later.

But the next generation of Li-ion batteries might do the trick. In late 2007, Nevada start-up Altairnano announced "nanostructured electrodes" that lengthen battery life, increase stability, and—this is very big—allow its batteries to recharge within a few minutes. Indiana-based EnerDel claimed to have a fully functional Li-ion battery pack all ready to go for the hybrid market. And Toshiba announced a "super charge ion battery" that recharges up to 90 percent of its energy in just five minutes and lasts a decade or more. Meanwhile, labs around the world are reporting dramatic progress on both safety and power. Chapter 24 mentions a few of the more promising breakthroughs.

Ultracapacitors

Wouldn't it be ironic, after all those lithium-ion breakthroughs, if batteries turned out *not* to be the solution? Well . . . meet the capacitor, a common electronic component that stores energy as positive and negative static charges on two electrodes separated by an insulator. It releases its charge almost instantly, as when you walk across a carpet in bare feet and touch a metal surface (or your unsuspecting spouse), producing a little spark. Pound for pound, capacitors hold just a fraction of the charge of a lithium-ion battery, but they're cheap, nonpolluting, can be charged quickly, and don't wear out. So the idea of scaling them up to battery size and beyond has always held an attraction. And lately some of the technical hurdles appear to have been cleared. The amount of electricity that a capacitor can store, for instance, is limited by the size of its electrodes—the greater the surface area, the more powerful the charge. This is exactly the kind of problem that engineers are good at solving, and in the past few years, several solutions have been developed, including giving electrodes a jagged and/or pitted nanoscale texture, thus increasing surface area without increasing size, and combining traits of capacitors and batteries to produce chemical/electric hybrid batteries. The result of this and other work is a new generation of "supercapacitors" that are now used in hybrid vehicles to capture the energy of braking and recharge the batteries. A GM truck model even uses a supercapacitor instead of a lead acid battery for starting.

Still, there are limits to how much power supercapacitors can store because existing insulators take up too much space in relation to the capacitor's charge to meet the power and size requirements of a hybrid vehicle. Enter EEStor, a secretive Texas company that recently announced a huge leap in performance with what is now being called an "ultracapacitor." EEStor uses a barium titanate insulator that it claims allows it to store twice the energy per unit of mass as a lithium-ion battery, at a lower cost. And this, remember, is with fast charging and zero pollution. Claims this radical are both common in hot industries and usually baseless, with the company or researcher making the claim generally disappearing without a trace.

So it was easy to dismiss rumors of EEStor's ultracapacitor when they first surfaced. But then ZENN Motor, after seeing a working model, bought 3.8 percent of EEStor for $2.5 million—valuing the whole company at $66 million—and announced plans to equip its next-generation electric cars with ultracapacitors. And in early 2008, defense contractor Lockheed Martin bought the exclusive international rights to EEStor's ultracapacitors for military and homeland security applications. So perhaps this is one of those rare too-good-to-be-true inventions that turns out to be both good and true.

Stationary Storage

For intermittent power sources like solar and wind, the ability to store excess electricity and make it available as needed spells the difference between producing baseline power—the most desirable kind—and being just a secondary source that the grid turns to after it has all the coal- and gas-fired plants it needs. Until very recently, the only commercially available form of stationary storage was a roomful of "deep cycle" lead acid batteries that were far too costly and high maintenance to be a viable large-scale solution. But lately, several more efficient stationary storage technologies have been developed. One of the most promising is a new generation of large fuel cells, which we will discuss at length in Chapter 10. Below are some of the other new technologies:

Flow Battery

Traditional batteries are limited by the finite amount of electrolyte they contain. That's okay for a laptop or even a plug-in hybrid because they're mobile and can only carry so much weight. But for a stationary application where weight and space are not so important, it's possible to create a battery that, instead of enclosing electrodes and electrolytes in a self-contained unit, has external tanks filled with electrolytes that circulate through the system, flowing as needed (hence the name "flow battery"). Because the external tanks make it possible to build flow batteries in pretty much any size, they're a possible solution for large-scale stationary storage. The larger the tanks, the more electricity the battery can store, and recharging is as simple as refilling the tanks. Several types of flow battery will be on the market in 2008, and according to the early reviews, they're cheap to build and easy to manage. One company that has attracted a fair amount of venture capital and plans to launch a line of flow batteries in 2008, called L-Cells, is Indian start-up Deeya Energy. From its marketing materials:

> The lifetime of a Deeya L-Cell is 7 years, after which it can be refurbished with minimal cost to run for another 7 years, *ad infinitum*. The L-Cells require minimal or no maintenance during this period. They are temperature independent and can be placed in an outside environment. Most importantly, they can be charged very fast. A 4-hour system can be charged in about 2 hours. Deeya L-Cells are effectively 3 times cheaper than Lead-Acid batteries, and 10–20 times cheaper than NiMH, Li-Ion, and Fuel Cell options.

In January 2008, Deeya received $15 million from a group of venture capitalists, which it will use to build a factory in India. Another flow battery maker, Canada-based VRB Power Systems, was actively marketing its batteries in early 2008, claiming "the lowest ecological impact of all energy storage technologies." By the time this book is released, these and several other brands of flow batteries should be generating comparisons with other kinds of stationary storage.

Flywheels

A flywheel is, like the name implies, a kind of flying wheel. It sits on a very low-friction support and, once set in motion, tends to continue, in effect storing the kinetic energy used to set it spinning. The energy is then recaptured and turned into electricity by slowing the wheel. For a flywheel to work, it has to be able to spin for a long time with virtually no friction, so modern versions are made of light but durable composites and spin in a vacuum to eliminate air friction. The newest designs use magnetic levitation to decrease friction even further, while some prototypes use high-temperature superconductor bearings.

On paper, flywheels are nonpolluting, cost-effective, and durable, which makes them a conceptually elegant way to store power generated by a solar or wind farm. The commercialization process has just begun, so by decade's end we'll know what role, if any, flywheels will play. An early entrant is Massachusetts start-up Beacon

Power, which offers a 20-megawatt storage system made up of 200 flywheels and associated gear that it claims can cost-effectively store the excess power from a wind or solar plant and then feed it back onto the grid as needed.

Compressed Air Energy Storage

For a wind farm lucky enough to be sited over an underground salt cavern or abandoned mine, it's possible to generate electricity at night, when the grid doesn't need it, and run a compressor that pumps air into a cavern. The next day, when demand is highest, the air is allowed to rush back out to raise the efficiency of a gas turbine, which generates electricity for sale at high peak rates. Unlike batteries, which wear out in a matter of years, underground caverns are effectively permanent. According to the U.S. Department of Energy's Sandia National Labs, compressed air energy storage (CAES) is a low-cost, environmentally benign way to store large volumes of power.

There are now two operational CAES facilities, one in Germany and one in Alabama, with at least two more planned. The first, due to go online in Iowa in 2011, will pump air into a cavern 3,000 feet underground and might be able to store about 20 weeks' worth of air. Another in West Texas is a collaboration of utility TXU and Shell WindEnergy that will store the nighttime output of a Shell wind farm. Other potential CAES sites are being explored in New Mexico and on the Gulf Coast. Nationally, the Electric Power Research Institute estimates that more than 85 percent of the United States has subterranean features that could support CAES storage.

Pumped Hydroelectric Storage

Recall from Chapter 5 that it's possible to use excess electricity to pump water from a lower to a higher reservoir and then, when more power is needed, let the water run back down through a turbine. There are over 100 pumped storage facilities in the world, the largest of which can put out over a gigawatt of electricity for days at a time. Pumped storage appears to have potential for offshore wind farms. A Netherlands-based energy consultancy recently proposed building an "energy island" in the North Sea containing a below-sea-level container that could be flooded to generate peak power and emptied by pumps run by nighttime wind power.

State of the Market

New entrants are piling in. In early 2008, Johnson Controls opened what it claims is the world's first factory dedicated exclusively to manufacturing lithium-ion batteries for electric and hybrid vehicles. Japanese electronics giants like Sanyo and Sony, which currently dominate the market for laptop and cell phone batteries, are gearing up for hybrids. And a slew of new American companies such as A123 Systems and Valence Technology are hoping to leapfrog established battery makers with superior technology. Right now the market is fluid, to put it mildly, since in early 2008 it was still not proven that any lithium-ion battery would work in plug-in hybrids. The story is the same (though a little less frenetic) with the other new energy storage solutions: A range of companies are introducing products aimed at one or more of these markets, and buyers of storage tech are evaluating them.

Table 8.1   Energy Storage Stocks

Company	Ticker/ Exchange	Headquarters	Market Value, 6/27/08 ($ millions)
Altair Nanotechnologies	ALTI/NASDAQ	U.S.	146
Capstone Turbine	CPST/NASDAQ	U.S.	622
Ceres Power Holdings	CWR/London	U.K.	261
Enersys	ENS/NYSE	U.S.	1,640
Johnson Controls	JCI/NYSE	U.S.	17,101
Maxwell Technologies	MXWL/NASDAQ	U.S.	243
Procter & Gamble (Duracell)	PG/NYSE	U.S.	184,650
Quantum Fuel Systems	QTWW/NASDAQ	U.S.	230
Saft Groupe	S1AEUR.PAp/Paris	France	781
Sanyo Electric	6764.T/Tokyo	Japan	4,669
Sony	SNE ADR/NYSE	Japan	44,450
Ultralife Batteries	ULBI/NASDAQ	U.S.	197
Valence Technology	VLNC/NASDAQ	U.S.	569

Energy Storage's Growth Prospects

The next few years will see a free-for-all in which batteries, capacitors, and all the rest scale up and slim down and generally become far more efficient. Then we'll discover what works where. The one certainty is that the market is huge. Global battery sales already exceed $55 billion annually, and with the advent of plug-in hybrids and the proliferation of wind and solar farms, demand for energy storage could easily double in just a few years. Once again, however, as of early 2008, it is not at all clear which companies or technologies will win. By 2010, the picture should be a lot clearer. In the meantime, a list of currently available energy storage stocks is presented in Table 8.1.

CHAPTER 9

Biofuels

MILES PER ACRE

Human civilization is maybe 10,000 years old, and for all but 200 of those years, we got most of our energy from plants in the form of firewood. The recent detour into fossil fuels is understandable: Oil and coal were cheap and abundant at first, and there weren't enough trees to power a modern global economy. But with the age of fossil fuels about to end, a case can be made that it's time to return to the old way of doing things, updated with modern technology. Plants, after all, are nature's solar energy storage devices. They convert sunlight into stalks and leaves that can, in theory, be tapped to make electricity or fuel. And since they sequester carbon when they grow, converting them to energy merely puts back what they've taken from the atmosphere. That is, "biofuels" are carbon neutral.

Returning to Our Roots

Biofuels also have other (albeit still theoretical) advantages. As agricultural products, biofuel crops should be less volatile than oil. If prices go up, we just plant more. And because most countries, the United States included, can grow their own biofuel crops and convert them to gasoline substitutes, biofuels would allow today's oil-importing countries to stop sending all their money to OPEC, and instead give it to their own tax-paying, incumbent-voting farmers. The result: energy and food security in one sweetly popular policy initiative.

But wait, there's more. It costs just a few hundred dollars to convert a conventional internal combustion engine to run on some biofuels, and since the infrastructure already exists for handling liquid fuels, replacing gasoline with the right biofuels wouldn't require a lot of new trucks or pipelines. Compared to the $3,000 or so per car cost of hybrids and the who-knows-what it will cost to convert to a full-blown hydrogen economy (see Chapter 10), biofuels look simple and cheap. Evolutionary rather than revolutionary—a return to our roots, so to speak.

Brazil is a good example of how this might work. It has spent the past decade developing the ability to turn sugarcane into ethanol, which can be used in place of gasoline. The Brazilian transportation system now runs primarily on this locally produced fuel, which is both cheaper than gasoline and immune from Middle East supply disruptions. So how do the rest of us get from here to there? The key is to find plants that

- Produce an acceptable amount of energy without unacceptable side effects.
- Can be "optimized" through the development of new, higher-yielding strains.

Then we have to figure out how to extract their energy ever more cheaply and in ever-larger amounts. In other words, the technology has to scale, and "miles per acre" has to soar. We're not there yet, but some of the approaches now being tried offer reason for hope.

Corn Ethanol: Farm Subsidy in Drag?

The first biofuel to be widely used in the United States was ethanol, an alcohol derived from corn. It was first because it's easy, rather than especially good. Corn is something American farmers know how to grow in vast quantities, and American truckers and railroads know how to ship. To turn it into ethanol, the corn is ground up and processed using heat, water, and enzymes to convert the liquefied starch to sugars, which are fermented into ethanol and carbon dioxide. The ethanol is then shipped to refiners, which mix it with their gasoline and sell it to gas stations.

From the U.S. government's standpoint, corn-based ethanol initially looked like a winner, for the reasons we previously covered: It would wean the country from imported oil and put more money into the pockets of farmers and distillers, many of whom live in crucial swing states. And because it comes from a plant, it was thought to be carbon neutral. As a result, the United States began encouraging ethanol production a decade ago by requiring refiners to mix it with their gasoline and by effectively banning competing gasoline additives.

It worked. "Big Corn" is now a power to rival Big Oil in the U.S. Farm Belt, and ethanol plants now operate in every corn-producing region. U.S. ethanol production soared from 1.6 billion gallons in 2000 to 7 billion gallons in 2007. And the amount of corn devoted to ethanol has tripled (see Figure 9.1).

Unfortunately, to call corn ethanol flawed is, to steal a line from humorist Dave Barry, like calling the sun "warm." Growing corn and turning it into ethanol is highly energy intensive at every step of the process. And because ethanol is a less efficient fuel than gasoline, it provides less power per gallon. The net result is that producing corn ethanol by current methods buys humanity little or nothing in the way of fossil fuel savings or CO_2 reductions.

And that's the good—or less bad—news. As corn is diverted to ethanol, corn prices are rising. Since corn sweeteners and starches are found in most processed foods, and corn is one of the main things growers feed their pigs, cows, and chickens, the higher prices are rippling through the food chain. And because farmland is being converted from other grains to corn (and soy in Europe to make

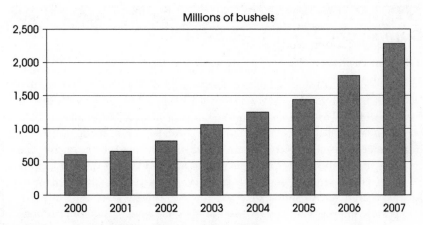

Figure 9.1   Corn Used in Ethanol Production
Source: Renewable Fuels Association

biodiesel), other agricultural commodities, like wheat and soybeans, are way up, too. The soaring price of wheat actually caused Italian consumers to stage a one-day pasta-buying strike in late 2007.

In the end, it was all for naught: When analysts finally got around to running the numbers, it turned out that for corn ethanol to replace a significant part of U.S. oil imports would require pretty much all the available farmland, thus sending food prices through the roof. *And,* icing on the rancid cake, because ethanol is corrosive, it can't be shipped in existing pipelines, nor can it be run in large concentrations in most of today's cars.

So are the massive subsidies now being lavished by Congress on Big Corn simply wasted money when there's neither time nor money to waste? Yes and no. Corn ethanol is clearly not a solution in and of itself, so the case can be made that we might be better off devoting less (or no) effort to it. On the other hand, the expense isn't as big as it seems because corn ethanol subsidies, by pumping up the price of corn and other grains, have lessened the need for payments under existing farm subsidy plans. According to some estimates, ethanol subsidies actually save the government more than they cost. And they've helped create a biofuel infrastructure that can, with a little tweaking, accommodate better fuels when they come along. So think of corn ethanol as a transition technology rather than the disastrous dead end that some claim.

Object Lesson: VeraSun

Subsidies Alone Won't Do It

Early in this decade, corn ethanol appeared to have all the attributes of a huge winner. It solved a big problem—our dependence on foreign oil—and it had the backing of the U.S. government, which appeared ready to force refiners to use ever-greater amounts of it in their formulations. So when South Dakota-based ethanol maker VeraSun went public in 2006, it was met with a fittingly enthusiastic reception. Its market cap on the day of its IPO was $3 billion, or nearly three times its annual revenue. And it delivered operationally—sort of. In its two years as a public company, its sales soared, just as you'd expect with the government mandating its product's use in every gallon of gas. But at the same time, several other things happened: First, ethanol companies were springing up all over the Farm

Belt to get in on the government's largesse, causing the supply of ethanol to soar and its price to fall. In the fourth quarter of 2007, VeraSun sold twice as much ethanol, year over year, but at an average price per gallon of 14 percent less. On the raw material front, corn was $3.81 a bushel, compared to $3.23 a year earlier. The result was a classic margin squeeze, with earnings falling from $0.27 a share to $0.04. While the business was deteriorating, the investment community was hearing about ethanol's many drawbacks and concluding that fuel made from food was a dead end. By early 2008, VeraSun's stock was down by about 70 percent from its post-IPO high. The lesson: Not everything sold as "green" is either green or a viable business. Some things just don't work, and the experts frequently miss the flaws early on.

Cellulosic Ethanol: Not Food

If all plants store energy in their cells, then why choose food crops for biofuel? There must be plenty of other plants that produce energy without driving up the price of pasta. And it turns out that there are. Everything from wood chips to grass clippings to "energy crops" like switchgrass and jatropha are potential biofuel sources. But unlocking their energy is tricky. Whereas corn starch is easy to break down into alcohol, the potential energy in many other plants is located in their cellulose, which, along with lignin, forms the tough cell walls of stalks and leaves. Because cellulose and lignin evolved to protect cells from the elements and predators, they don't break down easily. But nature has its ways. Soil bacteria use enzymes to digest plant matter, cows and other ungulates have second stomachs full of microorganisms that turn grass and leaves into energy, and termite guts work similar transformations on wood. So it's doable. The challenge is to do it cheaply and on an industrial scale.

In general terms, cellulosic ethanol is produced by first treating grass, wood chips, or whatever with chemicals to break down the cell walls and expose the cellulose. Then enzymes, called cellulases, are added to convert the cellulose to sugars. Add yeast or bacteria to ferment the sugars into ethanol, then refine and purify it, and you've got your fuel. Every step in this process is well understood, scalable, and cheap—except the one involving cellulase. The enzymes used today to make cellulosic ethanol are descended from a tropical fungus named *Trichoderma reesei* that was discovered during World War II, consuming soldiers' tents in the South Pacific. Today's selectively bred versions are faster, but not sufficiently so. Commercially produced cellulases are adequate for high-margin work like fading blue jeans, but they are far too slow and expensive to make commercial-scale fuel. So the race is on to find—or build—the perfect cellulase. Researchers are scouring rain forests and garbage dumps for microorganisms that may have already found a solution. Others are trying to evolve and/or engineer better microorganisms in the lab. And they're devoting serious resources to the search: Denmark-based Novozymes, the world's leading supplier of cellulases, has a team of over 100 researchers focused exclusively on cellulosic enzymes. The Holy Grail of this effort is a bug that does it all, eating cellulose and excreting ethanol or other fuels, a process called consolidated bioprocessing. And—par for the cleantech course—promising results are pouring out of labs around the world. Several groups claim to have lowered the cost of ethanol from $5 a gallon to $1 in the past few years.

Other researchers are going chemical rather than biological, using techniques borrowed from oil refining and petrochemicals to release the energy in cellulose, in some cases turning it into fuels like diesel that are easier to transport and use than ethanol. Variations of two general approaches are being tried: One mixes the material with steam to produce "synthesis gas" (also called syngas or synthgas), consisting of hydrogen and carbon monoxide. With additional processing, syngas can be converted to liquid fuels. The second approach involves creating a product that resembles oil that can then be refined into liquid fuel.

Biofuel Salad Bar

Assuming at least one of the many experimental processes works—and indications are that several will—the next step is to choose a biomass to turn into tomorrow's black gold. There are several leading contenders:

> **Switchgrass.** Here's a bit of irony: When Europeans arrived in the United States and began migrating westward, they

eventually came to the Great Plains, hundreds of miles of rolling hills and tall grasses. Deeming the grasses useless, they proceeded to plow them under to plant corn, wheat, and soy and paved the rest for highways and subdivisions. The grasses were relegated to the periphery of the farm economy or pockets of wild land. But now, as factory farms and suburbs drain the world of oil and natural gas, those grasses are getting a second look, and they're turning out to be one of the things that might save the factory farm and suburban lifestyle from extinction.

Take switchgrass, a big ugly plant that gets prettier the more you learn about it. One of the dominant grasses on the old Great Plains, it grows fast, can reach 10 feet in height, needs relatively little water, and can thrive in a wide range of environments and soils. A few farmers already grow it, either as forage for livestock or as ground cover to control erosion (its roots extend nearly as far below ground as its stalks grow above, which holds soil in place). It can be cut and bailed like hay using existing combines. And it's a hardy, adaptable perennial, so once established in a field, it can be harvested annually or semiannually for 10 years or more before replanting is needed. And because it has multiple uses—as ethanol feedstock, forage, and ground cover—a farmer who plants switchgrass knows he'll find a use for it.

Experimental switchgrass plots are yielding enough to make 1,000 gallons of ethanol annually per acre. And what isn't used to make ethanol can be burned to generate energy to run the process. Early results indicate that switchgrass can produce ethanol equal to about five times the energy required to obtain it. That's far better than corn. Switchgrass also removes considerably more CO_2 from the air than corn, sequestering it in its roots. In short, switchgrass has a lot of theoretical promise as an energy crop, and we'll soon find out if reality matches theory. Massachusetts-based Mascoma, a start-up formed to commercialize the research of Dartmouth professor and biofuel pioneer Lee Lynd, recently raised $60 million to build several plants, including one in Tennessee that will use specially designed microorganisms to convert switchgrass to ethanol. Production is slated to begin in 2009.

Forest Waste. The lumber business doesn't use anything close to the whole tree. Branches and bark are left on the forest floor during logging and sawdust and wood chips on the sawmill floor during processing. Figure out how to turn this wood into energy, and you've got a free feedstock that doesn't require synthetic fertilizer, usurps no farmland, and doesn't disturb the price of any other commodity. That's the rationale behind a Georgia biomass-to-fuel plant being built by Colorado-based Range Fuels. Range employs "a two-step thermo-chemical process" to produce cellulosic ethanol from pine chips and other waste from local softwood logging operations. By late 2008, the verdict will be in on whether this process lives up to billing, but the early claims are impressive. Range—which has the enthusiastic backing of major clean-tech venture capitalist Vinod Khosla, among others—describes the process as "self-sustaining, with virtually no waste products, very low levels of greenhouse gases, and high yields of clean ethanol."

Other Plant and Industrial Waste. California-based BlueFire Ethanol now operates several facilities in Japan that coat things like urban trash and wheat straw with sulfuric acid to free up the cellulose, and turn the resulting sugars into ethanol. The company claims the process works on pretty much any kind of agricultural waste, from energy crops to wood waste to paper and leaves. With funding from the U.S. Department of Energy, it's building an Irvine, California, pilot plant that will go online in late 2008. Factories, meanwhile, throw off all kinds of organic material that can theoretically be turned into fuel using processes similar to what works for plant cellulose. In 2007, GM took an equity stake in the Illinois start-up Coskata, and it is funding a demonstration plant to produce ethanol out of GM's factory waste and nonrecyclable car parts. Coskata's process is a cross between the biological and chemical approaches described earlier. It begins by turning waste into a syngas mixture of carbon monoxide and hydrogen and then feeds the gas to specially bred anaerobic microbes that turn it into ethanol. The GM plant will, the participants claim, turn otherwise useless waste into energy, while using relatively little water.

Biodiesel: Again, Not Food

Diesel fuel powers engines in which pressure rather than a spark causes combustion. It's big in Europe and, thanks to a new generation of quieter, cleaner diesel engines, might see dramatic growth in the United States and elsewhere. So a renewable source of this fuel would have a big potential market. Biodiesel's story is similar to that of ethanol: Today's version is made from vegetable sources like soy and palm oil. But that's a dead end, for a variety of reasons. First, these sources don't generate the yields per acre necessary to scale up and lower costs. Their trajectory, to use a term that's becoming popular in clean-tech investing, is insufficiently steep. Second, there are consistency problems when utilizing fuels from different feedstocks, which results in biodiesel with varying properties, quality, and consistency. One 2007 survey of biodiesel samples found that half of them failed to meet basic standards. Third, palm oil comes from the tropics, so ramping up production means cutting down rain forests that are far more valuable than a marginal bit of auto fuel. But the biggest problem is that soy and palm oil, like corn, are foods, and their diversion to fuel raises prices. Palm oil especially is a staple of Asia's poorest families, and its rising price is already causing real hardship.

But for every problem presented by palm- and soy-derived diesel, oil from jatropha, a hardy, drought-resistant perennial, appears to offer a solution. Jatropha grows on marginal land, so it doesn't compete with food crops. Not only isn't it food but it's inedible and is frequently used as a living fence to keep cattle in and sand out. It can survive for 50 years, and its seeds yield oil equal to 30 percent or more of their weight. Lots of big players are betting on its commercialization: In 2007, British Petroleum and British biodiesel producer Dl Oils formed a joint venture to plant nearly 3 million acres of jatropha in Africa, with the goal of meeting 18 percent of Europe's biodiesel needs by 2011. And California-based SE-Energy Technology is building the largest U.S. biodiesel plant, using primarily Mexican jatropha, in Virginia. In early 2008, millions of acres of jatropha were either growing or being planted around the world.

Biomass: Just Burn It

Once upon a time, biofuels like wood and cow dung were simply gathered and burned for heat, light, or energy. This was both straightforward and carbon neutral. Plants captured the carbon, fire released it, and nature stayed in balance. It was only when we started burning the stored carbon held in oil, natural gas, and coal that the balance was upset. So the idea of returning to the old ways of generating power has a simplicity that's attractive—assuming there's a fuel source that doesn't involve cutting down the world's remaining forests. A few possibilities have emerged in recent years, the most interesting of which is a tall decorative grass called miscanthus. Scientists have been growing test fields of it and have found that it yields acceptable amounts of energy and can be mixed with coal and burned in existing power plants.

State of the Market

Governments around the world continue to support corn-based ethanol and soy-based biodiesel with mandates and subsidies, despite their increasingly visible flaws. So production will continue to rise, and new plants will continue to be built. But soaring food prices and the realization that first-generation biofuels are not environmentally benign have forced a rethinking of the whole enterprise that will likely lead most governments to withdraw some of their support.

Table 9.1   Biofuel Stocks

Company	Ticker/ Exchange	Headquarters	Market Value, 6/27/08 ($ millions)
Archer Daniels Midland	ADM/NYSE	U.S.	21,200
Andersons	ANDE/NASDAQ	U.S.	753
Aventine Renewable Energy	AVR/NYSE	U.S.	199
Bunge	BG/NYSE	U.S.	12,820
BlueFire Ethanol	BFRE.OB/NASDAQ	U.S.	96
D1 Oils	DOO.L/London	U.K.	43
Green Plains Renewable	GPRE/NASDAQ	U.S.	48
Novozymes	NZYMb/Copenhagen	Denmark	6,035
OriginOil	OOIL.OB/NASDAQ	U.S.	59
VeraSun	VSE/NYSE	U.S.	710

The future lies with the next generation, and by the end of 2008, the data flowing from pilot plants should make it possible to identify some potential winners.

Biofuel's Growth Prospects

Given the progress that's being made on multiple fronts, it's likely that a decade hence, some combination of cellulosic ethanol, biodiesel, and biomass (along with other biofuels like butanol) will supply a significant part of humanity's energy. But the investment angle is not yet clear. First-generation biofuels aren't worthy of much enthusiasm, even though government mandates appear to guarantee a few more years of strong demand. And none of the half dozen promising next-generation biofuel processes and feedstocks have proven themselves commercially. This market, in short, is yet another work in progress, but a potentially big one. By 2010, it should be possible to build a portfolio of high-growth, moderate-risk biofuel stocks. In the meantime, Table 9.1 presents some of the biofuel stocks that were available in mid-2008.

CHAPTER 10

The Hydrogen Economy

A DREAM DEFERRED

For most of the past decade, small but influential groups of energy experts have been arguing that the time has come to abandon the whole fossil fuel experiment in favor of something better: hydrogen. The most abundant substance in the universe, it contains more energy per unit of weight than any other fuel. And it's clean: A hydrogen-powered fuel cell emits literally no harmful pollutants, just a dribble of pure water. A hydrogen-based economy, therefore, would be both clean and secure—and quiet, since fuel cell–powered vehicles are virtually silent. It's an attractive prospect.

Hydrogen ICE and Fuel Cells

The shortest path to hydrogen is also the most familiar. With a few upgrades, including a better-insulated fuel tank, specialized cooling equipment, fuel injectors, and valves, today's vehicles could be converted to burn hydrogen. Because hydrogen has a very wide combustion range, engines burning it can run smoothly in "lean" mode, producing easier starts and higher fuel economy. And because it burns cleanly, hydrogen internal combustion engines (ICE) meet the world's most stringent emissions standards. The BMW Hydrogen 7 concept car, for instance, goes 133 miles per hour, can travel 125 miles on a tank of hydrogen, and has a separate tank for gasoline if hydrogen isn't available. Most reviewers say it drives like its gas-burning counterpart—which is to say really well.

The downside of hydrogen ICE is efficiency. Because hydrogen requires energy to produce and store, it's less efficient from "well to tank" than gasoline. Internal combustion engines, meanwhile, are a relatively inefficient way to convert a fuel to power. Combine the two, and you get results that, while possibly acceptable in the near term, aren't a long-range solution. So think of hydrogen ICE as a transitional technology to drive the build-out of a hydrogen-based infrastructure.

Which brings us to the fuel cell—the real engine, so to speak, of the hydrogen economy. In much the same way that a battery brings different substances together to produce reactions that, in turn, produce electricity, a typical fuel cell exposes hydrogen to a catalyst (usually platinum) that splits the hydrogen into protons and electrons. A membrane allows the protons to pass unimpeded to combine with oxygen to form water. Electrons, however, can't cross this membrane and are forced to take a longer route through wiring outside the cell, producing electricity that powers an electric motor. The water vapor and waste heat are released through the exhaust. No greenhouse gases, no acid rain, no money flowing to nuclear-armed psychopaths. And because fuel cells operate like batteries, they can participate in vehicle-to-grid power systems, feeding power to the grid while their owners are at work. It's easy to see why so many people love this technology.

The other reason fuel cells are so interesting is that they're two to three times more efficient than internal combustion. This more than offsets the lower well-to-tank efficiency of hydrogen, producing a highly efficient vehicle that can cover twice the distance of a conventional car on the same amount of energy. In 2008, fuel cell concept cars were operating at efficiencies comparable to hybrids, with most industry observers predicting continued dramatic gains. Based on the progress of the recent past, this seems like a safe bet: In 1994, when Canadian fuel cell maker Ballard Power partnered with German automaker Daimler on a prototype fuel cell vehicle, the fuel cell took up the entire back of a van. A decade later, fuel cells were small enough to fit into a compact car without sacrificing passenger space, at a fraction of the 1994 cost. The U.S. Department of Energy calculates that the system cost for automotive fuel cells fell from $275 per kilowatt in 2002 to $95 per kilowatt in 2008 and projects a further decline to $60 per kilowatt in 2009.

The target is $30 by 2015, which is a bit lower than the current cost for a gasoline engine.

Today, virtually all the major carmakers have fuel cell vehicle programs. GM's Fuel Cell Development Center in New York and has a public goal of being the first company to sell a million fuel cell vehicles. Toyota is reportedly spending $800 million annually on fuel cells, and Daimler and Ford are collaborating on new versions of the technology.

The Hydrogen Road Map

From an engine standpoint, the path from here to hydrogen nirvana looks fairly clear: Start burning it in internal combustion engines now, and bring fuel cells online sometime in the coming decade. But the engine is just half the puzzle. The other half involves figuring out how to make enough cheap hydrogen and build a network of fueling stations. And not everyone is convinced that this is either possible or desirable. The Cato Institute, a highly respected libertarian think tank, dismisses the idea of a hydrogen economy as a fantasy, while others call it a smokescreen to avoid raising fuel efficiency in the here and now. Their argument is multifaceted, but it can be cooked down to the claim that at every stage of the process, hydrogen is simply too expensive, both economically and environmentally. Building out a whole parallel infrastructure of hydrogen production facilities and gas stations would cost hundreds of billions of dollars, and it would have to be done up front, before consumers will switch en masse to hydrogen cars. As it's now produced, hydrogen costs far more than gasoline and won't get cheaper when demand for it surges. And since the main way of making it involves burning natural gas, which produces CO_2, hydrogen does nothing to address global warming. One study concluded that converting to a hydrogen-based economy would double both net energy consumption and net greenhouse gas emissions. Better, say the skeptics, to skip the intermediate step of making hydrogen and just redesign cars to burn domestically produced natural gas.

The response of hydrogen's fans is just as multifaceted, but it can also be cooked down to a couple of basic arguments: The infrastructure will cost a fraction of the pessimistic estimates, and progress on all technological fronts will bring costs and environmental impact into acceptable territory within a decade. Since each piece is crucial, let's consider them in turn:

Cheap Hydrogen

Hydrogen is already being produced on a commercial scale by industrial gas makers like Air Products, Praxair, and BOC, which operate dozens of plants around the world where they mix natural gas and steam to "reform" about 60 million tons of hydrogen each year. Take a map of the United States and draw a 50-mile circle around every place where hydrogen is made, and you'd cover most of the population. Hydrogen produced this way and delivered by truck costs about $4 per kilo, which is the energy equivalent of a gallon of gas. So the problem isn't hydrogen's availability but its price. On that front, there's plenty of activity and a certain amount of guarded optimism. Scaling up existing plants and building more of them would probably generate economies of scale in production and transportation that might, all else being equal, knock a dollar or so off the gallon-equivalent price. But it would still leave the industry vulnerable to gyrations in the price of natural gas and charges that it contributes to rather than fixes global warming. The last point is a deal breaker, so the search is on for new hydrogen sources.

Electrolysis is one possibility. Run an electric current through water and it separates into hydrogen and oxygen. Unfortunately, hydrogen produced this way is more expensive than that derived from steam reformation, though it does become more attractive if the electricity source is cheap and/or environmentally benign. So as wind turbines and solar cells gain efficiency, setting up electrolysis plants to store excess peak power in the form of hydrogen has a certain green symmetry. Another interesting possibility is hydrogen "gas stations" where cheap rooftop solar panels would run on-site electrolysis facilities. Eliminating the need to transport hydrogen from distant plants would lower the cost a bit. Meanwhile, lots of new ideas for improving the economics of electrolysis are being pursued, many, of course, with "nano" prefixes. California start-up QuantumSphere, for instance, claims to have developed "highly reactive catalytic nanoparticle coatings" that increase the effective surface area of electrodes and raise the efficiency of the electrolysis process. The company predicts that its breakthrough will lower the price of hydrogen to competitive levels.

And now that people are looking, it turns out that hydrogen can be made in lots of other, less obvious ways. Penn State University researchers have coaxed modified versions of common bacteria to produce the gas. By varying conditions and foods and giving the bugs a small jolt of electricity, they claim to have achieved efficiencies exceeding both electrolysis and other biofuels like ethanol. In early 2008, they were looking into scaling the process up to commercial levels. Massachusetts start-up Nanoptek, meanwhile, has developed a "nano-engineered photocatalyst" made of a cheap material called titania that makes hydrogen out of water and sunlight. The company claims the process is low-cost and scalable, and has impressed both the Department of Energy, which recently renewed Nanoptek's research grant, and a group of venture capitalists, who invested $4.7 million in early 2008. To sum up, the odds of creating enough cheap hydrogen to supplant fossil fuels are pretty good. Not a lock, but favorable enough to keep going.

Hydrogen Infrastructure

Assuming that some of the above works and there's plenty of cheap hydrogen a decade hence, the question becomes how to make it available. Here again, there is disagreement on how much this will cost. The Cato Institute and others say hundreds of billions of dollars, while a study by energy consultant e4tech and London's Imperial College concluded that hydrogen could be added to 2,800 filling stations across the European continent for €3.5 billion over 15 years. Studies by GM and Shell put the cost of covering the most densely populated parts of the United States at $12 billion to $19 billion over 10 years. The general plan would be for municipalities and companies that operate centrally fueled fleets to go first, switching over to fuel cell buses and delivery trucks and building the requisite fueling stations. From there, through a combination of government programs and private-sector capital spending, pumps would be sited as needed. Spread these optimistic cost projections among energy companies (including the industrial gas makers), automakers, and various branches of government, and it's barely a blip on anyone's P&L. The conclusion: Probably doable.

Hydrogen Storage

Because hydrogen is so light, in its natural gaseous state it takes up a lot of space in relation to its energy content. To fit into a vehicle fuel tank, it has to be compressed to between 5,000 and 10,000 pounds per square inch. This requires energy and reinforced tanks, which in their current incarnations are both heavy and costly, a combination that detracts from the efficiency calculus. But again, this is not insurmountable. Current state-of-the-art fuel tanks can hold enough hydrogen to go 300 miles and appear to be quite safe. They cost more than gasoline tanks but not outrageously so, and as with everything else in the field, steady engineering progress will improve both price and performance. And some new storage ideas are under development, such as infusing hydrogen into certain metals that release it on command. So the storage question also appears to be manageable.

Alas, It's Not to Be

The technical barriers to shifting the transportation system over to hydrogen should be overcome within a decade. That, however, will probably be too late. Long before fuel cell vehicles are cheap and reliable enough to take off, the world will have shifted to plug-in hybrids and biofuels. Both will be here in a couple of years and can be serviced using the existing gasoline refining, transporting, and refueling infrastructure. And thanks to breakthroughs in battery technology, hybrid efficiency is improving almost as quickly as that of fuel cells— but from a cheaper starting point. So in the coming decade, it's possible that municipal and commercial fleets will choose fuel cells, but it's probable that the rest of us will go electric or biofuel. In recognition that the odds have shifted, the major makers of automotive fuel cells have scaled back and shifted their strategies, with industry leaders Ballard Power Systems now focusing on fleet vehicles like buses and forklifts, and Energy Conversion Devices deemphasizing its fuel cell division in favor of its much hotter thin-film solar group.

Object Lesson: Ballard Power

If It's More Than a Few Years from Market . . .

In the late 1990s, when technology was going to make the world a paradise, fuel cells fit the zeitgeist perfectly. They were green as green could be and, just like microchips, were getting smaller and cheaper every year. The big automakers were promoting upcoming concept cars with breathless hyperbole about zero pollution and clean skies and happy kids. Ballard Power, meanwhile, was the leader in automotive fuel cell technology, and it wasn't shy about its future. In a 1998 *Automotive News* article titled "Ballard Spreads Fuel-Cell Optimism," company executives pointed out that its partnerships with major automakers represented more than $1 billion in new investment. Ford had recently paid $200 million for a minority stake in Ballard, and Daimler, among others, would be building prototype fuel cell vehicles within a few years. "Ultimately, Ballard and its partners foresee a time when fuel-cell power plants will be comparable to conventional engines in size, weight, operating life, performance, range and refueling time. And Ballard is confident of bringing down costs—dramatically—once it goes into volume production. 'We're convinced that this will be cheaper than an internal-combustion engine,' [Ballard's automotive division president Neil] Otto said. 'I believe that with all my heart.'"

There was even the obligatory book, *Powering the Future: The Ballard Fuel Cell and the Race to Change the World,* which pegged fuel cells as the catalyst for the coming energy revolution. The investment web site Motley Fool reflected the mood in the investment press with an article that asserted "Whether you're an energy junky or not, whether or not the phrase 'platinum-coated polymer plastic membrane' thrills you, I recommend learning about the advent of fuel cells. . . . With a deregulatory atmosphere and political leadership committed to lowering air pollution, I suspect there are many, many billions of dollars of public-market value yet to be created by the industry . . . value for us to share in."

In the midst of the tech-stock bubble, statements like these were akin to throwing gasoline on a fire. Ballard's stock rose more than twentyfold

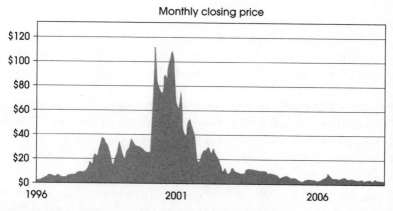

Figure 10.1   Ballard Power Stock Price (BLDP)

(*Continued*)

(*Continued*)

from its 1995 low, and by mid-2001, it was worth upward of $3 billion. Then, of course, the tech-stock bubble burst, and analysts started separating the viable business models like Cisco and Amazon from the majority that either didn't work or wouldn't for a while. And a few things became clear about Ballard: First and foremost, fuel cells were really, really expensive and not nearly durable enough to operate a car effectively. Upcoming prototype vehicles would cost several hundred thousand dollars and still not match the performance of a $15,000 Toyota Corolla. So even with dramatic annual improvements, fuel cells were a decade away from viability. Ballard, in short, was dead money. So whereas Cisco and Amazon eventually bottomed out, stabilized, and began rising, Ballard fell and kept falling, eventually returning to its 1995 low, which is pretty much where it languished in early 2008 (see Figure 10.1). The moral: Green is meaningless without a real, near-term shot at parity with existing technologies. Something that's more than a year or two away is a dangerous bet in a fickle market.

Stationary Power: This Decade's Fuel Cell Story

The fact that fuel cells won't be powering cars anytime soon doesn't mean the hydrogen story is over. It just means that, for now, the story isn't *mobile*. In stationary applications—where size, weight, and refueling convenience aren't such big concerns—fuel cells have some real advantages. They're clean and quiet, which makes them attractive for places like hotels and hospitals where green power and pleasant surroundings are key selling points. They're available 24/7, unlike, say, rooftop solar panels, which is a huge plus for facilities like prisons or grocery stores where power outages can be disastrous. And their reliability allows them to replace both baseline power and backup generators for some facilities.

Fuel cells are efficient as power generators go, converting about 47 percent of the energy in their fuel into electricity. That's better than a gasoline engine, and also better than grid-generated electricity, which dissipates as waste heat when it's generated and leaks from long-haul power lines on its journey from plant to customer. But stationary fuel cells can also use their waste heat to generate more electricity or to heat the surrounding structure. This raises the typical fuel cell's efficiency—the portion of a fuel's energy that makes it to the desired use—to 80 percent. So fuel cells offer double the energy from the same amount of fuel, which in some applications is enough to offset their still-high cost. And with fuel cells already competitive in this market, their ongoing improvement makes an immediate impact. United Technologies' UTC Power division, for instance, is planning a 2009 introduction of a next-generation "phosphoric acid" fuel cell that turns natural gas into hydrogen, which it uses to generate electricity. UTC claims that it will last 20 years and cost just $3.00 per installed watt. With early 2008 natural gas prices, that works out to electricity at $0.12 per kWh, which is comparable to grid-delivered power in some places. Connecticut-based FuelCell Energy, meanwhile, has a line of stationary fuel cells that can run on gases like methane produced as a by-product by wastewater treatment plants and landfills. Capture this gas and use it to run a fuel cell, and the result is cheap power with no new greenhouse gas emissions. With a little tweaking, the fuel cells can also be made to work with next-generation cellulosic ethanol and other biofuels, resulting in a completely domestically produced, carbon-neutral power source.

Table 10.1   Fuel Cell Stocks

Company	Ticker/ Exchange	Headquarters	Market Value, 6/27/08 ($ millions)
Acta	ACTAq/London	Italy	26
AFC Energy	AFEN.L/London	U.K.	27
Air Products	APD/NYSE	U.S.	20,780
Ballard Power Systems	BLDP/NASDAQ	Canada	369
Ceramic Fuel Cells	CFU/London	Australia	NA
Enova	ENA/AMEX	U.S.	91
Fuel Cell Energy	FCEL/OMX	U.S.	526
Hoku Scientific	HOKU/NASDAQ	U.S.	106
ITM Power	ITM.L/London	U.K.	66
Medis Technologies	MDTL/NASDAQ	Israel	126
Oxford Catalysts	OCG.L/London	U.K.	136
Plug Power	PLUG/NASDAQ	U.S.	221
Polyfuel	PYF.L/London	U.S.	14
Praxair	PX/NYSE	U.S.	29,600
Protonex	PTX.L/London	U.K.	81
United Technologies	UTX/NYSE	U.S.	59,510

Stationary Fuel Cell Growth Prospects

Stationary fuel cell growth prospects are pretty good, given their efficiency and ability to work with lots of different fuels (see Table 10.1). They compete with several other power sources, including natural gas cogeneration (see Chapter 14), grid-delivered electricity, and next-generation batteries. But they're definitely in the mix. This is a smaller, slower-moving market than cars, however. Existing buildings are already powered by other energy sources and will only change when their existing backup systems wear out or the price differential becomes compelling. New construction is an easier sell, but it makes up only a small part of the total building and industrial plant stock.

CHAPTER 11

Emissions Trading

CLIMATE CHANGE CAPITALISM

Most of the forces driving the shift to clean tech are pretty straightforward: Oil and gas are getting more expensive, solar and wind are getting cheaper, so capital flows accordingly. But global warming is a different, more complicated problem because it doesn't send direct price signals to the market. There's no *product* to value and trade. So the world's governments have decided to create a market in carbon emissions from scratch through "cap-and-trade" systems that work as follows: A government sets a total amount of greenhouse gases that it will allow certain sectors or the entire country to produce. That's the cap. Then it allocates among domestic businesses the right to emit certain amounts of greenhouse gas, generally based on some measure of past carbon production (or, let's be realistic, past campaign contributions). The allowances' owners can use them to offset their own carbon emissions, or they can sell them on specialized exchanges just like any other security. That's the trade.

The idea is to harness profit-seeking creativity in the service of the environment by making positive climate change a viable business. Under a well-designed cap-and-trade program, a utility, for instance, might build a wind farm that emits no CO_2 and use the resulting credit to cover an aging coal plant that would cost a fortune to upgrade. Or a paper company might upgrade a plant to reduce its emissions and sell its now superfluous credits (which are based on the plant's prior-year emissions) to offset the cost of the upgrade. The net result is a decrease in atmospheric CO_2 at minimal cost to companies, their employees, and their shareholders. A cap-and-trade world will, say its proponents, spawn a whole new, radically positive ecosystem: Entrepreneurs will scour the world for easy ways to reduce greenhouse gases and make a profit by trading or investing in the resulting credits. Investment banks and venture capitalists will fund projects based on expected returns. And mutual funds and hedge funds will build portfolios of such projects and the credits they generate. As you'll see shortly, even at this early stage of the emissions trading game, all of these things are happening.

A Little History

Emissions trading was first proposed back in the 1930s by the Technocracy Movement, a group dedicated to using scientific analysis to benefit society. The United States was the first to actually try it, implementing a sulfur dioxide (SO_2) trading system under the Acid Rain Program of the 1990 Clean Air Act. It seems to have worked: SO_2 emissions have since fallen by about half. In 2003, the Chicago Climate Exchange was formed to allow corporations to voluntarily trade greenhouse gas emissions allowances in the form of carbon financial instruments (CFIs), each representing 100 metric tons of CO_2 equivalent. This, too, has been a success: Early 2008 trading volumes were at all-time highs, with more than 24,000 contracts changing hands daily.

The big test began in 2005 when Europe created a continent-wide carbon cap-and-trade program similar to the SO_2 market in the United States. For each year through 2007, EU governments granted about 12,000 factories and power plants the right to emit a total of about 2.2 billion tons of CO_2 and set up an exchange on which excess credits (called European Union Allowances, or EUAs) could trade. And—in a twist that was to have interesting consequences—Europe allowed its companies to offset their own CO_2 with credits derived from green projects undertaken in other countries, called Certified Emission Reductions (CERs), as long as those credits were certified by the United Nations (UN) under a provision of the Kyoto climate change treaty known as the Clean Development Mechanism (CDM).

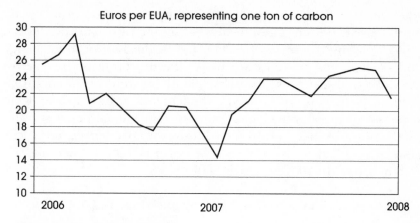

Figure 11.1   Carbon Prices
Source: European Climate Exchange

The first phase of Europe's program got mixed reviews. The compliance rate and trading volumes were both high, but European countries, as it turned out, issued carbon permits too generously. The result was a windfall for many companies, which simply cashed in their extra permits for a nice unearned profit. And European companies that did need to reduce emissions discovered that it was far cheaper to go to places like China and India and plant trees or retrofit ancient factories than to clean up their local European operations. So trading volumes surged, but the price of traded allowances plunged (see Figures 11.1), and European CO_2 emissions actually went up.

State of the Market

The rocky start wasn't surprising, since governments were trying to set carbon allocations without good data and so tended to error on the side of caution. Now, with the benefit of several years of experience, the fix is easy: Just issue fewer credits and lower the overall cap. And in the new round that began in 2008, that's what Europe did. By 2013, emissions are scheduled to fall by 14 percent from 2005 levels and then keep falling by more than 1 percent a year through 2020. And there will be no more free allowances for power companies. Beginning in 2013, utilities will have to buy all of their credits at auction or on the open market. The goal is to squeeze allocations over time and push up the carbon price by creating scarcity. When announced, the tighter caps had the desired effect, sending the price of carbon up on the European exchange and—a sign that the cuts are real—drawing protests from across the industrial spectrum. In early 2008, there were suits pending in the European Court of Justice in which at least five companies from various industries were claiming serious damage, and analysts were predicting a 50 percent drop in European coal-derived electricity generation by 2020. Now the whole world is joining the emissions trading game. In 2007 and early 2008,

- Australia's Financial and Energy Exchange began trading carbon credits.
- California passed a law obligating itself to cut greenhouse gas emissions by 25 percent by 2020 and agreed with four other Western states to set up a regional cap-and-trade system.
- The Mumbai, India, Multi-Commodity Exchange began a carbon futures trading program modeled on the Chicago Climate Exchange. Since India accounted for about a third of all CDM projects registered with the UN in 2007, this is expected to be a big, busy exchange.
- British Airways began offering customers the ability to offset their flight emissions by paying a little extra—between £1.50 and £16—for a ticket. The proceeds go to support a wind farm in China, a hydroelectric plant in Brazil, and Cambridge University research on the climate effects of aviation.
- Citigroup, JPMorgan Chase, and Morgan Stanley announced new "carbon principles" guidelines for lending to power companies, which they'll use to steer their clients to the most environmentally benign choices.
- The Brazilian Mercantile and Futures Exchange began conducting auctions of carbon credits.
- The insurance company Zurich North America began offering political risk insurance for carbon credit projects.

Perhaps the most interesting development of all is the Manhattan-based Green Exchange, which opened in March 2008. Created and owned by a group of global investment banks and emissions brokers, it's an attempt to turn carbon into a globally traded, fungible commodity like oil. This would be a big departure from 2007-style emissions trading, which took place in a series of discreet national or regional markets. Even the European Climate Exchange, the biggest of the original markets, wasn't open to firms based in India and China, two of the leading markets for emissions projects. Most emissions credits, meanwhile, were project-specific and therefore hard to value. "If you're buying from a small company in another country you don't know for sure if the project will perform," says Andrew Ertel, founder of Evolution Markets, a major emissions credit broker and part owner of Green Exchange. The goal of Green Exchange is to create a global market that is capable of tapping global pools of liquidity by creating and trading futures contracts for carbon that are backed by the full faith and credit of the exchange owners, thus guaranteeing delivery and performance. "If I sell a futures contract for a CER, the project risk is stripped out," says Ertel.

Emissions Trading Terms

Perhaps because it originated with government, the emissions trading business is rife with obscure, unhelpful acronyms. Unlike, say, exchange-traded fund (ETF) or National Football League (NFL), which tell you exactly what you're getting, even knowing what an emissions trading acronym stands for doesn't necessarily shed much light on its subject. But there's no escaping them if you want to understand this business, so here's a list of the major terms as of early 2008. No doubt by the time you read this, there will be many more.

- **GHG:** Greenhouse gas. Okay, this one isn't so bad.
- **EU ETS:** Emissions Trading Scheme, Europe's cap-and-trade program.
- **EUA:** European Union Allowance, the unit of measure for CO_2 emissions in the Emissions Trading Scheme. Each allowance represents one ton of carbon dioxide emissions.
- **CDM:** Clean Development Mechanism, the section of the Kyoto climate change treaty that awards tradable carbon credits to GHG emissions reduction projects hosted in developing countries. If a German company completes an emissions reduction project in India, for example, it would fall under the CDM purview.
- **CER:** Certified Emission Reduction, a credit issued under the CDM, measured in metric tons of CO_2 equivalent. The German

(Continued)

(Continued)

company in the foregoing example would receive CERs that it could use to offset its emissions at home.

- **ERU:** Emission Reduction Unit, similar to CER, except that the transaction is between two developed countries (referred to as Annex I parties) rather than between a developed and developing country. Each unit equals 1 metric ton of carbon equivalent.
- **CFI:** Carbon financial instruments, the contract traded on the Chicago Climate Exchange, representing 100 metric tons of CO_2 equivalent.
- **VER:** Verified Emission Reductions, the private-label version of emissions credits. Generally bought by companies that are voluntarily reducing their carbon footprint, for public relations or other reasons.
- **REC:** Renewable energy certificates, which represent 1 megawatt hour of electricity generated from clean renewable sources. They can be sold separately from the associated electricity and are frequently bought by organizations wishing to show support for clean energy. Some utilities, for instance, offer them to customers.

Object Lesson: EcoSecurities and AGCert

Life on the Bleeding Edge

As soon as the EU began its cap-and-trade experiment, it was clear to most observers that the demand for emissions credits was going to soar, and whoever could produce them consistently would make massive profits. Companies began forming and going public, and investors poured money into these ground-floor opportunities, the future Amazons and Microsofts of the emissions trading boom. But they don't call brand-new markets "the bleeding edge" for nothing. Early on, the definitions of emissions credits were still being worked out. Projects, meanwhile, required a lot of up-front capital and frequently involved new technologies and/or evolving local regulations. Here's what happened to two of the hottest of the first generation of emissions credit producers:

Oxford-based EcoSecurities is one of the first investment banks specializing in emissions credits. Say, for instance, you run a landfill that produces a lot of methane from rotting garbage. That's a problem for you and your neighbors, but it's also a potential asset, since methane is fuel. As a landfill operator, you have no idea how to collect methane and put it to profitable use, so you might call EcoSecurities, which would send in its EcoMethane Group to design, finance, install, and operate a system to collect the methane and either generate electricity or purify it for use in vehicles. EcoMethane would manage the documentation to gain carbon credits and market them to buyers. And voilà, a once-useless and annoying by-product of your business becomes a source of ongoing royalties, the environment gets cleaner, and EcoSecurities ends up with an addition to its already bulging portfolio of emissions credits. In early 2007, it claimed to have over 400 emissions reduction projects under development in 36 countries, using 18 different emissions reduction technologies. Just reading this paragraph makes one want to start buying EcoSecurities shares, and that's what a lot of European investors did, sending the stock—already richly priced at £200 in London—beyond £400 by mid-2007. Then it was revealed that several of the company's projects were having trouble getting through the UN's approval process. Without the UN's okay, the emissions credits were a lot less valuable, and EcoSecurities' profitability was impaired. One busted deal alone cost the company €9.2 million. Losses began to mount, and the stock price plunged. By April 2008, it was down by more than 75 percent from its high.

Dublin-based AgCert, meanwhile, had pioneered the practice of working with farmers to reduce their greenhouse gas emissions and then selling the resulting CERs. In 2007, it cut deals to deliver an aggressive number of CERs in 2008. But when its offset projects progressed more slowly than expected, it was left owing more credits than it could produce, without the capital to buy new CERs in the open market, where prices were rising. After negotiations with other trading firms for a bailout fell through, the once-hot company found itself in a possibly fatal cash squeeze. From its high of £240 in London trading, the stock crashed to £0.65 in March of 2008.

The lesson: Being a pioneer in a growing field is no guarantee of success. In fact, the first movers are seldom the eventual winners, either because they make beginner's mistakes or because powerful latecomers steal their market. Think of Netscape, which had the first true web browser but was crushed by Microsoft, and AOL, which had the biggest early online audience but couldn't figure out what to do with it. In emissions trading, developers were racing to bring projects to market, in some cases apparently without thinking through the technology or accurately forecasting the emissions reductions. The UN, meanwhile, was probably short of people capable of making fast, accurate judgments about new projects with esoteric technologies. The result was a speed bump for the market but a potentially fatal crash for some of its pioneers.

Private-Sector Players

A whole range of private-sector companies now see emissions credits as a growth market. For investment banks, the attraction of another big trading opportunity is obvious. But many of them are going further, actually initiating, financing, and managing projects to retrofit Indian factories, clean up Russian pipelines, and plant trees in Indonesia. This kind of "merchant banking" generates a river of fees that culminate (it is hoped) in trading profits and capital gains when the projects come to fruition and are sold. Each player is approaching the market in its own way: In 2007, Morgan Stanley bought 38 percent of MGM International, a Florida-based company that invests in emissions reduction projects. Credit Suisse bought 10 percent of Ireland-based EcoSecurities Group and said it may lend that company a billion euros for pollution investments. London-based hedge fund Man Group raised $382 million for a fund specializing in greenhouse gases at Chinese coal plants. Utah-based Blue Source LLC announced that it had amassed the biggest bank of pollution credits in the United States. German bank Dresdner formed a joint venture with Gazprombank, the banking arm of Russian gas monopoly OAO Gazprom, to invest in carbon reduction projects. The list goes on, but you get the idea: Emissions trading is a land rush reminiscent of the Internet circa 1997, with everyone trying to stake a viable claim. For specialized carbon-trading firms, meanwhile, 2008 is the year in which they have to achieve the critical mass necessary to survive the onslaught of the investment banks. Here are some of the more interesting newcomers:

- London-based **Climate Change Capital** (CCC) is a full-service investment bank focusing exclusively on emissions credits. In the same way that Goldman Sachs might help GM sell off a division, buy a competitor, or issue bonds, CCC helps companies raise money for projects that lower carbon emissions. It also advises governments and private-sector businesses on how best to implement green strategies. By the end of 2007, CCC claimed to have financed projects that will eliminate 70 million metric tons of greenhouse gases, or about the annual emissions of Denmark.
- Oslo-based **Point Carbon** is a very big, very slick consultancy, research house, and news aggregator for the carbon market.

Its analysts monitor the global market, compile indexes, and write reports, which are made available on a subscription or fee basis. Its web site offers analytic tools for professional traders, and it organizes and runs conferences that draw the major players in the industry. In early 2008, Point Carbon claimed more than 15,000 clients, "including the world's major energy companies, financial institutions, organizations and governments, in over 150 countries. Reports are translated from English into Japanese, Chinese, Portuguese, French, Spanish and Russian."

- New York-based **Evolution Markets** is a brokerage house and investment bank run by Andrew Ertel, one of the pioneers of emissions trading. In early 2008, Evolution was probably the world's leading emissions credit broker, with over 80 brokers and bankers staffing offices in New York, London, San Francisco, Calgary, and Buenos Aires. It now acts as a full-service investment bank, arranging financing for a project, helping to design the resulting credits to adhere to various regulations and meet the needs of buyers, and then placing the credits with customers.

Emissions Trading's Growth Prospects

Since governments have a big say in the price of carbon, and most governments desire a thriving market in emissions credits, it's reasonable to expect prices to remain high enough to stimulate plenty of activity. In coming years, new cap-and-trade systems and

Table 11.1   Emissions Trading Stocks

Company	Ticker/ Exchange	Headquarters	Market Value, 6/27/08 ($ millions)
Camco International	CAMIN.L/London	U.K.	154
Climate Exchange	CLE/London	U.K.	1,750
Econergy	ECG.L/London	U.S.	82
EcoSecurities Group	ECO.L/London	U.K.	222
Low Carbon Accelerator	LCA.L/London	U.K.	62
Umweltbank AG	UBKG/Frankfurt	Germany	130

exchanges will spring up and carbon will become a tradable commodity. Point Carbon projects a $565 billion market by 2020.

But for investors, this isn't yet a target-rich environment. The pioneers like AgCert and EcoSecurities (recall the Object Lesson a few pages back) are being crowded by the global investment banks, which bring vast resources to the table, along with a willingness to play rough. So look for many smaller, specialized players to be bought out and many others to fail. Since emissions trading will never be more than a sideline for Goldman Sachs or JPMorgan Chase, the question is which of today's "carbon plays" will be able to carve out and defend a viable niche (see Table 11.1).

CHAPTER

12

Smart Grid

THE NEW WIRED WORLD

Wiring up the developing world was one of history's great engineering feats. It allowed cheap power to flow continuously from efficient, centralized generating plants to every corner of every town. And—maybe a bit of a mixed blessing—it turned a society of early-to-bed candlelight readers into people who take for granted the ability to do whatever they want whenever they want in total comfort, regardless of the outside temperature or position of the sun. But then the utility industry just stopped. While the Internet was allowing merchants and hackers to trace our surfing habits down to the level of seconds spent staring at a web page, the electrical grid stayed one way, with power flowing out but no detailed information about usage flowing back. On the old "dumb" grid—which is still the norm in most places—information flow between electric utilities and their customers consists almost entirely of 12 meter readings a year and 12 monthly power bills.

So when the temperature spikes in August and people crank up the air conditioning and watch their plasma TVs in cool, well-lit rooms, the utility pumps out as much juice as it can—until it can't. Then it either buys power from neighboring utilities at extortionate rates or gives up and allows all or part of its network to go black. This is both annoying and really, really costly. The Electric Power Research Institute calculates that power outages cost U.S. business at least $50 billion a year. And Americans are among the lucky ones for whom outages are rare and brief. South Africa's mining and manufacturing sectors were brought to a virtual halt in early 2008 by widespread blackouts. And in Lahore, Pakistan, increasingly frequent outages were reportedly causing a run on batteries and backup power systems. It's the same story around the world. Grids are overloading and going down more frequently, in large part because power is being used inefficiently by people who have no real-time sense of what it's costing.

The direct cost of blackouts is just the tip of the inefficiency iceberg. In order to be prepared for periodic spikes in demand, utilities have to maintain peak power-generating capacity that's about twice what is needed on an average day. All those plants and lines sitting idle for most of their working lives are wildly expensive. And the gap between peak demand and supply is widening: The North American Electric Reliability Council expects peak electricity demand to rise by 18 percent, or about 13.5 gigawatts in the United States during the next decade, while peak generating capacity will grow by only 8.4 percent. And *then* there's the environmental impact: Despite the inroads now being made by solar and wind, the vast bulk of peak power generation comes from burning coal and natural gas, so the need to draw on such sources is a prime contributor to atmospheric CO_2. Today's grid, in short, is dirty, fragile, and expensive and not nearly flexible enough to manage, say, millions of rooftop solar panels and electric cars. But tomorrow's grid will be up to the task, as power companies, at last, build two-way communications capabilities. Here's how they'll do it:

Smart Metering and Demand Response

The meter reader—the person who walks from yard to yard checking each home's monthly electricity usage—is almost as much a part of American folklore as the mailman. It's a little disturbing, having a stranger wander through the back yard looking for the electric meter. But physically reading thousands of meters in a given territory is also an immense waste of time and effort. So—only a couple of decades after the invention of the cell phone—utilities have begun to install meters that can communicate wirelessly with the head office or with receivers in roving vans. In 2007, about 10 percent of U.S. homes were equipped with smart meters, but the total is growing fast. London-based market analyst Datamonitor predicts that smart metering will reach 89 percent penetration in North America and 41 percent penetration in Europe by 2012.

Once utilities and their customers establish real-time communication, lots of interesting things become possible. A utility can, for instance, install automatic controls on customers' water heaters, air conditioners, and other power-hungry devices and then remotely turn them off when demand spikes. Florida Power had half a million customers enrolled in such a program in 2007; customers agree to give the utility partial control over certain appliances at certain times in return for reduced bills. This is known as "demand response," because it's a voluntary reduction of electric *demand* in *response* to grid instability or high wholesale prices. Such a program might produce a net lowering of demand, as when an air conditioner is turned off for part of a day and isn't needed once the sun goes down. Or it can shift demand from peak to off-peak hours, as when a hot water heater is turned off at noon and then reheats the water later in the evening. Either way, the utility avoids having to build and maintain as much peak generating capacity, and, if it's done well, customers hardly notice a thing.

Even bigger savings are possible when customers do notice, and a communications system that lets utilities see what a customer's appliances are doing in real time also gives the customer, in theory, the same view. So on the horizon are smart meters that will show customers how much juice they're using per hour and what it costs. A Canadian company called Blue Line Innovations, for instance, now offers a $150 power cost monitor that looks like a digital electric clock, but instead of the time, shows the owner's monthly power bill. Switch on a given appliance, and you instantly know how much it's costing you. In a typical house, the air conditioner might bump power consumption from $0.03 an hour to $0.10. A toaster oven might cost $0.30 an hour and a microwave $0.40, while an electric clothes dryer might be a dollar or more. Now, combine this kind of appliance-by-appliance understanding of power consumption with new utility pricing schedules that vary with the time of day and overall power demand, and you have a powerful behavior modification program. People confronted with those big digital real-time meter readings will be a lot more likely to turn off the lights when leaving a room, snuggle under a blanket in winter, and limit the amount of time the kids play Halo on the plasma TV. It's not exactly a retur to our pioneer roots, but it is a few tentative steps away from the profligate, clueless suburban stereotype.

Apply this kind of demand response and customer monitoring to the whole grid, and pretty soon you're talking real money. Energy consultancy Pacific Northwest National Laboratory (PNNL) calculates that moving to smart grid technology will eliminate the need for $46 billion to $117 billion in conventional utility infrastructure. The term for this avoided capacity is "negawatts," as in negative watts. That is, eliminating the need for a new plant is functionally the same thing as building one—except that negawatts are utterly clean and extremely cheap. PNNL estimates that $600 million of smart appliances capable of adjusting demand to grid conditions could provide reserve capacity equal to power plants costing $6 billion. Bytes, as they say in this business, are cheaper than iron.

Another attraction of the smart grid is that detailed data on which appliances are using how much electricity allows a utility to finance efficiency improvements for its customers and then claim carbon reduction credits that can be traded on the exchanges mentioned in Chapter 11. With the old dumb grid, the reductions flowing from new appliances and other upgrades couldn't be verified, giving a utility less incentive to make such investments. But information validated by real-time readings will soon be worth big bucks, increasing the incentive for utilities to help their customers to go green.

State of the Market

Early on, the smart grid market was dominated by giants like IBM, Itron (an early leader in utility meters that is moving up the technological food chain very successfully), and Echelon, which makes network infrastructure gear and software. But now that it's taking off, an array of newcomers are introducing innovative ideas. Here are some of the more interesting examples:

New Jersey-based Comverge recently signed a deal with Connecticut Light and Power Company to create 130 megawatts of ⸱⸱ꞁ peaking capacity" by installing demand response gear like ⸱mostats and load control switches in customer homes ⸱es. Once in place, the system will allow Comverge to back on usage during peak periods and then sell the negawatts to the utility. Comverge's managed capacity exceeded 1.5 gigawatts in early 2008, making it, in a strange sort of new economy way, a major power producer without actually generating any power.

Massachusetts-based EnerNOC focuses on commercial energy customers, "aggregating demand reduction" by tying backup generators and industrial equipment into a network that utilities can draw on as needed. In exchange for committing to reduce their electrical demand by a certain percentage when needed, customers get a monthly "capacity payment" from EnerNOC. In addition, they earn a "curtailment payment" every time EnerNOC actually pushes the button. In early 2008, EnerNOC claimed 700 demand response customers, representing nearly 1,000 megawatts in potential electricity savings.

Perhaps most ambitious of all is the platform being rolled out by Virginia-based GridPoint, which enables utilities to "reshape the load curve" by directly managing a network of distributed energy sources to lower peak and raise off-peak demand. This is the kind of system that will be needed when vehicle-to-grid and other distributed sources become widely available.

Table 12.1   Smart Grid Stocks

Company	Ticker/ Exchange	Headquarters	Market Value, 6/27/08 ($ millions)
American Superconductor	AMSC/NASDAQ	U.S.	1,470
Chloride Group	CHLD/London	U.K.	1,364
Comverge	COMV/NASDAQ	U.S.	276
EnerNOC	ENOC/NASDAQ	U.S.	342
Echelon	ELON/NASDAQ	U.S.	453
International Business Machines	IBM/NYSE	U.S.	164,900
Itron	ITRI/NASDAQ	U.S.	3,090
Power Integrations	POWI/NASDAQ	U.S.	959
Umweltbank AG	UBKG/Frankfurt	Germany	130

Smart Grid's Growth Prospects

Dramatic. Most of the world's power grids will be upgraded in the coming decade. That means millions of smart meters and related gear, and numerous openings for new technologies, services, and business models. Because the smart grid offers so many technological points of entry, start-ups are flooding this space with everything from broadband-over-power-line services that allow utilities to monitor their power flows while offering customers high-speed Internet, to chipsets that power networks of smart appliances, to meters that more efficiently transmit data to and from utilities. The market they're creating is vastly more interesting than the old dumb grid, and should spawn some great growth stocks (see Table 12.1).

PART

III

OTHER CLEAN
TECHNOLOGIES

13

Water

LIQUID GOLD

If running out of energy seems unlikely for inhabitants of a planet that's bathed in sunlight, a water shortage is even more counterintuitive. Seen from space, the earth is mostly water. Two-thirds of its surface is blue, which implies that our main problem should be too much water and not enough land. But *water* isn't really the issue— fresh water is. Most of the earth is covered with seawater, which is too salty for drinking or irrigation, while most fresh water is locked up in the polar ice caps. The rest, a relative pittance, resides in lakes and flows through rivers that are steadily replenished by rain and snowmelt. And in the past century, we've put this water to increasingly purposeful use, irrigating farms and supplying a population that—as a result of all the new food and drink—has tripled.

Just as a century of cheap oil produced an energy-intensive economy, the illusion of unlimited water led us to embrace "necessities" that require shocking amounts of water. According to the U.S. Geological Survey, it takes 1,851 gallons of water to acquire and refine a barrel of crude oil and 684,000 gallons of water per acre per year to keep a golf course green. The average American family uses 21,600 gallons of water on its lawn each year. Table 13.1 lists the water content of some of life's other staples.

Table 13.1   Gallons of Water Required

Production of	Gallons of Water*
Pound of potatoes	65
Pound of wheat	150
Pound of rice	300
Pound of sugar	400
Pound of cheese	650
Pound of beef	800
Quart of milk	1,000
Bushel of corn	1,750
Barrel (42 gallons) of beer	1,500
Pound of coffee	2,650
Ton of steel	62,600

* Water intensity estimates vary widely. Depending on the source, for instance, a pound of beef can require anywhere from 12,000 gallons to 500 gallons (the latter estimate is from the Cattleman's Beef Board). I've erred on the side of caution here, presenting numbers from independent conservative sources.

Meat Eating, Beer Swilling

As Fred Pearce puts it in his scary, evocative book *When the Rivers Run Dry,* "I figure that as a typical meat-eating, beer-swilling, milk-guzzling Westerner, I consume as much as a hundred times my own weight in water every day." And now the rest of the world wants the same lifestyle. China's meat demand is doubling every 10 years. Poultry consumption in India doubled in the first half of this decade. According to the UN, world population is expected to grow 10 percent by 2020, but demand for beef, pork, and chicken will rise 25 percent. The calculus is simple: In today's world, the higher your income, the more energy and animal protein—and therefore water—you tend to consume.

And the equalization process has a long way to go. The average American eats 56 pounds of meat annually, while the average Chinese or Indian eats about a fourth as much. For the latter to catch up to the former will require a lot more pasture land and animal feed, which means a whole lot more water. Will there be enough? Probably not, from conventional sources. Over the past century we've gotten very good at damming or diverting rivers and draining lakes to irrigate fields, sometimes in amazingly unlikely places like deserts and dry prairies. Early on, it worked. Crop yields soared, people were fed, and they had babies who were also fed. But now the rivers in many places are maxed out, while water needs continue to rise as people move from cold, wet climes to warm and dry ones. The result: growing water problems in a rising number of places. Here are a few representative examples:

The Forgotten River. With a name like Rio Grande, the river that forms part of the Texas–Mexico border should be, well, Grande. And until recently it was. The fifth-longest river in North America and among the 20 longest in the world, it flows nearly 2,000 miles from the Colorado Rockies to the Gulf of Mexico. But the land it runs through is otherwise very dry, and over the years, its neighbors have dammed and diverted it to irrigate farms growing water-intensive crops like cotton and alfalfa. Each diversion leaves less for those downstream, and by the end of its course, there is often not much left. Another snippet from *When the Rivers Run Dry*:

> Climbing the levee by the river at the end of his last field, Bishop shows me the problem. The once mighty Rio Grande is now reduced to a sluggish brown trickle. In its middle stretches, the river often dries up entirely in the summer. All the water has been taken out by cities and farmers upstream. "The river's been disappearing since the fifties," says Bishop, who has farmed here since then. There hasn't been a flood worthy of the name since 1978. For 200 miles upstream of Presidio, there is no proper channel any more. They call it the forgotten river . . . Bishop's land brings with it legal rights to 8,000 acre-feet of water a year from the river—enough to flood his fields to a depth of more than three feet, enough to grow almost any crop he wants. But in recent years he has taken only a quarter of that. Even when he gets water, "it's too salty to grow anything much except alfalfa." But that's all academic now. Yields got so low, the farm went bust.

The Rio Grande's slow death leaves cities like El Paso with a lot of potentially thirsty citizens. In response, they're buying up properties from farmers for their rights to underground water reserves. But "water ranching" is only a temporary solution, because the aquifer that Texans are drawing down is running dry as well.

Ogallala Aquifer. Sitting under parts of South Dakota, Nebraska, Wyoming, Colorado, Kansas, Oklahoma, New Mexico, and Texas is a body of water that, if it were on the surface, would dwarf the Great Lakes. Known as the High Plains Aquifer or the Ogallala Aquifer, it spans about 175,000 square miles and contains one of the largest quantities of fresh water anywhere. And it's relatively close to the surface and easy to reach. Once farmers discovered this seemingly inexhaustible source of water, they turned desert and prairie into hugely productive corn and soybean fields. According to the U.S. Geological Survey, approximately 27 percent of the irrigated land in the United States is in this region, and about 30 percent of the groundwater used for irrigation in the United States is pumped from the Ogallala Aquifer. Dry, mountainous Colorado is now the thirteenth-largest corn-producing state. Nebraska, with little surface water, is pretty much synonymous with farming, and it is now moving into corn ethanol in a big way, with all that that implies for future water use. Perhaps wildest of all, the Texas panhandle is now a thriving dairy farming region, with locals growing their own alfalfa to feed a cow population that has ballooned in this decade from about 20,000 to 140,000 and will, according to local officials, increase by 20,000 annually for the next five years. One of the attractions, according to the Lubbock Online web site, is that "the climate is ideal—low humidity and less rainfall—which aids swift evaporation and limits runoff into the few streams in the region." In other words, the fact that there's no surface water to speak of is a selling point for this water-intensive industry.

But the Ogallala, like Saudi oil, has turned out to be finite after all. It is now being pumped at a rate 14 times greater than it can be replenished, and in some parts it is down more than 100 feet from its original level. Recent studies have found the water level to be dropping by three feet to five feet a year in some sections, while other parts are already dry.

U.S. Snowmelt. Much of the American West gets its fresh water from mountain snowpack. In winter, snow accumulates on mountain slopes, and in spring, it melts and flows down to replenish rivers and lakes. Colorado, Utah, Wyoming, New Mexico, Arizona, Nevada, and Southern California get much of their fresh water from the Colorado River, which is fed by the Rockies. Northern California gets most of its water from snowpack in the Sierra Nevada mountains. These states are booming, as people relocate for the dry air and gorgeous scenery. California's Department of Finance recently predicted that the state's population will rise to 60 million by midcentury, from 36 million today.

But the available water is already spoken for, having long since been divvied up among the surrounding states for their farms, factories, and towns. And now the total available amount seems to be shrinking. As winters get warmer, less snow accumulates on mountainsides, leaving less to melt in the spring. The snowpack in the Sierra Nevada is already at its lowest level in 20 years, and in 2007 the Colorado River was at one of its lowest levels on record. If the climate models that predict continued warming are correct, by 2050 half of the remaining western U.S. snowpack will disappear. Consider what this means for, say, Las Vegas, one of the fastest growing cities in the United States in one of the most unlikely places: the middle of the Nevada desert. Metro Vegas is now home to 1.8 million people, but to get a sense of its incongruity, you have to fly over it on a clear day. Surrounding the city are vast green rectangles divided into smaller squares. Those are subdivisions that went up during the housing boom of the past decade. The tiny blue dots next to many of the houses are swimming pools.

The city's main water source is Lake Mead, a narrow, 110-mile-long lake fed by the Colorado River. At full capacity it holds 28 million acre-feet of water, which makes it the country's largest reservoir. But the recent inflow from the Colorado isn't keeping up with outflows and evaporation, and by 2007 Lake Mead was down to 49 percent of capacity, or about 100 feet below its past high-water mark. This is perilously close to the level of the Las Vegas Water Authority's intake pipes, so the authority recently hired an engineering firm to drill a deeper intake pipe near the bottom of the lake, and is planning a multibillion-dollar pipeline to ship in groundwater from less populous parts of the state.

A Global Water Shortage

The United States, because it's rich enough to engineer its way around most water problems and buy some breathing room for those it can't solve, is actually in relatively good shape. Other countries have more immediate, less easily delayed, problems. For example, India's "green revolution" is by most standards one of the past century's great success stories. Once a country where tens of millions of people existed on the edge of starvation, it is now nearly self-sufficient in food, thanks largely to the irrigation of vast fields of rice, alfalfa, sugarcane, and corn. Because India's rivers weren't up to this task, its farmers and villagers have gotten the necessary water by digging wells, millions of them, to tap what once seemed like an inexhaustible underground aquifer. But now, predictably, underground water levels are dropping, rendering old wells inadequate and forcing farmers to dig deeper and use more electricity to pull water to the surface. As municipal wells run dry, towns are bidding for water on the open market, and for many farmers, it's now more profitable to sell water to distributors than to use it to grow crops. Meanwhile, in some parts of India, as water levels drop, fluoride—which occurs naturally in the granite rocks that underlie much of the country—has begun to contaminate wells, and literally millions of people are now suffering from various kinds of fluoride-related bone growth deformities. And—this being India rather than Las Vegas—there's no immediately apparent fix. The groundwater is poisonous, the surface water is polluted by human and industrial waste, and filtering or otherwise treating either water source is prohibitively expensive. In many parts of India—and China and the rest of Asia—the green revolution is about to be replaced by something else, as yet unnamed but far less pleasant.

A few more examples:

- In the southern African state of Swaziland, the rainy season used to start in September but lately has been coming in October or November and dropping considerably less rain. Water levels in the Maguga Dam, the country's largest reservoir, were at one-third of capacity in 2007, causing the government to impose water rationing on its citizens.

- In Australia, the worst drought in recorded history recently ended, but water levels in rivers and reservoirs remain low. Restrictions on water use, hitting primarily farmers, are projected to remain in place for years.
- The Andes glaciers that supply most of Peru's water and electricity are disappearing, leaving the growing population along the country's desert coast with increasingly precarious water and power supplies.

The list could go on to fill up the rest of this book, but the point is clear: Rising populations are bumping up against a shrinking supply of fresh, clean water. The International Water Management Institute estimates that about a fifth of the world's population, or more than 1.2 billion people, already lives in areas with insufficient supply. The UN expects that figure to rise to fully two-thirds of the world's population within 20 years. The result will be ugly, which is to say full of opportunities. One of the most interesting is desalination.

Desalination

For centuries, it has been technically possible to turn seawater into fresh water, a process known as desalination. Until recently, this could only be done at a price that was far higher than the nearly free water available from rivers or aquifers. But as the cost of traditional water goes up and technology makes desalination cheaper, the technology is approaching "aquifer parity"—the point at which it is, to an increasing number of people, worth the price. Here are the three main forms of desalination:

Vacuum Distillation. Take seawater, which is a mixture of things that vaporize at different pressures, and lower the pressure to the point at which the most volatile components evaporate. Generally the most volatile substance is water, which becomes steam and is captured and turned into fresh water. With the most common vacuum technology, multistage flash distillation, seawater is heated in a container known as a brine heater and then flows to another container where the surrounding pressure is lower. The sudden exposure to low pressure causes the water to boil rapidly, or "flash" into steam. Repeat this process at progressively lower pressures, and eventually most of the water becomes steam, which condenses into clean water. Multistage flash distillation is energy intensive, so it's most cost-effective when paired with power plants that generate waste heat to raise the seawater's temperature.

Reverse Osmosis. Now take some seawater and instead of lowering the ambient pressure, raise it—a lot. Then put it next to a semipermeable "hydrophilic" membrane that lets fresh water through but blocks salt and other dissolved substances. This is the reverse of the normal osmosis process, which is the natural movement of a dissolved substance from an area of high concentration to low. For example, if you separate fresh water and saltwater with, say, a coffee filter, the salt will migrate across until both sides are equally saturated. In reverse osmosis, the fresh water migrates and leaves the salt behind. Membrane systems are a bit less energy intensive than multistage flash distillation, so the resulting water costs less.

A current example of reverse osmosis is a plant being built by Connecticut-based Poseidon Resources in Carlsbad, a seaside town north of San Diego. The $300 million plant will take water directly from the Pacific, run it through filters to get rid of dead fish and seaweed, and then pump it under high pressure through membranes to remove the salt. The expected output is 50 million gallons of drinking water a day, enough to supply about 100,000 homes, at a cost of about $950 per acre-foot. That's higher than the $700 or so that local agencies now pay for their suddenly precarious water, but still not bad when you consider that an acre-foot is 325,851 gallons, enough water for four profligate Americans for one year. The desalinated price is less than a penny a gallon.

Solar Desalination. The simplest form of desalination is to heat seawater with sunlight until it evaporates and then condense the steam into fresh water. Small-scale solar stills used to be common but went out of style when electricity became cheap and water plentiful. But now, as those trends reverse and solar power plants are springing up everywhere, it's coming back into style. Recall from Chapter 3 that a consortium of European and Middle Eastern investors is planning to build a series of solar thermal plants in North Africa that will supply power to Europe. The plan also calls for capturing the superheated steam that drives the plants' turbines and using it to desalinate seawater. The result: potentially massive amounts of fresh water as a by-product of the solar thermal plants' operation. Enough to make those North African deserts bloom.

State of the Desalination Market

According to the International Desalination Association, 13,080 desalination plants produce more than 12 billion gallons of water a day worldwide (see Figure 13.1). Most are in places like the Middle East, where water is scarce and energy cheap. Saudi Arabia, not surprisingly, now accounts for about a fourth of the world's desalination capacity and intends to spend $40 billion in the coming two decades on water projects. But as the cost of water goes up, desalination is becoming an option for dry regions around the world. In California, there are now more than 20 desalination plant proposals

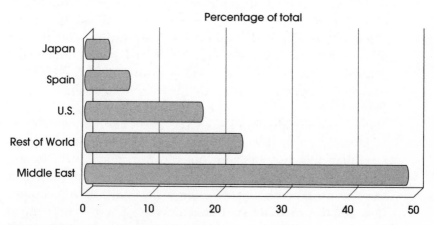

Figure 13.1   Desalination Capacity
Source: Global Water Intelligence

working their way through various bureaucracies. If all are built, they'll produce water equal to 6 percent of the state's 2000 urban water demand. Israel and Singapore have large desalination plants, and Australia, which is both dry (generally and because of a severe recent drought) and surrounded by ocean, is building a bunch of them. The city of Perth has been operating a seawater desalination plant since 2006 and is in the process of building another, with Sydney and several other cities following suit. The Perth plant is powered partially by energy from a nearby wind farm, while the Sydney plant will be powered entirely by renewable sources. When powered this way, desalination plants are popular with voters. A proposal to raise water rates to cover the full cost of a proposed desalination plant near the Australian city of Adelaide got a 60 percent vote of confidence in a recent phone poll.

And this is all with existing technology, which is, of course, about to be upgraded by some potentially radical breakthroughs. Among them are the following:

- **Nanotube Membranes.** Researchers at Lawrence Livermore National Laboratory have created a membrane made of carbon nanotubes, which, as the name implies, are tiny little tubes made of carbon, 50,000 times thinner than a human hair and with extremely smooth surfaces. The researchers embedded the nanotubes in a ceramic membrane, where they act as pores, allowing water molecules through but blocking anything more than six water molecules across. What makes these membranes so interesting is that they allow water to flow more quickly than conventional membranes, which means that lower pressure—and therefore as much as 75 percent less energy—is needed to create a decent flow. The result: cheaper water.
- **Nanocomposite Membranes.** UCLA researchers have developed "a cross-linked matrix of polymers and engineered nanoparticles" that draw in water ions but repel organic molecules and bacteria that tend to clog up conventional membranes. Again, this lowers the amount of energy necessary to force water through the membrane. Initial tests suggest the new membranes consume 50 percent less energy, which might reduce the total expense of desalinated water by as much as 25 percent.

Water Management

When something is plentiful and cheap, there's little incentive to use it wisely. And with water, which has been nearly free for the past century, the amount of waste is breathtaking. Old pipes leak, water treatment systems do an inadequate or too costly job, homes and businesses have no idea what water costs and so don't make an effort to conserve. A 2007 European Commission report on water issues noted that Europe wastes at least 20 percent of its water. And if Europe is this bad, the U.S. number must be closer to 50 percent. (I'm just guessing here, but since we're the most profligate with everything else, why should water be an exception?) But, as always, the more egregious the problem, the more profitable the market. As the world confronts its water issues, dozens of companies are offering solutions. Here are some promising categories:

Smart Water Meters. Today's water system is just as dumb as the
old electrical grid. Users have no idea how much it costs
to water the lawn, wash the car, or run the dishwasher at
noon versus midnight, so they do whatever they like and use
a lot more water than they would if they actually understood the price or saw the cost add up in real time. So one
obvious way to rationalize water use is to install smart water
meters that allow water companies to impose pricing structures that differ depending on usage or time of day and show
consumers how much they're spending. Smart meters will
also enable municipalities to monitor consumption trends
in order to enforce restrictions on certain types of usage,
such as lawn irrigation, in times of drought. In one recent
U.K. test, metering resulted in a 9 percent drop in water
consumption.

Frequently, smart water meters are part of a package that
includes other utility efficiency gear. Typical is the February
2008 project in which Tallahassee, Florida, contracted with
Honeywell to install a smart metering network consisting of
22,000 meters and related equipment from North Carolina-
based Elster Integrated Solutions for electricity, natural gas,
and water. When the system goes live in 2009, the meters will
communicate wirelessly with local utilities, detect gas and
water leaks, and give customers detailed usage information.

And it will serve as the platform for next-generation demand management programs. The players in this market are mostly the same as in electricity metering. They're included in the list at the end of this chapter.

Water Management and Infrastructure. These days, when water has been used by a modern factory or home, it flows to a treatment plant where it might pass through an "advanced aeration, sequence batch reactor and membrane bioreactor system," and then to other tanks to be treated with "ozone, ultraviolet and chlorine disinfection systems" or filtered through reverse osmosis membranes, about which you've already read. The resulting pure water goes back into aquifers, on crops, or to factories for new industrial processes. The round trip involves a wide variety of equipment and facilities, all of which are made by public companies with increasingly global reach. ITT, for example, generates more than half of its sales from things like pumps, filters, and processing tanks. And Watts Water Technologies describes its business as "backflow preventers for preventing contamination of potable water caused by reverse flow within water supply lines and fire protection systems; a range of water pressure regulators for both commercial and residential applications . . . point-of-use water filtration and reverse osmosis systems for

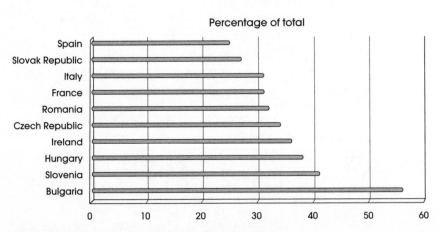

Figure 13.2   Water Losses in European Systems
Source: European Environment Agency

both commercial and residential applications." This isn't as easily grasped or as sexy as desalination, but it is crucial technology that virtually every major water user is willing to buy.

Meanwhile, many of today's cities have been around for a long time, which means the pipes carrying water to and from homes and businesses are older than most current residents. Because water pipes are invisible, unless they flat-out break, their maintenance tends to take a back seat to higher-profile services like garbage collection and policing. So drips, leaks, and general decay are endemic (see Figure 13.2).

State of the Water Management Market

This is a huge, sprawling sector with players ranging from specialized equipment makers to multibillion-dollar utilities. So it's hard to generalize, other than to say that demand is rising for most categories of goods and services and the most successful companies are coming to be seen as classic growth stocks.

Desalination and Water Management's Growth Prospects

Impressive across the board. Seawater, like sunlight, is free and virtually unlimited, so the arrival of cost-effective desalination will set off a decades-long boom. Because desalination plants are utility-scale projects, the players, as in wind power, tend to be large and global. General Electric and 3M are leading suppliers of filtration technology. Citigroup's Sustainable Development Investments unit is a big investor in Poseidon, which was formed in 1995 by former General Electric executives. Spain's Acciona S.A. and Germany's RWE AG are the main builders of desalination plants. One of the few small-cap growth vehicles in this space is Consolidated Water, which operates 13 reverse osmosis plants on various Caribbean islands.

And with cities increasingly strapped for cash just as water becomes an issue they can't ignore, they're either completely privatizing water systems or forming partnerships in which private companies build and/or operate parts of systems. France is furthest along: It has a history of private water system management dating back to the 1800s and is home to two of the world's leading water companies, Veolia Environment and Suez. But now virtually every major city and most major businesses are in the market for equipment and services

Table 13.2 Water Stocks

Company	Ticker/Exchange	Headquarters	Sector	Market Value, 6/27/08 ($ millions)
Acciona	ANA.MC/Madrid	Spain	Desalination	14,136
Consolidated Water	CWCO/NASDAQ	Cayman Islands	Desalination	283
Danaher	DHR/NYSE	U.S.	Water treatment	24,482
Danone	DANO.PA/Paris	France	Bottled water	31,824
Doosan Heavy Industries	034020.KS/Korea	South Korea	Desalination	8,781
Echelon	ELON/NASDAQ	U.S.	Water meters	454
Gammon India	GAMM.BO/Bombay	India	Infrastructure	492
General Electric	GE/NYSE	U.S.	Desalination	261,740
Halma	HLMA.L/London	U.K.	Leak detection	1,528
Itron	ITRI/NASDAQ	U.S.	Water meters	3,029
ITT	ITT/NYSE	U.S.	Water equipment	11,270
Leighton Holdings	LEI.AX/Australian Exch.	Australia	Desalination	14,288
Nalco	NLC/NYSE	U.S.	Water treatment	3,120
Nestle	NSRGY.PK/Pink Sheets	Switzerland	Bottled water	159,000
Roper Industries	ROP/NYSE	U.S.	Water meters	5,920
Rotork	ROR.L/London	U.K.	Water equipment	1,924
RWE	RWEG.F/Frankfurt	Germany	Desalination	61,500
Suez	LYOE.PA/Paris	France	Water services	82,050
Thermax	THMX.BO/Bombay	India	Water treatment	1,041
Veolia Environment	VE/NYSE	France	Water services	25,750
Watts Water Tech	WTS/NYSE	U.S.	Water equipment	890

that will conserve and stretch existing water supplies. So every category of water management, from utility-scale services and waste treatment plants to advanced pipe materials, pollution detection products, and water management algorithms, will see rising demand for at least the rest of this decade. As Table 13.2 illustrates, water, like solar, offers investors a wide range of possibilities but requires time and effort to make sense of the jumble of technologies, business models, and market niches. As you'll see in Chapter 19, there are entire mutual funds devoted to just this industry.

14

Green Building

SUNNY AND COOL

Fuel-efficient cars are nice, but most people spend their days in buildings, bathed in artificial light and breathing conditioned air. According to the EPA, buildings account for about 68 percent of U.S. electricity consumption, 39 percent of total energy use, and 38 percent of total carbon dioxide emissions. Yet during the Age of Unlimited Energy, most homes, factories, and office complexes were constructed with energy efficiency and environmental impact as afterthoughts. Design was about aesthetics or up-front cost. Building placement was about curb appeal or logistics rather than the relationship to sun, wind, and shade. And when thought was given to energy efficiency, the result was often counterproductive, as when office buildings are sealed so tightly that their internal air becomes dirtier than that of the surrounding city. Most of today's buildings, in short, are energy hogs designed, built, and furnished in ways that are problematic for both their inhabitants and the environment.

But here again, that's about to change. As energy costs rise and more people figure out that livability is valuable, "green building" is suddenly in. And right on cue, technologies and techniques are being developed or resurrected that will make tomorrow's buildings not just energy efficient but, in some cases, energy negative, meaning that they will produce more energy than they consume. Meanwhile, changes that make a building green frequently have benefits that go way beyond lower power bills. Houses with cleaner air and better light make for happier, healthier families. Schools with better ventilation and more comfortable temperatures report higher test scores. Green commercial buildings report fewer sick days, better worker productivity, and lower turnover. All of this translates into higher resale values and increased incentives to build green.

Defining Green Building

Standardizing and codifying green building is a lot harder than simply singing its praises. It's not immediately or intuitively obvious what a given attribute accomplishes and which, in a project with a limited budget, will give the biggest green bang for the buck. Are triple-glazed windows better than advanced lighting controls or superefficient insulation? How does nontoxic carpet stack up against a layer of sod on the roof? How much more can you charge (or should you be willing to pay) for a given basket of green upgrades? In response, building organizations around the world have devised rankings and certifications aimed at standardizing their product. In the United States, the main certification is based on the Green Building Council's Leadership in Energy and Environmental Design (LEED) rating system. Building attributes are assigned points, and the points are added up to produce a LEED rating on a scale that runs from "Certified" through Silver, Gold, and Platinum.

Since energy efficiency is the main financial selling point of green building, let's start with a look at what buildings do with the electricity they consume. Something like half goes to motors that cool space and food and run industrial machinery. About a sixth goes to heating space and water. Lighting is 20 percent—25 percent if you include the heat given off by incandescent light bulbs that has to be air conditioned away. And myriad smaller categories like cooking and electronics use appreciable amounts of power. Each has massive room for improvement, and each interacts with some or all of the others. So taking a traditional building design and making it green is a puzzle with pieces that vary in size, price, and complexity. The art—and the investment opportunity—lies in combining them in effective, profitable ways.

Windows and Bulbs

Most of the other clean-tech stories in this book are forward looking: A new technology like lithium-ion batteries or thin-film solar comes along that revolutionizes current practice in easily quantified ways.

Bigger charge, higher efficiency, lower cost per watt, and so on. But with green building, the story is more complex, with practices that were once common now being rediscovered and reintegrated into modern designs, while technology is taking these old ideas in radically new directions. Consider the commonsense but still profound idea called "daylighting." This is simply the orientation of a building and its windows to use incoming natural light to warm and illuminate as much interior space as possible. In pre-central-heating days this was obvious, but in the past half century it fell into disuse. Homes and office buildings were aligned according to arbitrary subdivision or office park road maps, and windows were placed and sized with aesthetics rather than function in mind. Now daylighting is making a comeback, as windows are once again sited where they do good rather than just look good. Meanwhile, new technologies are taking this concept and running with it.

> **Light Pipes.** A window or skylight can admit only the light that shines directly into it, and only for a limited internal distance. In a decent-sized building, that leaves a lot of dark interior space. Enter the light pipe, also known as a light tube, solar pipe, daylight pipe, or solar light pipe, which captures light on the roof or side of a building and transports it to the interior. Some use mirrors to bounce the light along, while others transmit it over optical fiber. Some distribute light along their entire length, while others bring the light to a specific point. One new version uses a light sensor called a heliostat to track the movement of the sun to maximize the amount of light entering the tube at all times. And—this ranks very high on the coolness, if not the LEED scale—tracking systems can be set to capture moonlight as well as sunlight. Light pipe systems can also be combined with light sensors and fluorescents to automatically maintain a constant light level.
>
> **Better Windows.** Glass isn't a very good insulator. To feel the truth of this, just walk over to a nearby window and touch it. Then touch the wall next to it. You'll probably notice that the wall is pretty much room temperature, while the window feels more like the outside. That's because a thin sheet of glass, or even two sheets with an air pocket between them, is a far less efficient insulator than layers of drywall, wood, and fiberglass

insulation. As a result, windows are "thermal holes" that let too much of the outside in and the inside out. The average home loses nearly a third of its heat or air conditioning energy through its windows, which in the United States alone is estimated to cost about $30 billion a year.

Today's top-of-the-line windows are triple glazed with heat-reflecting materials and insulated with layers of gases like argon that block heat far better than air. They're such good replacements for old-style windows that they can pay for themselves in 2 to 10 years, depending on the climate. In new buildings, they make it possible to install smaller, less expensive heating and air conditioning systems and still have a more comfortable internal environment.

But triple-glazed windows will soon be surpassed by electrochromic (EC) windows, which have coatings that allow them to darken and lighten in response to low electric voltage. Combine this capability with light sensors and smart grid control systems, and the result is a window that operates as part of a coherent climate control system that will, in theory, save both lighting and air conditioning energy while cutting down on glare and hot spots as the sun passes by. Theory is getting closer to practice: In 2008, a research team at the University of California–Berkeley, developed prototype EC windows that they estimate cut total annual lighting energy costs by around half compared to currently available windows while reducing peak power demand for cooling by about 20 percent. The gains are higher in sunny climes and greater for large windows than for small ones.

Better Bulbs. Daylighting, even the high-tech version using light pipes and EC windows, only works during the day, so a big part of a building's energy use will always be artificial light. And since the typical home's electric light still comes from inefficient incandescent bulbs, much can be done to raise efficiency with existing technologies. The first simple, currently available fix is to replace those old, inefficient incandescents with compact fluorescent bulbs that emit more light on less power, and don't get as hot. Think of them as "negawatt" power generators: By replacing a 75-watt incandescent with a 14-watt compact fluorescent, you get the same amount of light but save 61 watts, which is functionally the same as building a plant that generates that much power. Estimates vary on the cost of this kind negawatt generation, but everyone who looks into it concludes that it's really, really cheap. And consumers seem to get it: Sales of compact fluorescents are growing nicely. But because they contain highly toxic mercury, they have to be handled carefully and can't be recycled. So they're only partially green, and therefore just a transition technology.

LEDs. Here's where the lighting story gets really interesting. Light-emitting diodes (LEDs) are semiconductors that emit light when exposed to an electric current. They've been around for a century and have been used commercially since the 1960s in specialized niches like instrument indicators and traffic lights. They've always had some intriguing theoretical advantages, such as long life (50,000 hours versus 1,000 hours for an incandescent bulb), very low heat, and low power demand. But the early versions didn't cheaply scale up to light bulb size and only emitted colored light.

Lately, researchers have managed to bring down costs and adjust light wavelengths. And now a handful of LED makers, including Cree, Philips, Nexxus Lighting, and (as always) General Electric, offer LEDs priced low enough to generate rising sales, which is lengthening production runs and bringing down prices further. Meanwhile, labs around the world are reporting breakthroughs that might speed the cost decline. To take just one of many possible examples, in early 2008, Glasgow University scientists reported a cheap, fast method for making large numbers of microscopic holes on the surface of LEDs that increase their brightness without increasing energy consumption. The researchers claim that their process will bring LED prices down to a point at which they'll become the dominant form of indoor lighting.

OLEDs. Right behind LEDs are OLEDs, organic light-emitting diodes, which are plastics that can be molded and even sprayed onto surfaces and convert electricity to light. Today's OLEDs are too expensive and fragile for the lighting market, but because they're thinner and brighter than current flat-panel displays, they're becoming the screen of choice for cell phones and are now being scaled up for TVs. In December 2007, Sony introduced an 11-inch OLED TV with a 3-millimeter-thick display and picture quality that had reviewers raving.

One study predicts that the OLED market will grow from $280 million in 2008 to $3 billion in 2013. This huge market potential is driving research on better production methods, bringing OLED lighting closer to commercial viability. General Electric recently unveiled a 2-foot-square OLED panel that emits as much light as an 80-watt incandescent bulb and expressed optimism that fluorescent-level efficiency was coming soon. It's a safe bet that within a decade OLED wallpaper will be lighting rooms around the world.

Light Management Systems. Combine small, cheap light and motion sensors with demand control systems, and you get a building that's capable of managing its own lights in ways that cut power while improving livability. Commercial buildings, for instance, can monitor the amount of sunlight coming in and adjust window tints and artificial lights to maintain a constant light level. Or they can turn lights on and off automatically when people enter or leave a room. Done well, these kinds of lighting control systems can cut energy used for lighting in commercial buildings by nearly one-half (see the Cooper Union profile on page 155 for a real-world example).

Other Green Building Technologies

The story is the same throughout the building industry. Everything is being redesigned for efficiency and every product is being aimed at a suddenly environmentally aware customer base. It would require the rest of this book to cover the whole field, but here are a couple of examples:

Superefficient Appliances. Refrigerators and washers with better insulation and more efficient motors are on the way. In 2007, Department of Energy and appliance industry researchers demonstrated a refrigerator that uses less than a dime's worth of power per day. Other labs and manufacturers are developing "horizontal-axis" clothes washers that use about half the energy of existing models, water heaters that double as dehumidifiers while using less energy than either stand-alone appliance, and heat pumps that work in colder weather and use half the energy of the most efficient gas furnaces.

Green Building Materials. "Rapidly renewable" materials like bamboo and straw are seeing renewed interest, as are recycled metals and nontoxic glues and dyes. Among the investible ideas is a form of polystyrene from German chemical giant BASF that can be made into blocks to build walls that are strong, lightweight, and superinsulating. And keeping with the old-is-new-again theme, consider "thermal mass" substances like adobe that store heat in the day (keeping it from getting inside) and then release it at night when the desert rapidly cools, thus stabilizing a building's internal temperature. Like daylighting, thermal mass is seeing renewed interest, both in traditional and high-tech forms. Engineers at Oak Ridge National Laboratory in Tennessee, for instance, have developed "phase-change" materials that, when placed in an attic, melt while soaking up daytime heat. At night when the outside temperature drops, the material resolidifies and releases its heat into the atmosphere. Oak Ridge claims to have found phase change materials that can absorb 10 times as much heat per unit of volume as water.

The Joy of Co-Gen: Portrait of a Green Building

In Lower Manhattan's East Village, amid the nineteenth-century straight-line earth-tone architecture, something radically different is going up. A new academic center commissioned by Cooper Union, a venerable art, architecture, and engineering college, will, when completed in early 2009, face the street with a shiny latticework skin that curves to reflect light at varying angles. As the college web site puts it, "To further dissolve the boundaries between inside and outside, a semi-transparent screen of stainless steel spans the entire width of the building along Third Avenue, slanting and strategically breaking to allow views into and out from the building."

But the unusual look is the least of this building's differences. Approximately 75 percent of its occupiable space will be lit naturally with daylight, reducing the need for artificial light. Sensors in each room will monitor incoming light and dim or brighten interior lights automatically, and turn lights off when a room's occupants leave. A related system will manage airflow in classrooms and labs. "In a lab, the code says if you're working with chemicals you need twelve air changes an hour, which means you're replacing 100 percent of the room's air every five minutes," says

(Continued)

(*Continued*)

Clark Wieman, Cooper Union's planning director. "If that's happening constantly you're heating and cooling a lot of air." So the new system will sense when labs are empty and drop the air flow to four changes an hour.

Part of the building's heating and air conditioning will come from water circulating through radiant ceiling panels. "This is almost unheard of in the Northeast," says Wieman. "But water is more efficient than air for transporting heat. We visited some buildings in Canada and Amsterdam where it works well." About a fourth of the roof will be covered with plants, which will be irrigated with rainwater collected in tanks. The foliage will mitigate the building's heat island effect while reducing the flow of storm water into Manhattan's sewer system. And a second rainwater collection tank will offset water use in lower-floor bathrooms.

This design would be enough to earn the building a LEED Gold rating. But in his research, Wieman found that a co-generation system would both save energy and make LEED Platinum a possibility. "Co-gen" involves generating power on site and using the resulting waste heat to do other useful things, which dramatically raises the building's energy efficiency. In Cooper Union's case, the system pipes in natural gas to run a turbine that provides the building's baseline electricity and generates waste heat to warm the building or, through an absorption chiller, cool it. "The ability to put waste heat to work is the magic bullet," says Wieman. "A typical building might be 35 percent efficient in terms of how many incoming BTUs are actually used; 65 percent is waste. With a co-gen plant the efficiency goes up to 80 percent or more." The impact on overall "greenness" is equally dramatic. Without co-gen, the building would be about 25 percent cheaper to operate than its typical neighbor. With co-gen, it's 42 percent cheaper, according to computer models that predict energy use. The result is a short payback period and a lower long-term operating cost—and significantly more LEED points. A building can receive up to 10 LEED points for energy efficiency, as measured by a Department of Energy model that compares a proposed building's energy performance to that of a standard building. Daylighting and radiant heating were worth four or five LEED points, says Wieman. "But by adding co-gen, we got ten. These additional points put us in shooting range of LEED Platinum."

State of the Market

Green building is being adopted by everyone from architects to builders to appliance makers. But it's less of a revolution than a mass conversion. Upstarts, by and large, are not displacing entrenched interests; the players are the same, and the numbers (in terms of

Table 14.1 Green Building Stocks

Company	Ticker/ Exchange	Headquarters	Sector	Market Value, 6/27/08 ($ millions)
3M	MMM/NYSE	U.S.	Light pipes	48,950
BASF	BASF/Frankfurt	Germany	Building materials	6,225
Cree	CREE/NASDAQ	U.S.	LEDs	2,120
Comverge	COMV/NASDAQ	U.S.	Lighting controls	277
Eastman Kodak	EK/NYSE	U.S.	OLEDs	4,180
EnerNOC	ENOC/NASDAQ	U.S.	Lighting controls	342
General Electric	GE/NYSE	U.S.	OLEDs	261,740
Honeywell	HON/NYSE	U.S.	Building controls	36,510
Johnson Controls	JCI/NYSE	U.S.	Building controls	17,010
Orion Energy Systems	OESX/NASDAQ	U.S.	Lighting controls	268
Sumitomo Chemical	4005.T/Tokyo	Japan	OLEDs	10,423
Universal Display	PANL/NASDAQ	U.S.	OLEDs	458

construction spending, housing starts, industry employment, etc.) are in line with those of past years. There are few large wind farm–type installations that signify a radical break with the past. Just a lot of more livable, efficient buildings.

Green Building's Growth Prospects

Huge, as green building techniques, materials, and systems go mainstream. A decade hence, most new structures in the developed world and many in the developing world will incorporate green systems and materials. Since construction is one of the largest global industries, the numbers involved will be big and will grow rapidly. But at the moment, there aren't a lot of pure-play green building stocks. The makers of lighting/climate control systems earn most of their profits in other markets, as do the makers of green building materials. Construction firms, even those specializing in green building, are dependent more on the credit markets and the state of the general economy, which in early 2008 were dismal. The main pure plays are the LED and OLED makers like Cree and Universal Display, but as Table 14.1 illustrates, they're up against global giants.

15

Agriculture

EIGHT BILLION MOUTHS TO FEED

That the world's farmers and fishermen are able to feed 6 billion people is remarkable. That they'll have trouble feeding the 8 billion likely by 2030 is undeniable. Consider the following facts, some of which appeared in other chapters, some of which are new:

- Deserts are spreading, which is degrading farm land in some of the poorest and least able to adapt parts of the world.
- The amount of water available from rivers, lakes, and underground aquifers is declining, and the replacement—desalinated seawater—is considerably more expensive.
- Irrigated land is being poisoned by salt buildup.
- Current farming methods cause the gradual erosion of topsoil, which reduces the amount and quality of available farmland a bit more each year.
- The practice of planting just a few highly productive varieties of most crops leaves them vulnerable to diseases like the potentially devastating wheat fungus that is now threatening Europe's farms.
- Commercial fish populations are declining in some parts of the ocean and crashing in others, while demand for fish is soaring.

Add it all up, and it's more likely that business as usual will produce a *decline* in food output rather than the necessary huge increase. Which means, once again, that the companies with the solutions are tomorrow's growth stocks. This chapter presents a range of technologies that (maybe because of the universal appeal of food) are especially interesting, if not always immediately investable. Some, like genetically modified crops, are available today, while others, like lab-grown meat, are a long way off. But taken together, they have the potential not just to stave off a Malthusian nightmare but to dramatically improve all of our diets.

Genetically Modified Plants

As water and synthetic fertilizers become more expensive, agriculture has no choice but to adapt. Farmers will stop spraying water on their fields and shift to techniques like drip irrigation, which applies water in smaller amounts at the root zone, where it's most beneficial. They'll use pesticides and fertilizers more carefully. And, despite their perhaps reasonable misgivings, they'll buy and plant genetically modified (GM) seeds that produce higher yields with less water, fertilizer, and pesticide. Research into new crop varieties is now a huge business, and agricultural biotech—the science of genetically altering crops for various advantages—is exploding. This is not universally seen as a good thing; in fact, it's not clear to many critics that genetically modified plants and animals deserve to be viewed as clean tech. The arguments against take two general forms: First, because GM crops are new additions to the gene pool and food chain, their long-term effects on the ecosystem and consumers are unknown. What if they transmit genetic traits to nearby crops or wild relatives? If certain traits turn out to have unintended consequences, we won't be able to call them back, and the damage may be irreversible. Second, GM foods are unnatural and creepy, and therefore unappetizing.

The first of these concerns, at least, is legitimate. But because it's outweighed by the high probability that desperate times are coming, farmers and consumers are likely to put aside their misgivings in favor of what works in the here and now. Europe has banned GM foods almost entirely, but the rest of the world has proved more hospitable. In 2007, 10 million farmers were planting genetically altered crops worldwide. Nine million of those farmers were in the developing world, which now accounts for 40 percent of global biotech acreage. In the United States, GM seed accounts for 73 percent of corn, 87 percent of cotton, and 91 percent of soy production. And the trend line is steepening: By 2015, more than 20 million farmers in 40 countries are projected to be growing genetically altered crops.

Farmers and plant breeders have, of course, been modifying crops for centuries by selecting and sowing seeds from plants with desirable traits in the hope of passing those traits on to the next generation. In the process, they modified the genetic makeup of crop plants to the point that current varieties often bear only a passing resemblance to their wild ancestors. Such crossbreeding was a blunt instrument because it involved thousands of genes, only a few of which were responsible for the desired traits. But with the discovery of DNA (deoxyribonucleic acid) in 1953, scientists began to realize that all cells operate on the same basic principles and share the same language. All contain DNA that tells them, among other things, which proteins to make in what quantities. From there, it didn't take long to figure out that moving a snippet of DNA from one cell to another would cause the second cell to start behaving like the first. Now it's possible to figure out which genes do what and insert them into a plant to produce a version that's identical to its ancestor except for one new, genetically engineered trait—such as the following:

- **Pest Resistance.** Some GM plants produce pesticides in their cells that kill the bugs that used to eat them. "Bt" crops, for instance, produce a protein derived from a common soil bacteria, *Bacillus thuringiensis,* that's toxic to some insects. Free from predation, the plants thrive with fewer pesticide applications, increasing per acre yields and saving the farmer time and money.
- **Herbicide Resistance.** Farmers used to spray herbicides on their fields before their crops sprouted. This killed the weeds but didn't harm the crops. Once the crops were growing, however, the weeds got more of a free ride. But with "Roundup Ready" crops, which are modified to withstand the popular herbicide Roundup, farmers can kill weeds anytime they want without hurting their crops. Fewer weeds means more food and water for crops and bigger yields.

- **Drought Tolerance.** The ability to grow in dry climates or survive if seasonal rains fail would be huge. It's not here yet, but everyone is working on it. Missouri-based Monsanto claims to have a drought-tolerant corn nearly ready for market, with soybeans and cotton in the pipeline. German multinational Bayer CropScience is working on drought-resistant strains of canola, rice, cotton, and corn.
- **Salt Tolerance.** When groundwater is used to irrigate thirsty crops in dry regions, salt tends to build up in the soil, eventually ruining it. This is a huge problem worldwide, and as rising seas infiltrate groundwater, coastal agricultural land may become increasingly contaminated. In early 2008, California-based Arcadia Biosciences was reportedly licensing a salt-tolerant variety of alfalfa and working on rice, cotton, tomatoes, and canola. Chinese researchers, meanwhile, reported progress with both drought- and salt-tolerant rice.
- **Enhanced Nitrogen Absorption.** The better a plant is at pulling nutrients like nitrogen from the ground, the less synthetic fertilizer it needs. This is potentially huge from both a financial and environmental perspective, and everyone is working on it.
- **Fast-Growing Trees.** ArborGen, a South Carolina biotech company, claims to have modified pine trees to grow to marketable size in 18 years rather than the current 30 and to have created a low-lignin eucalyptus tree that is better for pulping. If successful, such "transgenic" trees will allow existing forestry operations to produce more wood on the same land, relieving some of the pressure on old-growth and rain forests. Reducing the amount of lignin, meanwhile, would improve the economics of both paper and biofuels.
- **Coming Soon: Multiple Traits.** Early on, biotechnologists were able to manipulate only one gene at a time. But in the past few years they've learned how to work with multiple genes and are now mixing and matching them to produce crops with portfolios of new traits. By 2010, Monsanto and Dow Chemical plan to release a strain of corn called SmartStax with eight engineered traits, including protection against several corn pests and a tolerance for certain herbicides. Soon after that, they plan to add drought resistance and enhanced nitrogen absorption.

State of the Market

The market for GM crops is so new and specialized that only a few companies operate there on any scale. Monsanto is the dominant player, and through a combination of innovation and legal hardball, it has managed to alter farmers' buying and planting habits. Instead of buying seeds from four or five seed companies, farmers have begun to narrow the list down to one or two, with Monsanto usually at the top. As a result, its sales are soaring and its profit margins are widening. In early 2008, the consensus among analysts called for sales growth of better than 20 percent a year for the following three years. But now competition is heating up, as Dow Chemical's AgroSciences division and Swiss-based Syngenta, the world's biggest agrichemicals company, are both bringing out GM seeds. Dow's "Herculex" corn resists an array of harmful insects, while Syngenta is introducing Roundup-tolerant corn.

Agribiotech's Growth Prospects

Genetic engineers are just beginning to figure out how to mix and match genes to produce useful plants. So barring a major Frankenfood incident, next generation GM crops will extend their advantages over traditional varieties and will come to dominate agriculture. But the small number of players (see Table 15.1) limits investors' choices, so this sector doesn't require a lot of thought or offer much advantage to in-depth study.

Table 15.1   Agribiotech Stocks

Company	Ticker/ Exchange	Headquarters	Market Value, 6/27/08 ($ millions)
Bayer (Bayer CropScience)	BAYG.F/Frankfurt	Germany	60,900
Dow Chemical (AgroSciences)	DOW/NYSE	U.S.	32,410
DuPont (Pioneer Hi-Bred)	DD/NYSE	U.S.	38,450
Monsanto	MON/NYSE	U.S.	70,430
Origin Agritech	SEED/NASDAQ	China	136
Syngenta	SYT/NYSE	Switzerland	29,972

Vertical Farms

Take a stroll through the local grocery store and notice how much of what you're seeing comes from just a few miles away. Chances are it's less than 10 percent, with the rest coming from other states and frequently other continents. Getting this stuff—say fruit in the off season that's grown in a different hemisphere—from field to store requires a lot of energy, raising the cost of both food and oil, while polluting at each stage of the process. Meanwhile, the amount of good farmland around most cities is shrinking as a result of urban sprawl, stretching supply chains even further.

So why not solve both problems at once by building vertical farms right in the middle of cities, says Dickson Despommier, a 67-year-old microbiologist at Columbia University. Every major city, after all, has hundreds of abandoned buildings, most with water and electricity hookups. Convert them to hydroponic farms and you use no new land, while producing food that has virtually no commute. Or build new state-of-the-art skyscraper farms from scratch: A 30-story farm covering one city block would, estimates Despommier, produce enough food to feed 50,000 of its neighbors each year, with no pesticide runoff or other agricultural waste.

The technology that makes this kind of radical break with current practice possible is hydroponics (from the Greek *hydros,* water, and *ponos,* labor), a time-tested way of growing plants in liquid nutrient solutions. Soil, it turns out, is just a placeholder for the minerals and inorganic ions that plants absorb through their roots. Water does just as good a job, and for decades people have been growing certain crops hydroponically. In the state-of-the-art version proposed by Despommier, the plants will travel by automated conveyer belts past grow lights and through nutrient-rich solutions. Because such a farm would capture and reuse the water that evaporates from crop leaves, it would theoretically use just a fraction of the water that an outdoor farm of the same size uses, while producing dozens of varieties of fruits and vegetables. Further down the road, Despommier envisions genetically engineered and selectively bred plants that are perfectly suited for the environment (a nice tie-in with Monsanto et al.). Plant waste might go into an on-site biofuel distillery that produces part of the energy to run the farm. In some climates, the rest of the energy might come from rooftop solar panels. The benefits of making each city partially self-sufficient in food are legion. A shorter supply chain means less oil use and less CO_2 in the atmosphere. It means less farmland and more forest, again producing a cleaner environment. It means less water being pulled from rivers, lakes, and aquifers. And it means fresh vegetables available year-round to people who today don't eat nearly as well as they should. The vertical farm blends a whole lot of green ideas into one very attractive concept.

Vertical Farms' Growth Prospects

Is it doable at market prices? Not yet. The first few buildings would require serious subsidies, though not out of line with what is now being directed to solar power in some countries—or to current subsidies for traditional farming. In early 2008, it appeared that Despommier would have a chance to build a prototype, thanks to research grants from various sources. "Ten years from now," he predicted in a 2007 interview, "there will be vertical farms throughout the world. I guarantee it." At the moment there's nothing to invest in here, but if the concept works, it's easy to imagine a whole constellation of companies running such farms, making specialized gear and designing new plant varieties. So put vertical farming in the 2012 file.

Aquaculture: Blue Revolution

The problems caused by our attempts to put roast beef and chicken teriyaki on the table are nothing compared to the consequences of our growing taste for fish. Today's oceans are crawling with football-field-sized factory ships trailing miles of netting that sweep up sharks, dolphins, turtles, and whatever else is out there. We're so good at large-scale fishing, and so lax in deciding who gets to take how much, that the oceans have become a textbook example of the tragedy of the commons, the parable illustrating the point that when it's in everyone's short-term interest to take as much as possible, eventually there's nothing for anyone. Once virtually unlimited populations of cod, haddock, and halibut are crashing, and increasingly desperate factory trawlers are encroaching on each others' territories and moving down the value chain, taking less attractive fish and smaller members of popular species. The UN estimates that 28 percent of fish stocks worldwide are either overfished or nearing extinction and another 47 percent are near the limits of sustainability. According to the U.S. National Oceanic and Atmospheric Administration, in waters off the United States, roughly a third of fish stocks are in jeopardy. A University of British Columbia study predicts that many large species will be all but gone from the North Atlantic region within a few decades. Yet demand for fish, thanks to the developing world's growing middle class, is doubling every two decades, which means we'll have to somehow come up with almost twice as much fish by 2025.

The traditional response to rising seafood demand has been to raise fish in concrete tanks near inland water sources or in huge nets in bays along the seacoast. This is already a very big business, producing about 40 percent of the fish consumed each year world-wide. But it has a whole host of unintended consequences. Diseases run rampant in such close quarters and have to be knocked back with massive doses of antibiotics. Fish that have been genetically altered to grow fast and otherwise thrive in crowded enclosures are escaping and polluting wild gene pools. Inland fish farms require expensive pumps and filters that have to operate continuously; a power outage means a lost crop. And as anyone with an aquarium knows, fish are really dirty. A school of 200,000 salmon produce nitrogen and phosphorous that's equivalent to the sewage of a city of 20,000 people; the pollution generated by so many fish in such a small space is fouling waters for miles around large shore-based farms. But the biggest problem is that this is generally waterfront property we're talking about. As such, it's worth more for home sites and hotels than for aquaculture. In a battle between farmers of any kind and the well-off seeking gorgeous views, the farmers always lose. So in the future, there simply won't be enough room for fast-growing shore-based fish farming. It's possible, then, that the world of 2020 will be one in which only the well-off eat fish and the mul-titudes who traditionally depend on fish but aren't rich will be out of luck—and out of protein. Unless we find new ways of producing fish. Here's one possibility.

Open Ocean Aquaculture

Fish farming's main drawback is that it's done in close quarters. Shore-based pens are fenced and stationary, and are generally located in a placid body of water like a bay without swift currents or big waves. Because the water doesn't move fast enough to carry away the waste and food particles that commercial quantities of fish generate, the area gets dirty, the fish get sick, and both neighbors and customers complain. Meanwhile, there's this big ocean right nearby, with thousands of miles of open water capable of absorbing anything a single school of salmon can throw at it. So why not put the farms out to sea?

For over a decade, a Seattle company called Net Systems has been selling huge SeaStation model enclosures that make it possible to site fish farms miles from shore, where currents guarantee a continuous flow of clean seawater. The enclosure is a rigid cage that's wide in the middle and tapered at the top and bottom, covered with "predator-proof" netting made of Spectra, a superstrong polyethylene fiber used by NASA to tether spacewalking astronauts. Current models are in the range of 50 feet high by 80 feet wide, which is big enough to hold tens of thousands of fish. A steel cylinder runs from the bottom of the cage to the top and is capped by a pump that forces air in and out of the cylinder to raise or lower the enclosure. Depending on the mix of air and water, the cage floats on the surface or sinks from 40 feet to 60 feet, where even in surface storms the sea is placid. Another company, Maine-based Ocean Farm Technologies, is developing a line of spherical geodesic enclosures that operate basically the same way, though, it claims, with cost and scalability advantages.

The theoretical advantages of open ocean fish farming are many: The enclosures are virtually invisible from shore—all you see is a single buoy. Ocean currents keep the fish healthy without the need for antibiotics, and the size of the ocean minimizes the impact of fish waste. Attracted by the possibilities, universities and governments around the world are running feasibility tests. The U.S. government and the University of Hawaii are operating a prototype open ocean fish farm anchored in 100-foot waters 2 miles off Hawaii's Ewa Beach. The researchers fill the cage with 70,000 baby moi, a local delicacy, feed and monitor them, and harvest them when they're grown—at a cost that's estimated to be comparable to current market price. Other studies, most using Net Systems enclosures, are ongoing in at least 10 other countries.

Two private companies are already farming this way: Puerto Rico-based Snapperfarm raises cobia 2 miles off the local coast in Net Systems and Ocean Farm Technologies enclosures. According to Snapperfarm, strong currents refresh the enclosures' water over 1,000 times per day, which keeps the fish healthy, allowing it to market its cobia as "all natural, free of hormones, pigments, drugs, and antibiotics." Studies by the Universities of Miami and Puerto Rico have, again according to the company, found no significant environmental impact. Hawaii-based Kona Blue Water Farms, meanwhile, operates a hatchery and offshore farm system that raises Kona Kampachi, a "sushi-grade Hawaiian yellowtail" in pens half a mile off the Kona, Hawaii, coast. Here again, brisk currents keep the fish healthy without drugs.

The offshore farming concept appears to have potential for shellfish, too. The University of New Hampshire and some local fishermen have successfully convinced mussels to grow along lines suspended from buoys far from shore. The shellfish filter water for microorganisms and require no other food or drugs, and because the deep water is calmer, they develop thinner shells and more meat, making them more marketable than their close-to-shore cousins.

Mobile Farms

The ocean is big enough to accommodate a lot of offshore fish farms. But the real payoff from the development of this technology comes with the addition of one more capability: mobility. Take a giant fenced enclosure, fill it with fingerlings in Florida, and send it out to drift slowly in the Gulf Stream or another of the ocean's many predictable currents. Program a self-powered computerized navigation and feeding system to keep the enclosure on course and the fish fed. The ocean supplies clean water and whisks away waste, and after nine or so months, the fully grown fish arrive at a European port, ready for market. Then the enclosure is refilled with fingerlings from a local hatchery and heads on to its next port of call.

This kind of capability is being developed in several places. The University of New Hampshire is working with Net Systems to develop a 20-ton buoy that will automatically feed and monitor fish for weeks at a time, while MIT engineers are designing a huge enclosure, three times the size of current models, called the Ocean Drifter. As envisioned, it will be powered by three electric thruster motors attached to the rig's steel equator that are run by a diesel generator mounted atop the central spar and steered by software. Test results should be coming in by late 2008.

There are two potential problems here. First, since open ocean aquaculture proponents envision specially designed fish that thrive in this kind of environment, genetic pollution will be a risk, just as it is for shore-based farms. Already, Massachusetts-based Aqua Bounty

Technologies claims to have figured out how to switch on a growth-regulating gene in fish, leading to hybrid salmon, trout, and tilapia that reach market size twice as fast and convert feed into body mass more efficiently. As with GM plants, the era of GM fish appears to have arrived, and we can only hope for the best. Meanwhile, farmed fish are generally fed pellets that contain fish meal, so the process partially defeats its own purpose, requiring fish to make more fish. But that's the kind of fix the market can provide. Several companies are working on fish-free pellets, and early testing indicates that fish thrive with the new meal.

Aquaculture's Growth Prospects

We'll know soon if this is feasible. If it is, there's room out there for thousands of enclosures, producing all the fish a hungry populace could ever want, at prices that will put those factory trawlers with their 20-mile driftnets out of business. Investment opportunities will include enclosures and related gear, genetically modified fish, fish food, and large-scale fish farming business models. And seafood restaurants, which will enjoy declining costs relative to their steakhouse competitors. At least until the following technology pans out . . .

Lab-Grown Meat

Back in the old days—the really old days, when we were hominids on the savanna competing with leopards and baboons—meat was the ultimate luxury. Rich in protein and fat, a bellyful of antelope would all but guarantee another few days of vigorous life. So our ancestors evolved the compulsion to gorge on meat when it was available, and they passed this compulsion down to us. The problem is that meat is now available 24/7, so we eat a lot of it. And as the billions who hardly ever get meat suddenly find themselves with some extra cash, they're opting for more frequent drumsticks and pork chops. As a result, global meat consumption is up dramatically.

Unfortunately, fattening up a cow and then slaughtering it is one of the least efficient ways to turn sunlight and water into nutrition. According to the U.S. Department of Agriculture, it takes 4.5 pounds of animal feed—usually corn—to produce a pound of chicken, 9.4 pounds of corn for a pound of pork, and 25 pounds of corn per pound of beef. Half of the corn produced in the United States is used for animal feed, which explains why, as meat demand spikes worldwide, grain prices are soaring as well. And because growing corn is water and energy intensive, this also explains in part the shortages that seem to be developing in those markets. Then there's the greenhouse gas angle: Growing a pound of beef puts about as much CO_2 into the air as driving the average car 200 miles. According to one study, the animals we raise for meat account for one-fifth of all the CO_2 produced by human activity. And recall from Chapter 13 that a pound of beef requires 800 gallons of water. Meat, in short, may not be the main cause of our many looming resource shortages, but it's right up there.

Left to itself, the market will solve the meat dilemma by raising the price of everything associated with it until, once again, only the rich can afford it. That's happening now and seems likely to continue for the next few years, but it's hardly ideal. Much better would be to use our growing understanding of biology to find ways to make meat without going through the rigmarole of growing the corn, feeding the cow for two years, cutting, packaging, and shipping the meat. Scientists have, in fact, been working on lab-grown meat for years. The idea is that by industrializing the process, it might be possible to grow unlimited amounts of designer meat with minimal inputs and little pollution. So far, no one has figured out how to turn tissue cultures into anything resembling a T-bone steak. But as stem cell expertise in particular and biotech in general accelerate, some promising avenues are opening up.

The lab-grown meat story begins in 2001, when scientists at New York's Touro College were asked by NASA to explore ways of producing food on future spaceflight missions. They successfully grew goldfish muscle in a nutrient broth, which led a group including Henk Haagsman, a professor of meat sciences at the Netherlands' Utrecht University, and local sausage company Stegeman to try the same thing with pork. Their method involves adding pig muscle cells to thin membranes immersed in a growth medium. The cells multiply to form thin layers of meat tissue. It works, but only in a very limited sense. The resulting meat doesn't have the consistency of pork or ham because it hasn't been flexed the way living muscle is. And natural meat is infused with blood vessels, connective tissue, and fat, which the researchers aren't even attempting to add yet.

And the growth medium, fetal bovine serum, is so expensive that lab-grown meat is at least $1,000 a pound.

But hey, early solar panels had their limitations, and look how far they've come. Lab-grown meat is likely to travel the same falling cost/rising quality path until it reaches some level of acceptability, and ideas abound for getting from here to there. Hawaii-based biotech firm Tissue Genesis is attaching self-assembling muscle tissue to three-dimensional anchors that cause the cells to develop into long fibers similar to real muscle. Haagsman and many other researchers are looking for cheaper growth media, better cells, and more efficient "bioreactor" designs. The ultimate goal is a single facility in which bioreactors create cells and growth media and then combine them to produce meat.

Cultured Meat's Growth Prospects

Strictly science experiment for another few years. Then a slow ramp-up, leading to the possibility of a big global market with an extensive supply chain and many public companies. There's nothing here for investors in the short run, but it's worth understanding and following for what it might someday become.

CHAPTER 16

Green Materials

LIGHTER, STRONGER, CLEANER

Look up from this book for a second and notice your surroundings. Unless you're in a forest or at the beach, chances are, much of what you're seeing is composed of man-made materials like steel, concrete, plastic, and glass. Brought together in various shapes and configurations, they form civilization's bone structure. They're all good at what they do, and very, very cheap. But they're also flawed, contributing in one way or another to the problems discussed in earlier chapters. The steel in auto frames is heavy, which means cars use more gas than they would if they weighed a thousand pounds less. Plastic comes from petroleum, and it frequently contains chemicals that leach into food and groundwater. Concrete is hugely energy intensive to produce. But for each problem, there exists a solution in the form of new materials that do the same job without the attendant drawbacks. As they move from lab to market, the result will be lighter cars that stretch a gallon of gas (or a battery charge) farther than current models, safer and more fuel-efficient aircraft, plastics that biodegrade in landfills and don't leach nasty chemicals, and microchips that do more with less power.

Amory Lovins, chief scientist at the Colorado-based green think tank Rocky Mountain Institute, has been preaching the advantages of advanced materials for decades. In early 2008, he wrote in *Newsweek*,

> In 2000 my team designed an ultrasafe carbon-fiber SUV that needed 10 to 20 times fewer body parts and no body shop (the

parts snapped precisely together without jigs, robots or welders). It didn't require a paint shop because color can be molded into the composite. The car yielded 72 percent fuel savings, repaying the $2,511 extra retail cost in one or two years.

To varying degrees, the mainstream automakers are buying into Lovins's vision. Ford recently announced a plan to trim between 250 and 750 pounds from each of its cars through the use of lighter, stronger body parts. Mitsubishi Motors' i-MiEV concept car weighs 265 pounds less than if it were made with traditional materials. Toyota's 1/X concept hybrid is one-third the weight of a Prius and uses half the fuel, yet it has the same interior volume. It's the same in every other industry, which means that virtually everything we build and use a decade from now will be enhanced and generally cleaned up by lighter, stronger, more stable materials. But this field, more than any other in the clean-tech world, is the province of scientists and engineers, which makes it hard to penetrate. For an idea of just how hard, check out the web site of a trade magazine like *Advanced Materials*. In early 2008, a visitor would have found the following under the heading "Advances In":

- Self-Assembly of Ligand-Free PbS Nanocrystals into Nanorods and Their Nanosculpturing by Electron-Beam Irradiation
- Tailoring the Optical and Catalytic Properties of Gold-Silver Nanoboxes and Nanocages by Introducing Palladium
- Nanoscale Patterning and Electronics on Flexible Substrate by Direct Nanoimprinting of Metallic Nanoparticles
- Chemical Nanostructures of Multifunctional Self-Assembled Monolayers
- Sequence-Dependent Fluorescence of DNA-Hosted Silver Nanoclusters
- Fabrication of Elastomeric Wires by Selective Electroless Metallization of Poly (dimethylsiloxane)

Nanocages? Silver nanoclusters? Self-assembled monolayers? See what I mean? Advanced materials are a little tougher for the non-engineer to grasp than, say, wind power. But buried in this haystack of technical verbiage are the core products of a whole generation of growth companies. So investors with a scientific bent might find the effort worthwhile. As for this chapter, there's no central narrative here. Instead, there are lots of smaller stories flowing into a river of new molecules and processes with properties that were once the province of science fiction novels, followed by a few company names. The rest will be up to you.

Carbon Fiber

Carbon fiber consists of long, thin sheets of graphite-like carbon that are stronger than steel but lighter than aluminum. Thomas Edison is said to have invented it in 1879, and in 1961, Japanese researcher Akio Shindo developed the modern version, called polyacrylonitrile carbon fiber, after which several companies began producing it for specialized, expensive products like golf clubs and fishing rods. In the late 1980s, Japanese manufacturer Toray mixed carbon fiber with an epoxy resin to create a carbon-reinforced plastic called "prepreg," which found its way into high-end sailboats, bike frames, and Formula One race cars. This version of carbon fiber offered some huge weight and strength advantages for aircraft manufacturers, and recently Boeing gave it a big break by designing the upcoming 787 Dreamliner with carbon-fiber composites. The Dreamliner's promised combination of fuel efficiency and range has translated into a deluge of advance orders, which means demand for carbon fiber will soar. In response, the main suppliers are gearing up. Cytec Industries, Toray Industries, and Kawasaki Heavy Industries will now start making it on an industrial scale, which will push down prices and make carbon fiber attractive for more uses, possibly including midrange cars. Toray, in fact, aims to become the world's first company to mass produce car parts made of carbon fiber and hopes to more than double its sales to the automobile industry in the coming decade. Carbon fiber has also replaced fiberglass in the current generation of wind turbines. Missouri-based Zoltek, the leading supplier of carbon fiber for that market, landed large long-term orders from turbine makers Vestas Wind Systems and Gamesa in 2007.

Bioplastics

The old guy in *The Graduate* was right. Plastic was the future. Durable, light, malleable, and cheap, it's everywhere today, from food packaging to toys to computer keyboards. But lately its imperfections have become as apparent as its strengths. It's made from oil, with all the downsides that implies. To achieve its most valued characteristics, it is frequently impregnated with chemicals that have turned out to (1) leach from toys and containers once thought to be inert, and (2) cause developmental defects and possibly cancer (more about this soon). And it doesn't biodegrade, instead lurking for decades in landfills and floating around in the ocean. So a replacement for petro-plastic would solve several problems and find a big, willing market.

One possible solution is to make plastic from plants instead of oil. Today's "bioplastics" are produced in a process similar to that for producing ethanol—by fermenting corn starch and feeding it to specially designed microorganisms that excrete polymers, which are then turned into films, sheets, and fibers, just like petroleum-derived plastic. Because plants sequester carbon when they grow, turning them into plastic puts less carbon into the atmosphere. And bioplastics don't require the dangerous additives that are striking such fear into parents these days. On the minus side, bioplastics can't be recycled along with traditional plastics because they're not compatible. But this is a temporary problem; the recycling industry is working with bioplastic producers to make it easier to tell the two kinds of plastic apart. So as the amount of bioplastic in the marketplace rises, the recycling infrastructure will develop along with it.

Current bioplastics are more expensive than petroleum-based commodity plastics, but they are becoming cost competitive at the high-performance end of the market. They're seeing rising demand in niches like drug capsules, electronics, and car parts. Cargill's NatureWorks joint venture makes a popular corn-based bioplastic that's used in water bottles, among other things. Toyota is building bioplastic plants and intends to make its own auto body parts. And Massachusetts-based Metabolix recently partnered with Archer Daniels Midland to introduce a bioplastic called Mirel that biodegrades in any environment where microbes are present, including soil, industrial or home compost, septic systems, and the ocean. Target stores now offer gift cards made of it. At about 2 billion pounds a year, the high-end plastics market is big enough to offer plenty of near-term growth for newly developed bioplastics. But this generation of bioplastics will never replace oil. As with corn-based ethanol, the fact that they're made from food is a deal breaker, because their popularity drives up prices at the grocery store, penalizing the world's poor and destabilizing the global economy (and raising bioplastic manufacturing costs). But as with biofuels, starting with corn helps build an infrastructure that can adapt to other feedstocks as they become available. Metabolix, for instance, is genetically engineering switchgrass, oil seeds, and sugarcane to produce bioplastic in their cells. Once this becomes possible on a commercial scale, the next step is to set up dual-process bioplastic and biofuels plants. "We'll grow the biomass crops, extract the plastic and use the residual 90 percent as a source of biofuels," says Dr. Oliver Peoples, founder and chief scientific officer of Metabolix. "There's more to be done, but we're way beyond proof of concept." Before the middle of the next decade, he predicts, crops containing bioplastic will be grown on a commercial scale.

Ceramics

Ceramics are inorganic, nonmetallic materials with crystalline or partly crystalline structures formed at high temperatures. The earliest ceramics were clays that were made into pottery and tiles. The more modern versions include silicon carbide and boron nitride, and are used pretty much everywhere for pretty much everything, from engine heat shields to artificial bone to magnets. Ceramics seem to be especially big in cars:

- Recall from Chapter 8 that EEStor's new ceramic ultracapacitor will, if it works as promised, make electric vehicles commercially viable.
- Ceramic brakes that weigh 5 pounds each versus 20 to 30 pounds for old-style cast iron brakes are now commonly offered on high-end sports cars and will soon work their way down to midrange cars.
- Illinois-based Corning recently introduced a next-generation ceramic substrate for vehicle catalytic converters that is lighter than existing substrates, leading, according to the company, to "reduced fuel consumption and increased engine power through low exhaust system back pressure."
- German conglomerate Evonik Industries makes a ceramic separator that fits between the electrodes of next-generation lithium-ion plug-in hybrid batteries. The ceramic material has a higher melting point and greater mechanical strength than existing separators, which, according to Evonik, gives

batteries longer life and enhanced safety, both crucial for plug-in hybrids.

Composites and Laminates

In the same way that metallurgists once discovered that blending a bit of carbon into molten iron produced steel, today's engineers are discovering that existing, well-understood substances can be mixed and matched to produce materials with new, sometimes radically different characteristics. There are dozens of composites and laminates on the market. Here's one to illustrate the idea: In late 2007, U.S. aluminum company Alcoa and a group of Dutch researchers announced that they had developed an aluminum fiber laminate that they claim can make aircraft wings nearly impervious to metal fatigue. They sandwiched layers of glass fiber and epoxy between thin layers of aluminum and then glued them to thicker aluminum layers by a proprietary bonding material. The result, called CentrAl—an abbreviation of central reinforced aluminum—is stronger than the carbon fiber now used in Boeing 787s and 20 percent lighter. A large wing made of CentrAl would weigh about 300 pounds less than one made of carbon fiber and would be easier to repair and maintain. If a large transport aircraft like Lockheed Martin C-130 had wings made of CentrAl, it would, claim the researchers, cost $20 million less to maintain over the plane's lifetime.

Nanomaterials

For all you science fiction fans out there, researchers around the world are producing tiny particles and fibers with almost magical levels of strength and conductivity. Most of these materials are still in the lab because they turned out to be easier to invent than to make in commercial quantities. But that's changing, as nanofabrication techniques inch closer to viability. When they cross the line, look for a flood of lighter, stronger, greener nano replacements for familiar materials. Two of dozens of possible examples:

> **Carbon-Impregnated Plastic.** One problem with strong but tiny particles is that they have to be glued together to form a bigger structure, which makes the structure no stronger than

the glue. But in late 2007, University of Michigan researchers announced a "brick-and-mortar" technique for scaling up nanomaterials that solves this problem. They deposited alternating atomically thin layers of polyvinyl alcohol "mortar" and "bricks" of strong carbon-based nanoparticles. The overlapping structure transfers the strength of the carbon to the whole structure, producing a material as strong as steel, but ultrathin and—get this—transparent. The U.S. Defense Department is reportedly examining it for body armor and aircraft components.

Mass-Produced Nanotubes. Carbon nanotubes are 1,000 times smaller in diameter than conventional carbon fibers. Extremely strong with extraordinary conductivity, they have a huge number of potential uses—if they could just be made cheaply in commercial quantities. In early 2008, a New Hampshire company called Nanocomp Technologies claimed to have taken a big step in that direction by producing 3-foot by 6-foot sheets of carbon nanotube material. These "nanotubes" are actually a millimeter long, versus the typical tens of microns. But the material's strength-to-weight ratio and electrical and thermal conductivity "exceed those of many other advanced materials by orders of magnitude," according to the company.

Green Materials' Growth Prospects

A decade from now, most things will be lighter, stronger, and cleaner, and many companies will be profitably supplying the new materials that make this possible. But the pace of innovation makes specific predictions about which materials will end up where highly risky. Right now, the two with the clearest prospects are carbon fiber and bioplastic. (See Table 16.1.)

- **Carbon fiber** should see fast growth in aerospace, continued growth in wind turbines, and gradual penetration of the high-end auto market. But it's still far too expensive for mass-market cars, so the price will have to fall dramatically before carbon fiber replaces steel and aluminum in your Chevy. Most of the major carbon fiber makers are diversified giants like Cytec and Kawasaki Heavy Industries, though there are a few relatively pure plays like Toray and Zoltek.

Table 16.1 Green Materials Stocks

Company	Ticker/ Exchange	Headquarters	Material	Market Value, 6/27/08 ($ millions)
Allegheny Technologies	ATI/NYSE	U.S.	Specialty metals	6,110
Archer Daniels Midland	ADM/NYSE	U.S.	Bioplastic	21,200
Cereplast	CERP.OB/NASDAQ	U.S.	Bioplastic	92
BioSolar	BSRC.OB/NASDAQ	U.S.	Bioplastic	56
Corning	GLW/NYSE	U.S.	Ceramics	36,930
Cytec Industries	CYT/NYSE	U.S.	Carbon fiber	2,620
Hexcel	HXL/NYSE	U.S.	Carbon fiber	1,850
Kawasaki Heavy Industries	7012.T/Tokyo	Japan	Carbon fiber	4,574
Metabolix	MBLX/NASDAQ	U.S.	Bioplastic	229
Rohm & Haas	ROH/NYSE	U.S.	Variety	9,290
Toray	3402.T/Tokyo	Japan	Carbon fiber	7,531
Zoltek	ZOLT/NASDAQ	U.S.	Carbon fiber	845

- **Bioplastic** has two possible growth paths. The conservative view calls for double-digit annual growth rates from a very low base through 2012 or so. Then, if bioplastics derived from nonfood plants prove to be viable, growth will accelerate as they compete effectively in a wide range of applications. The aggressive growth scenario requires a longer look at the stuff that's in traditional plastics. It turns out that what were once thought to be inert juice bottles and baby pacifiers actually release minute amounts of substances called phthalates and BPA (Bisphenol A) that appear to function as "endocrine disruptors," with some truly terrifying effects. In animal studies, these substances have been shown to cause developmental and reproductive disorders ranging from miscarriage to malformed testicles. And after decades in the food chain, they saturate our kids' bodies. If these and other endocrine disruptors turn out to be as dangerous as the early results imply, the legal and regulatory ramifications for petroleum-based plastic are deadly. In that scenario, bioplastic will find a more open field and might become one of the great growth businesses of the next decade. It's not yet clear how to invest in bioplastics, however. Besides Metabolix, there are a handful of emerging companies with interesting ideas. But they face chemical and agribusiness giants like Archer Daniels Midland, Dow, and Cargill, which see bioplastics as a natural extension of their existing businesses.

Beyond carbon fiber and bioplastic, green materials as an investment theme becomes a bit nebulous. Virtually all the big-name tech conglomerates are doing cutting-edge work in advanced materials, and they all have breakthroughs to crow about. But for the General Electrics and 3Ms of the world, materials are sidelines, and certainly not a reason to buy their stock. A few years from now the story may be very different, as breakthroughs now in labs are commercialized. I'll go out on a limb and predict that within five years there will be at least ten profitable growth companies making specialized bioplastics and carbon nanotubes.

CHAPTER

17

Pollution Control

TRASH IS A TERRIBLE THING TO WASTE

Give people a century of cheap energy, unlimited water, and abundant forests, and it's no surprise that the result is a throwaway society. That's no excuse, but it does explain how we got here. Packaging—and products themselves—were just so cheap that it was simpler to toss and replace them than to design and build things that last. According to the U.S. Energy Information Administration, the typical American produces about 5 pounds of trash a day, and the nation as a whole about 260 million tons per year. And the rest of the world is nearly as profligate. Garbage dumps outside cities like Buenos Aires and Mumbai are themselves cities, with nightmarish parallel ecosystems of families who spend their days and nights combing through mountains of refuse for enough scraps to eke out another day of existence.

Meanwhile, the things we throw away are neither gone nor forgotten. Industrial chemicals that saturate everything from magazine pages to discarded toys leach into groundwater, and nonbiodegradable plastics float on the surface of the ocean until they're eaten by unsuspecting turtles or sea birds. And the garbage that *is* biodegradable ferments into methane and other greenhouse gases that distort the atmosphere.

Now contrast this system with that of the natural world, where refuse, whether feces, dry leaves, or the remains of a lion kill, is processed by scavengers, insects, and microorganisms or is broken down by the elements and returned to the food chain. Every creature's

183

waste is another's vital raw material. Viewed through nature's lens, the throwaway society is outrageously inefficient, since most of what we throw away contains energy that could be used, among other things, to improve the lives of the people now sifting through it for a living. Thankfully, that day is just about here, as a series of new technologies capable of either eliminating waste or putting it to use hit the market. This decade will see the birth of "waste-to-energy" as a viable industry that's both big and, since its energy source—garbage—is free, potentially very profitable.

Waste Is Energy

Burning trash to generate electricity—or just to get rid of it—is already a common practice. Incinerators are everywhere, and according to the Solid Waste Association of North America, there are now 89 waste-to-energy facilities in the United States that burn landfill trash to produce power. In total, they generate 2.7 gigawatts of electricity, enough to power about 700,000 homes. This is renewable energy, but by and large, it's not green. Despite tightening emissions rules, the typical incinerator still puts coal plant levels of CO_2 into the air, along with unacceptable amounts of industrial chemicals from the materials being burned. Some greener variations are more interesting:

   Reverse Polymerization. Put paper, old tires, plastic, or pretty much any other kind of common trash into a chamber filled with nitrogen rather than oxygen, then zap it with microwaves, and something interesting happens. The material heats up, but without oxygen it can't burn. Instead, molecular bonds break, converting the materials to simpler compounds of lower molecular weight—without releasing dioxins or other toxins. The process exceeds the tightest European emissions standards and produces oils and carbon residue that can be used as fuel. Canadian firm Environmental Waste International is marketing a reverse polymerization process for several different waste streams, including medical waste (it recently sold one machine to the pharmaceutical firm Abbot Labs) and tires.

   Gasification. Recall from Chapter 9 that forest waste can be turned into syngas, which is either processed into other fuels or burned directly to run a turbine. Massachusetts start-up Ze-gen is trying something similar with debris from construction and demolition sites, passing the material through molten metal, which dissociates it into hydrogen and carbon monoxide. The syngas is then burned to power a steam turbine, which produces more than enough power to run the plant. In theory, the process produces far less greenhouse gas than either incinerating the trash or allowing it to become methane in a landfill. If Ze-gen's plant works as promised, it (and about a thousand other entrepreneurs with similar ambitions) will extend the process to other waste streams, turning landfills and transfer stations into power plants and garbage into cheap energy.

Biogas Harvesting. When you bury organic material—or dump it in ponds, as livestock farms tend to do—it doesn't just sit there. Bacteria feast on it, multiply, and excrete a combination of methane and carbon dioxide. Landfills, waste treatment plants, and pig farms all produce gas in this way. Capture it and use it to run a turbine, and you've got yet another source of carbon-neutral power. Already, the United States has over 400 landfills with gas-to-energy plants, with 50 more under construction in early 2008. And many more are coming. North Carolina has over 1,100 farms with enough pig manure to justify a power plant, while California has over 900 sufficiently large dairy farms.

Plasma. Run an electrical current through a container of ionized gas and you get 30,000-degree lightning in a bottle. When tires, old chemical weapons, scrap metal, or pretty much anything else is exposed to this kind of heat, molecules break apart into constituent atoms, producing a few pieces of glassy stone and syngas that can be used to power the machine. The theoretical value of such a process for the waste disposal business is obvious: Just create a big plasma-torch chamber, feed in the trash, and poof—that's the end of the garbage issue. Obviously it's not that easy, or there would be no need for this chapter. But plasma's fans claim that it does indeed have this kind of potential—if the cost can be lowered a bit. Plasma-torch disposal is currently twice as expensive as incineration or landfill disposal in most places. So it's only economical where landfill space is extraordinarily tight and air quality standards too stringent for incineration. Parts of Europe and Japan qualify on both counts, and plants are operating there and doing what they promise. Meanwhile, labs around the world are researching ways to lower plasma's cost.

Object Lesson: Startech Environmental

Cash in Hand Is Worth a Dozen Unfunded Contracts

Back in 1998, I was a columnist for a web site called TheStreet.com, which was at the center of the tech-stock media feeding frenzy, and tips from strangers with inside information on can't-miss start-ups were pouring in. So when a man claiming to be an accountant who worked with "angel investors" called, I listened politely as he told me about a company with a revolutionary way to turn garbage into clean electricity. "It's going to be hot, hot, hot!" were his exact words. I made some notes, mildly intrigued by the perpetual motion machine idea of unlimited clean energy from trash, the freest of free fuel sources. Recalling the scene from *Back to the Future* in which the professor returns from 2020 and dumps some banana peels and coffee grounds into his car's on-board nuclear plant, I looked up the company, Connecticut-based Startech Environmental, and found that, sure enough, it claimed to be using plasma to convert trash into more than enough hydrogen to run its machines. The U.S. government had assessed its pilot plant and pronounced it effective, and orders were in hand from Japan, Poland, and New Jersey. Its stock had soared from single digits into the 20s, and, well, the premise was just so hot, hot, hot that I bought a lot, lot, lot.

Then came the speed bumps. The pilot plant, it turned out, hadn't performed quite as well on the government tests as the company claimed, and financing for the initial orders (which hadn't included big nonrefundable deposits) was taking longer than expected. But no problem, potential buyers were flying in for demonstrations on a daily basis and going away impressed. More orders were imminent. But those orders also ran into various difficulties, and the stock began to drift downward. Then the tech bubble burst, and the decline became a freefall. I sold out, except for a thousand shares that still languish in my IRA at around $1 as of early 2008. Startech is still around, still receiving orders (the latest from a company in Poland), and—who knows?—may yet become a major force in clean tech. But now it will have to prove itself with real orders that produce real cash. The lesson: Revolutionary technologies are a dime a dozen. The vast majority will either fail completely or take far longer to pan out than the inventors promise. So be willing to forgo the initial share price pop in order to ensure that a new technology has real traction in the marketplace, as evidenced by actual cash flow.

Table 17.1   Waste Management Companies

Company	Ticker/ Exchange	Headquarters	Market Value, 6/27/08 ($ millions)
Alkane Energy	ALKN.L/London	U.K.	39,460
Allied Waste	AW/NYSE	U.S.	4,930
Covanta Holding	CVA/NYSE	U.S.	4,040
Environmental Power	EPG/NYSE	U.S.	66
Environmental Waste International	EWS.V/Toronto	Canada	12
StarTech Environmental	STHK.OB/NASDAQ	U.S.	22
Waste Management	WMI/NYSE	U.S.	18,270

Waste-to-Energy's Growth Prospects

All the processes mentioned here are becoming more efficient just as
environmental restrictions on incinerators and landfills are tightening around the world. So in the aggregate waste-to-energy will see dramatic growth in coming years, though in early 2008, it isn't yet clear
which technologies will be the eventual winners. U.K.-based Alkane
Energy, the leader in methane generation plants, is a solid choice in
that segment. But as with so many other clean technologies, the innovative smaller players (i.e., the potential growth stocks) face competition from deep-pocketed giants (see Table 17.1). Garbage firms Waste
Management, Allied Waste, and Covanta, for instance, operate dozens
of traditional incineration plants and recycling operations and will
no doubt aggressively adopt new waste-to-energy technologies as they
become viable.

PART

IV

INVESTING IN A
GREEN BOOM

CHAPTER 18

Bubbles and Bear Markets

Some clean technologies will be very big, and many won't. But for investors, this may not matter if predictions of a clean-tech bubble turn out to be true. Because in bubbles, quality—and the arduous security analysis that uncovers it—doesn't matter. While a bubble is inflating, everything, no matter how pie-in-the-sky, goes up. And when a bubble bursts, everything, no matter how solid, goes down. In 1998, for instance, time spent comparing Amazon.com and Cisco with the dozens of other tech stocks flooding the marketplace was wasted because they all soared. And in 2000, research was also wasted because they all tanked. If a 1990s-style bubble is coming, then our job as investors is pretty easy: load up on a random selection of clean-tech stocks and prepare to sell after they rise by an arbitrary but extremely large amount. But if clean tech is not destined to be a bubble—or if it's going to be a different kind of bubble—then we face a more interesting analytical challenge.

So let's start by recognizing that a bubble is more than just a big increase in the valuation of some narrow sector. An asset's price can soar for legitimate reasons and still be fairly valued. For something to be a bubble, a rising price must be accompanied by two things:

1. Traditional business practices being tossed aside in favor of "innovations" that look suspiciously like scams but, in the heat of the mania, are embraced by everyone still on the field

2. Regular people making fortunes doing things that professionals used to find difficult

During the housing bubble, an example of the first was zero-down, adjustable-rate mortgages, and an example of the second was landscapers and taxi drivers quitting their jobs to become condo flippers. Housing was clearly a bubble.

So will clean tech follow the housing bubble/dot.com script? Well, in early 2008, money does seem to be flowing freely. Venture capitalists are funding a lot of untested technologies, and many solar stocks are tracing bubble-like arcs. On the other hand, there are fundamental differences between clean tech and the dot.coms. For one thing, in the 1990s, the Internet was uncharted territory. It was being created before our eyes and seemed to have unlimited potential. Because there were no metrics against which to value a new idea like America Online or Yahoo!, analysts (no doubt under pressure from investment bankers down the hall) simply made up measures like "eyeballs" and assigned them arbitrary, sometimes astronomical values. The result was a disconnect between stock price and earnings potential that made all manner of bizarre behaviors possible.

Clean tech, on the other hand, addresses the needs of existing markets. Electricity is already being produced and valued in the real world, so a new power source has to meet an existing benchmark to be taken seriously. That's why wind and solar, which are cost competitive with existing power sources, are doing so well, while fuel cells, which are far more expensive than internal combustion engines, are not. And some of the major clean-tech players are large, well-known companies. Sharp is the largest producer of solar panels, while General Electric is a leading maker of wind turbines and just about everything else. They're real, can be valued by traditional measures, and are growing at steady, positive rates.

The verdict? Clean tech that works has an extraordinary run ahead of it. Solar, you'll recall, now generates less than 0.05 percent of the United States' electricity. So it can theoretically grow at high double-digit rates until most of us are too old to care about the stock market—and it will still just be getting started. But clean-tech *stocks* are tethered to reality. Solar and wind power companies will always compete with other measurable power sources, ranging from biofuels to hydrogen to each other, which will restrain investors' enthusiasm and prevent the kind of analytical and operational flights of fancy that characterize bubbles. So clean tech is not the return of the dot.coms. There will be plenty of hype and dramatic price moves, but in the coming bull market it will be possible, through diligence and judgment, to pick winners and losers from a parade of great stories.

The other crucial question involves timing. Great technologies are only great investments if the overall economy and stock market are behaving well. That's not always the case, and it's quite possible that the global economy in general and the U.S. economy in particular are in for a rough patch that might complicate the green investing process. Consider the following.

Bear Market of 2008?

As this is written in early 2008, the U.S. housing market is imploding and the dollar is falling versus gold, oil, and most foreign currencies. The budgets of the U.S. federal government and most states are deeply in deficit, with spending cuts and/or tax increases inevitable. And Wall Street is in chaos. Venerable investment bank Bear Stearns has collapsed, and hedge funds, mortgage lenders, and homebuilders are closing their doors on a daily basis. But this turmoil is just the surface manifestation of a more serious illness that might unsettle the financial markets—and make optimistic investment themes like clean tech a hard sell—for several years. To put it bluntly, we've made a mess of the global financial system, and it's crucial for would-be clean-tech investors to understand how we got here and how big the coming dislocations might be. So let's take a brief detour into the world of finance for a look at why the United States and possibly the global economy are in such precarious shape.

Rise and Fall of Paper Currency

Our story begins long ago and far away, when our ancestors first figured out how to trade for what they needed. Makers of arrowheads exchanged them for animal skins, gatherers of medicinal herbs offered them in return for goats, and so on. But this "barter" system was unwieldy, for a lot of obvious reasons. (What if you really needed a goat but the goat guy didn't need arrowheads?) So every society eventually designated something to serve as a go-between, a unit of measure in which other things could be priced, and a store of value that would make it possible to save for future consumption. In other words, they invented the concept of money. Over the centuries, our ancestors auditioned virtually everything for this role: sea shells, tea, pigs, children, slaves. Each had a brief run and was abandoned as too fragile or variable or prone to escape. Eventually, most societies settled on bits of worked metal called coins. These were durable and could be made in identical bits that simplified calculation. Different metals could, based on their rarity and beauty, serve as large and small denominations. And because there was a limited amount of each metal, they tended to hold their value pretty well. Eventually, through a long process of competition and elimination, gold, silver, and copper emerged as the winners. And they functioned as money for several thousand years.

By the nineteenth century, the global economy was booming, thanks in part to the fact that everyone recognized and accepted gold and silver coins (along with paper notes that circulated as representations of precious metals in government vaults) as legitimate money. Known as the classical gold standard, the system worked because the limited supply of gold and silver—about 2 percent more each year was dug from the ground—kept prices stable, while the metals' universal acceptance made cross-border trade easy. Economic growth, as a result, was steady and progress was taken for granted. But the days of "sound money" ended when the chaos of the twentieth century—two world wars with the Great Depression in between—forced governments to print as much paper currency as was necessary to buy tanks and planes and food. The balance between precious metals and paper currency was broken.

As the rubble of World War II was being cleared away, the leaders of the victorious powers cobbled together a monetary system known as Bretton Woods, named for the New Hampshire town in which it was negotiated. Under this plan, the dollar—the currency of the only country not decimated by the war—was convertible into gold at the request of other governments, while the exchange rates of the world's other major currencies were linked to the dollar. The global financial system, in other words, depended on the United States operating in a financially sound manner, not borrowing too much or otherwise taking on obligations that would force it to print more paper currency than there was gold to back it up.

But confronted with an expansionist enemy in the Soviet Union and increasingly visible poverty at home—and encouraged by the seemingly unlimited global demand for dollars—the United States chose both "guns and butter," fighting wars in Korea and Vietnam while establishing huge new social programs at home. And it printed as many new dollars as it took to cover the resulting costs. The supply of paper dollars began to outstrip the supply of gold in Fort Knox. And eventually, even the countries that had eagerly soaked up dollars in the past began to fret about the effects of so much paper. They presented their dollars to the U.S. Treasury and asked for gold in return. In 1971, this run on the dollar became so serious that President Richard Nixon "closed the gold window," breaking the link between the global financial system and gold. Suddenly, there was nothing limiting the ability of governments to increase spending and encourage their citizens to borrow. The world's currencies were just paper, based on nothing more than the promises of elected leaders and the willingness of individuals to believe. That's when everything changed.

Blowing Bubbles

When the world went off the gold standard, the United States was in relatively good financial shape, with modest debt and a stable relationship between new borrowing and new wealth creation. That is, Americans were a productive, somewhat frugal people who tended to borrow wisely for things that produced useful, marketable stuff. But with the global supply of currency soaring, it became easier for baby boomers—who began turning 30 in the 1970s—to adopt debt as a way of life and to elect leaders who behaved the same way. The United States began to borrow more and more, and to invent ever-more-complex ways to create credit out of thin air. Government policy became wildly expansionary, with soaring deficits and interest rates low enough to entice individuals and companies to borrow and speculate. Wall Street, both responding to and driving this new appetite for debt and risk, began to inflate a series of financial bubbles—pockets of the economy that appear to be capable of growing forever and therefore attract huge amounts of capital. Prices of bubble assets soar, and the most aggressive speculators get rich beyond reason.

Then the bubble bursts, and everything falls apart. In the 1980s it was junk bonds, in the 1990s it was tech stocks, and in this decade it was housing. Each bubble was bigger than the last and left the system with more residual debt. The result is illustrated in Figures 18.1 and 18.2. Figure 18.1 shows U.S. per capita household debt soaring from

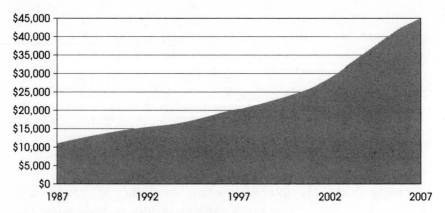

Figure 18.1   U.S. Per Capita Household Debt
Source: Federal Reserve, U.S. Census Bureau

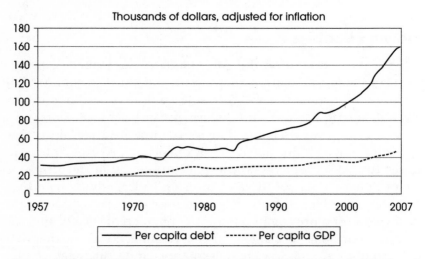

Figure 18.2   Total Per Capita Debt and Gross Domestic Product
Source: Federal Reserve, U.S. Census Bureau

$11,000 in 1987 to $45,000 in 2007. Figure 18.2 is a society-wide view of total U.S. debt and gross domestic product (GDP). Note that until the 1970s, they track closely as new borrowing produced commensurate amounts of new wealth. Then the lines begin to diverge, with debt growing faster than wealth until the gap becomes a chasm. By the end of 2007, U.S. debt was three times GDP, up from two times in the 1980s, and it took $5 of new debt to create $1 of new GDP.

Meanwhile, Wall Street was responding to this abundance of paper currency by taking "financial engineering" to undreamt-of levels of complexity (and absurdity). Here are two major examples.

Securitization

Back in, say, 1980, if a bank wrote a mortgage or a car loan, it expected to keep that loan on its books until the borrower paid it off. The bank had little choice because no one wanted to buy such nonstandardized, hard-to-analyze loans. Because they had to live with the consequences of their lending decisions, banks tended to be cautious. They required 20 percent down payments on mortgages and looked closely at customers' ability to pay back consumer and business loans. That's one reason debt grew relatively slowly back then. But in the mid-1980s, Wall Street's financial engineers figured out that they could buy consumer loans and mortgages from banks and bundle them into "asset-backed securities" that pension funds around the world would happily buy (since everyone was hungry for bonds denominated in dollars, the currency of the world's economic superpower). Suddenly, banks were able to sell the loans they originated for cash, which they could then use to make more loans. This relieved banks of the need to scrutinize their customers, since they no longer had to live with the results of their lending decisions. In other words, it was no longer the banks' money.

The result was a lending frenzy in which pretty much anyone with a pulse could get a home mortgage or a car loan or a credit card. Home prices soared because of all the new buyers who were suddenly able to get mortgages. Homeowners discovered that they could borrow against their rapidly appreciating homes to buy the luxury cars and PlayStations that other countries so graciously offered to sell. By 2006, home prices and household debt had both risen to unsustainable levels, and the housing bubble burst, causing the problems that afflicted the economy in early 2008.

Derivatives

Pension funds and other institutional investors were anxious to buy asset-backed bonds, but they sometimes wanted extra assurance that those exotic securities would perform as promised. So they bought an obscure form of insurance, called credit default swaps, or CDS, in which an underwriter—usually an investment bank or hedge fund—agrees to cover any losses that a given bond might incur in return for a modest annual fee. This is a reasonable-sounding idea, but in bubbles, reasonable things tend to be taken to excess and beyond. Speculators began to treat credit default swaps as tradable instruments, bundling them into new kinds of asset-backed securities and then writing new insurance on those bonds. And because there was no regulator limiting the amount of swaps that could be written on a given company's debt to the actual amount of the debt, hedge funds began writing insurance far in excess of the underlying loans. By one estimate, in 2005, $25 billion of insurance was outstanding on $2 billion of auto parts maker Delphi's debt. As Figure 18.3 illustrates, the total notional value (i.e., the face value of the debt insured) of credit default swaps soared from $12 trillion (that's right, *trillion*) in 2000 to over $60 trillion in 2007. Bear Stearns, just before it collapsed, was revealed to have $2.5 trillion of credit default swaps, most of which were hidden from its stockholders in off-balance-sheet entities.

And—here's where it gets really scary—unlike insurance companies, which keep reserves against the possibility that they'll have to pay off on their policies, the hedge funds (private, unregulated investment companies) writing credit default insurance don't keep reserves. They just take each year's premiums into income and pay

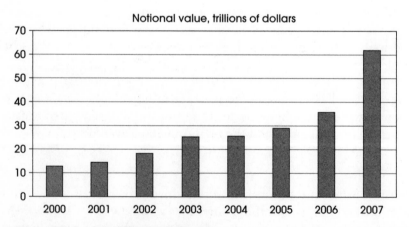

Figure 18.3   Credit Default Swaps
Source: Bank for International Settlements

bonuses on these "profits." So as corporate bonds begin to default because of lower consumer spending and the past decade's overbuilding of condos and shopping malls, the hedge funds that promised to make good on those loans are dying. They're dumping their remaining securities to raise cash, which is pushing down the prices of those instruments, triggering more selling, and so on. The next couple of years will probably see a massive die-off of hedge funds and other leveraged speculators. And since hedge funds borrow from banks in order to implement their leveraged strategies, banks that suffered through the housing/asset-backed securities debacle in 2007 may have another crisis on their hands in 2009.

Unfunded Pension Liabilities

Believe it or not, the debt numbers cited earlier don't include the largest of the U.S. government's obligations, which are the unfunded liabilities of Social Security and Medicare. This is the amount the United States needs to have saved today to cover the promises it has made to future retirees. And as baby boomers start retiring and new benefits like Medicare prescription drug coverage are added, the number has been soaring. From an already breathtaking $20 trillion in 2000, it jumped to $50 trillion in 2007 (see Figure 18.4). The result is that, perhaps very soon, the federal government will face the choice of either cutting benefits for boomers, who have never been shy about

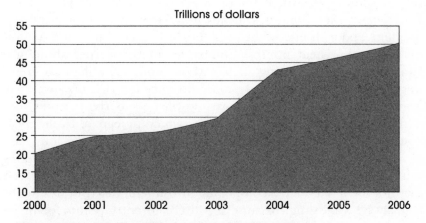

Figure 18.4   U.S. Government Unfunded Liabilities
Source: U.S. Treasury Department

voting their own self-interest, or raising taxes on workers to levels that would bankrupt many of them. Or—the most likely course of action—printing as many new dollars as it takes to cover these obligations, even if it means that each dollar becomes a lot less valuable, which regular folks know as inflation. That's the course the United States seems to have chosen, based on the aggressive interest rate cuts and debt buybacks now being implemented in early 2008.

Deep Financial Trouble

There are other festering problems, including the mounting cost of U.S. global military commitments and the trillion or so dollars of unfunded state and local pension obligations, but by now the picture of a country—and possibly a world—in deep financial trouble is pretty clear.

What exactly does "deep financial trouble" mean for clean tech? To begin with, excessive debt and massive "malinvestment" in stores, office buildings, and houses that never should have been built will lead to a period during which people who can't cover their debts will go bankrupt, and then the creditors of the first group will go bankrupt, and so on. The result will be falling prices for homes, commercial real estate, and financial stocks, which, in turn, means lower tax revenues for governments that will then have to cut spending and lay off workers.

As all this plays out, fewer investment projects, big and small, will be affordable, which might affect the market for clean tech. Fewer new office buildings means fewer next-generation windows. Suddenly poor homeowners will be less likely buy solar panels or geothermal heat pumps. Companies more worried about survival than about reducing their carbon footprint will forgo green upgrades for a few years. Investors who once felt rich because their homes and stocks were both soaring will be sobered by their sudden loss of wealth. They'll shift their remaining capital to the most conservative possible options, like Treasury bills and precious metals, and shy away from new technologies. If this book hits the shelves during such a time (and I'm afraid that it might), then clean tech may not seem like such a compelling investment idea. But this might actually be a blessing, because it will create entry points for many clean-tech stocks that, with a few years of hindsight, will look like gifts from a benevolent market god. And it will give us time to pick just the right companies and strategies. So as you choose among the approaches outlined in the next few chapters, be aware that timing is crucial. Buying a great stock at a bad time is a fast way to lose money, as solar stock investors discovered recently. Those who bought shares in a leading solar panel maker like Sun Power in early 2007 had the ride of their lives, while those who waited until late 2007 had an equally memorable but less enjoyable experience. So if the markets are in the throes of a financial crisis when you read this, you have three choices:

1. Conclude that your favorite clean-tech stocks have been beaten down by all the external bad news and load up in the expectation that going forward they'll outperform the typical stock.
2. Remain on the sidelines until the dust clears and normal economic times return.
3. Begin a program of "dollar cost averaging" in which you buy small, regular amounts of high-quality clean-tech stocks. If you're a bit early and they go down further, that's okay because you'll get more shares each time you buy, lowering your average price.

Which of these three approaches is best depends on how close the global financial system is to addressing its problems. Are banks cleaning up their balance sheets by writing off bad debts and booking the losses? Have builders cancelled enough projects to bring the supply of homes and shopping malls back in line with demand? Are governments reining in their spending and taking other steps to stop the decline of the dollar? (As I see this last question in print, it seems unlikely to the point of absurdity, but it is what has to happen.) If the answer to most of these questions is yes, then clean tech might soon have a nice stiff market wind at its back. If the answer is no, then clean tech stocks will have to overcome an unfavorable environment for a while longer—but might become extraordinarily cheap in the process.

Which Strategy Is Right for You?

Now that we've put clean tech in perspective, let's consider some ideas for profiting from its (eventual) bull market. There is no single correct strategy for such a broad, diverse swath of the global economy, but for each investor, there are approaches that fit both temperament and resources. So as you go through the next few chapters, read them not in terms of right and wrong but of comfort and discomfort. What feels best, given your level of financial expertise, tolerance for risk, and available capital? And as always with specific companies or mutual funds, note that the lists in this section are examples that illustrate a thought process, not specific recommendations. Much will have changed in the months (or years) between this writing and your reading, so you'll want to use the resources listed in Chapter 24 to find the stocks that best fit your chosen strategy.

CHAPTER

19

Green Mutual Funds

By now you have a sense of the breadth and complexity of clean tech: hundreds of companies with dozens of technologies operating all over the world, with shares trading on about a dozen different exchanges. This is not retailing or commercial real estate, where a few hours of study yield a grasp of the basics and a sense of where to put your money. Clean tech is a much bigger, more complicated animal. Which means the vast majority of people reading this book—who presumably have lives beyond investing—should not be trying to separate clean-tech winners from losers with their life savings. Far better to hand the responsibility off to a professional who spends all day and most of each night sorting through the dynamics of biodiesel versus lithium-ion versus hydrogen storage, and let him or her spread your risks around.

Many Shades of Green

But which money manager? This, at least, is a relatively straightforward question, since in early 2008 there were just a handful of options. Table 19.1 lists the available actively managed green mutual funds. The subsequent tables present snapshots of each fund, including its 10 largest investments as of the end of 2007. (See Tables 19.2 to 19.7.) Let's begin by noting that both socially responsible (SRI) and clean-tech funds are frequently lumped under the "green" heading, but as you can see by comparing the portfolios of, say, the Guinness Atkinson Alternative Energy (Table 19.2) and Sierra Club (Table 19.4) funds, they operate with very different philosophies.

Table 19.1 Green Mutual Funds

Company	Ticker	Assets ($ millions)	3-Year Avg. Annual Rate of Return	Expense Ratio (percent)	Turnover (percent)	Market Value of Average Stock ($ millions)
Guinness Atkinson Alternative Energy	GAAEX	159	NA	1.98	22	2,156
New Alternatives	NALFX	295	19.37	1.25	40	6,336
Sierra Club Stock Fund	SCFSX	46	3.32	1.37	40	23,242
Spectra Green	SPEGX	19	17.48	1.24	132	13,335
Winslow Green Growth	WGGFX	415	13.50	1.31	113	897

Note: All figures as of 2/1/08.

Table 19.2 Guinness Atkinson

Guinness Atkinson Alternative Energy Fund

Tel: 800-915-6566   **Web:** www.gafunds.com/funds_alternative_energy.asp

Profile: A broad selection of the major alternative energy names. Relatively high management fees but low turnover. Highly recommended.

Top 10 Holdings 12/31/07

Company	Ticker/Exchange	Headquarters	Sector	Market Value, 6/27/08 ($ millions)
Vestas Wind Systems	VWS.CO/Copenhagen	Denmark	Wind	24,650
Renewable Energy Generation	RERWE.L/London	U.K.	Wind	223,720
Conergy	CGYG.F/Frankfurt	Germany	Solar	719
Q-Cells	QCEG.F/Frankfurt	Germany	Solar	7,669
SolarWorld	SWVG.F/Frankfurt	Germany	Solar	5,076
Solon AG	SOOG.F/Frankfurt	Germany	Solar	1,110
Gamesa	GAMbl.MC/Madrid	Spain	Wind	11,580
PNOC Energy Development	EDC.PS/Philippine	Philippines	Geothermal	1,730
Energy Company of Minas Gerais ADR	CMIG4.SA/Sao Paolo	Brazil	Utility	12,004
Ormat Technologies	ORA/NYSE	U.S.	Geothermal	2,030

Table 19.3 New Alternatives

New Alternatives Fund

Tel: 800-441-6580   **Website:** www.newalternativesfund.com

Profile: Globally diversified (over half its holdings were headquartered outside the United States in 2007) and sharply focused on alternative energy. Highly recommended.

Top 10 Holdings 12/31/07

Company	Ticker/Exchange	Headquarters	Sector	Market Value, 6/27/08 ($ millions)
Vestas Wind Systems	VWS.CO/Copenhagen	Denmark	Wind	24,650
Q-Cells	QCEG.F/Frankfurt	Germany	Solar	7,669
Gamesa	GAM.MC/Madrid	Spain	Wind	11,580
Renewable Energy	REC.OL/Oslo	Norway	Solar	12,998
Ormat Technologies	ORA/NYSE	U.S.	Geothermal	2,030
Schneider Electric	SCHN.PA/Paris	France	Electronics	NA
Acciona	ANA.MC/Madrid	Spain	Wind	14,015
Abengoa	ABG.MC/Madrid	Spain	Solar	2,694
Orkla	ORK.OL/Oslo	Norway	Conglomerate	14,061
EDF Energies Nouvelles	EDF.PA/Paris	France	Power generation	162,540

Table 19.4   Sierra Club

Sierra Club Fund

Tel: 866-897-5982　　　　**Web:** http://sierraclubfunds.com

Profile: Runs large-cap companies through 22 screens designed to weed out bad corporate citizens, then buys equal dollar amounts of the 100 largest.

Top 10 Holdings 12/31/07

Company	Ticker/Exchange	Headquarters	Sector	Market Value, 6/27/08 ($ millions)
Genzyme Corporation	GENZ/NASDAQ	U.S.	Biotech	19,410
Apple	AAPL/NASDAQ	U.S.	Consumer electronics	154,000
Express Scripts	ESRX/NASDAQ	U.S.	Health care	15,831
Microsoft	MSFT/NASDAQ	U.S.	Software	250,250
Google	GOOG/NASDAQ	U.S.	Internet	167,950
Aflac	AFL/NYSE	U.S.	Insurance	29,910
Medco Health Solutions	MHS/NYSE	U.S.	Health care	23,690
United Health	UNH/NYSE	U.S.	Health care	31,490
State Street	STT/NYSE	U.S.	Finance	16,210
Gilead Sciences	GILD/NASDAQ	U.S.	Biotech	48,130

Table 19.5 Spectra Green

Spectra Green Fund

Tel: 800-711-6141

Website: www.spectrafunds.com

Profile: A wide variety of high-quality large cap companies but a dearth of pure-play clean tech, despite the "green" label.

Top 10 Holdings 12/31/07

Company	Ticker/Exchange	Headquarters	Sector	Market Value, 6/27/08 ($ millions)
Microsoft	MSFT/NASDAQ	U.S.	Software	250,250
Deckers Outdoor	DECK/NASDAQ	U.S.	Footwear	1,790
BorgWarner	BWA/NYSE	U.S.	Auto tech	5,240
Apple	AAPL/NASDAQ	U.S.	Consumer electronics	154,000
Yahoo!	YHOO/NASDAQ	U.S.	Internet	27,790
Cisco Systems	CSCO/NASDAQ	U.S.	Networking equip.	136,750
eBay	EBAY/NASDAQ	U.S.	Internet	36,500
Endeavor Acquisition	EDA/NYSE	U.S.	Apparel	NA
Iconix Brand	ICON/NYSE	U.S.	Apparel	709
Cummins	CMI/NYSE	U.S.	Auto tech	13,220

Table 19.6   Winslow Green

Winslow Green Growth

Tel: 888-314-9049   **Website:** www.winslowgreen.com

Profile: A mixture of alt-energy and "good citizen" companies.

Top 10 Holdings 12/31/07

Company	Ticker/Exchange	Headquarters	Sector	Market Value, 6/27/08 ($ millions)
LSB Industries	LXU/AMEX	U.S.	Water	405
Green Mountain Coffee	GMCR/NASDAQ	U.S.	Coffee	914
First Solar	FSLR/NASDAQ	U.S.	Solar	21,590
Bankrate	RATE/NASDAQ	U.S.	Financial serv.	689
EnerNOC	ENOC/NASDAQ	U.S.	Smart grid	357
Chipotle Mexican Grill	CMG/NYSE	U.S.	Restaurants	2,690
United Natural Foods	UNFI/NASDAQ	U.S.	Food	521
Biomarin Pharmaceutical	BMRN/NASDAQ	U.S.	Pharmaceuticals	2,860
Orion Energy	OESX/NASDAQ	U.S.	Lighting	271
LSI Industries	LYTS/NASDAQ	U.S.	Lighting	168

Table 19.7 Green Exchange-Traded Funds

Fund	Ticker	Assets ($ millions)	Index	Expense Ratio (percent)
Claymore S&P Global Water Index	CGW	345	50 Leading Water Companies	0.72
Market Vectors Global Alternative Energy	GEX	208	Ardour Global Alternative Energy	0.65
PowerShares Cleantech	PZD	115	Cleantech Index	0.71
PowerShares Global Wind	PWND	NA	Clean Edge Global Wind Energy	NA
PowerShares WilderHill Clean Energy	PBW	1,732	WilderHill Clean Energy	0.70

A socially responsible fund like Sierra Club is open to pretty much any company that's a good corporate citizen—or at least not a bad one. By this standard, Google, Microsoft, and Aflac are all acceptable investments because they treat their workers well and don't pollute. That's a good thing; various studies have shown that the best corporate citizens tend also to be winning investments, and every well-rounded portfolio should include such stocks. But this book is about the *technologies* that will solve humanity's environmental and economic problems, and socially responsible funds can't automatically be assumed to contain a lot of clean tech. Spectra Green (Table 19.5), for instance, owns mostly good corporate citizens and very little clean tech, so it's not what we're looking for. Winslow Green Growth (Table 19.6), despite the similar name, offers a mix of smaller-cap clean tech and socially responsible companies, and so is a reasonable choice for investors wanting to kill two birds (clean tech and SRI) with one stone. Another of Winslow's funds, Green Solutions, is brand new as of this writing but looks even more promising, with a focus on global clean-tech leaders.

Here are some other things to consider when choosing a fund:

Global Diversification. With most sectors, it's possible for U.S. investors to build a completely acceptable portfolio of domestic companies. Not so with clean tech. Many of the leaders in solar, wind, and several other niches are headquartered in Europe or Asia, and many of their stocks don't trade in the United States (though that's not the hurdle it once was, as you'll see in Chapter 22). A mutual fund with the ability to buy foreign stocks has a big advantage in that regard. The New Alternatives Fund, for instance (Table 19.3), invests about 60 percent of its capital in companies based outside the United States.

Expenses. Mutual fund managers charge their investors management fees that are calculated as a percent of assets. If you've invested $10,000 with XYZ Fund and its expense ratio is 1 percent, then you'll pay $100 per year for their services. Generally, more complex sectors have higher fees. The manager of a long-term Treasury bond fund deals with relatively a simple subject and therefore can't get away with charging much. But running a tech fund—especially clean tech, which is both complicated and global—requires a great deal of analysis, as well as frequent travel to visit companies around the world. You'd expect them to charge more than the average fund, and you'd be right—though in the scheme of things, and considering the potential gains that will accrue to good judgment, the major clean-tech funds' fees are reasonable.

Turnover. Mutual funds are constantly buying and selling, and turnover is the number that gauges how much action a given manager generates, expressed as a percentage of the overall portfolio. A turnover rate of zero means the manager never sells anything, while a rate of 100 percent means that in a typical year he sells and replaces everything. Generally speaking, if an industry is going to do well, frenetic buying and selling tends to be wasted effort, though there are many funds with both high turnover and good returns. So this is more about temperament than quality. Are you comfortable with and willing to pay for lots of action, or are you more attracted to the kind of buy-and-hold investing practiced by legends like Warren Buffett, who famously claims that his preferred holding period is "forever"?

Green Exchange Traded Funds

In the mutual fund world, a debate has been raging for years over whether actively managing money is even necessary. Critics of traditional mutual funds point out that in a typical year, 80 percent of actively managed funds underperform their target indexes after expenses. Far better, say the critics, to simply buy a bunch of stocks that represent a given index or sector and leave them alone. Such a portfolio will do as well as the index, and because it will cost next to nothing to run, after expenses it will beat most actively managed funds. Early on, the vehicle of choice for this kind of passive investing was the index fund, a concept that made Vanguard one of the leading mutual fund managers. Then came the exchange-traded fund (ETF), which combines the index fund concept with the trading characteristics of a stock. Whereas a mutual fund is priced at the end of the trading day when its component securities are totaled up and can only be traded at the end-of-day price, an ETF holding the same securities can be bought and sold like an individual stock whenever the markets are open. It can also be shorted like a stock, and many

ETFs have options that allow for spreads, straddles, and hedges that are impossible with mutual funds. The five clean-tech ETFs profiled in Table 19.7 should easily outperform broad indexes like the S&P 500 or Russell 2000 in the coming decade. So for most people, buying several such funds is all that's necessary to beat the market.

The downside of the kind of broad diversification offered by mutual funds and ETFs is that their returns will tend to cluster toward the middle of the pack. That is, they'll do about as well as clean tech in general (which, again, should be very well), but less well than the sector's biggest winners. So if you have the time and inclination to construct and manage your own portfolio, there's a chance to outperform even the clean-tech averages. And—no small thing—picking your own stocks is a lot more fun than letting someone else do it for you. The chapters that follow offer a variety of strategies for breaking clean-tech into bite-sized pieces and constructing potentially high-reward portfolios.

CHAPTER 20

Clean Tech in Bite-Sized Pieces

The first step in building a clean-tech portfolio is figuring out where to begin—and that's not as simple as it sounds. Without a strategy for winnowing a field this vast into manageable, bite-sized pieces, an investor risks being paralyzed by the sheer scope of the challenge. So let's start with the observation that in the stock market, as in real estate, location is paramount. San Francisco-based bank Wells Fargo recently analyzed the sources of its trust department's investment returns and found that 75 percent came from sector allocation, and only 25 percent from stock picking. In other words, if you choose the right categories, you've done most of the work. Real-world examples of this principal are easy to find: Between 1998 and 2000, a portfolio of randomly chosen tech stocks outperformed the average electric utility, and vice versa in 2001; between 2002 and 2006 financial stocks were the place to be; and between 2006 and 2008, the average solar stock far outdistanced the average fuel cell stock. So our first goal is to identify the handful of green technologies with the best near-term growth prospects. In 2008 that list would appear to include solar, wind, geothermal, water, and smart grid, and to exclude batteries, biofuels, and fuel cells, which will emerge in 2010 and beyond.

This chapter offers several strategies for building portfolios from the most promising categories. Each can work quite well as an investor's sole approach. But they're not mutually exclusive and can be refined and combined in ways limited only by your time and ambition.

Green Utilities

One of the advantages of renewable energy is a stable price. Sunshine and wind are always free, so the cost of the power they generate changes only with the cost of maintenance and capital equipment, which is generally not much. And this advantage should increase as fossil fuel price gyrations become more violent. Take coal, the fuel that runs most large power plants. While soaring oil prices have been getting all the headlines, surging coal demand from China and the rest of the developing world sent its price up by 150 percent between 2006 and mid-2008 (see Figure 20.1). And if anything, the squeeze is likely to intensify, as China's power plant building boom accelerates.

Meanwhile, virtually all major governments are adopting policies like carbon taxes and cap-and-trade programs that penalize fossil fuels. This presents both opportunities and challenges for electric utilities, the companies that generate and sell electricity. They're generally able to pass along part of their rising fuel costs to customers, but it's unlikely that they'll be able to pass on the entire increase in coal's price. So electricity generated with renewable sources now looks much better in comparison, costing the same year after year while yielding tradable emissions credits.

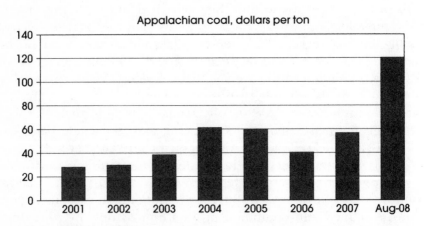

Figure 20.1   Coal Price
Source: NYMEX

The greenest utilities are also embracing smart grid technology. Minnesota-based utility Xcel Energy, for instance, just announced a plan to make Boulder, Colorado, a "Smart Grid City" by installing 50,000 new smart meters at a cost of about $100 million. And as you read in Chapter 12, Florida Power had demand response gear installed in over half a million homes in 2007.

All else being equal, electric utilities that generate more power from renewable sources should be safer and more profitable than their fossil fuel–dependent competitors. And their shares should have more upside potential, both because renewable energy will command a "stability premium" and because a growing number of green mutual funds will prefer such stocks. A portfolio of green utilities would be, in short, a conservative, relatively high-yielding way to play the shift to renewable energy.

To identify U.S.-based green utilities, a good starting point is a list compiled by the Department of Energy's National Renewable Energy Laboratory (NREL) of U.S. utilities that have the biggest "green power programs." These programs allow customers to pay a bit extra, usually $0.01 to $0.05 more per kWh, in order to buy power generated from renewable sources. NREL counts hydro as renewable power, which isn't ideal because so many dams are problematic for salmon runs and other parts of local ecosystems. But overall, it's a pretty good snapshot of which utilities are moving most aggressively into renewable sources and marketing the power most effectively to customers. Table 20.1 lists several relatively green U.S. utilities.

Table 20.1   Green U.S. Utilities

Utility	Ticker	Market Value, 6/27/08 ($ millions)
FPL Group	FPL	25,920
OG&E Electric Services	OGE	2,880
PG&E	PCG	13,710
Portland General Electric	POR	1,420
Puget Energy	PSD	3,180
Xcel Energy	XEL	8,510

Meanwhile, Across the Pond . . .

European utilities are further along in renewable power than their U.S. counterparts, thanks to European governments' early embrace of solar and wind. Iberdrola (Spain) is the world's biggest wind power generator and one of the leaders in solar. It derives nearly 15 percent of its power from renewable sources. EDF (France), Enel (Italy) and E.ON (Germany) are all following similar strategies, building renewable capacity as fast as possible. With good reason: Recall from Chapter 11 that in the next phase of the European emissions reduction program, power companies will be required to buy all their greenhouse gas allowances, raising the cost of coal and natural gas dramatically and making renewable power that much more valuable. A survey by Spanish consultancy Emerging Energy Research found that Europe's top 20 utilities plan to double their renewable power capacity by 2011. The Energy Information Administration calculates that coal and natural gas supply nearly half of Europe's current power, with nuclear and hydro accounting for most of the other half and renewables at less than 5 percent. Half of this 5 percent is wind, while solar, despite its fast recent growth, is still miniscule. So there's plenty of room for growth. See Table 20.2 for a list of relatively green European utilities.

Clean-Tech Leaders

In a typical bull market, a sector goes through a series of stages that correspond to the emotional states of its investors. Early on, buyers are cautious because they don't know the business and haven't heard of the companies—and more than likely are still nursing wounds

Table 20.2   Green European Utilities

Utility	Ticker/Exchange	Headquarters	Market Value, 6/27/08 ($ millions)
EDF	EDF.PA/Paris	France	162,540
ENEL	ENEI.MIB/Milan	Italy	56,568
E.ON	EONGn.DE/Xetra	Germany	117,050
Iberdrola	IBE.MC/Madrid	Spain	61,947
Renewable Energy Generation	RERWE.L/London	U.K.	223,720

from their last bout of financial enthusiasm. So to the extent that they invest in the new sector at all, they tend to choose big, solid companies with recognizable names. As money flows into these stocks, two things happen: First, their prices go up, which makes their early investors feel more adventurous and draws the attention of new investors, who notice the stocks on various "top performer" lists, look into them, and like what they find. Second, it widens the disparity in valuation between the field's leaders, which are being bid up by new investors, and the smaller, less well-known players that have so far been ignored.

That's the first stage. The second stage begins when the increasingly confident investors who made a killing with the leaders begin looking around for the next big winner. They compare the valuations of the smaller stocks to those of the leaders, discover that the little guys are very cheap, and start piling in, sending their prices through the roof.

Where is clean tech in this cycle? That depends on what has happened between this writing and your reading. But let's assume that it's late 2008 or early 2009 and the U.S. economy is closing the book on a year most investors would rather forget, with lower stock prices, anemic corporate earnings, and some big, scary crises of the Bear Stearns variety. Solar and wind stocks have been caught in the general downdraft, and most other clean technologies have yet to peak investors' interest. If that's your world, then clean tech is beginning stage one, with most people either unfamiliar with the growth prospects of these companies or too wounded by what's happened to their mutual funds to contemplate betting on something new. So the leaders are nice and cheap, and the most logical way to approach this sector is to build a portfolio of the biggest, highest-profile clean-tech companies in the expectation that they'll be noticed first when investors' animal spirits start to revive. These are the companies that are identified with their segments, the names a broker pulls up when an investor calls and says "I want some wind (or solar or smart-grid) stocks." In other words, the visible end of the supply chain, well-known and big.

Table 20.3 is necessarily a bit arbitrary, since far more than 10 companies can legitimately be called clean-tech leaders. And as with all references to specific companies in this book, it's a snapshot of a particular point in time. Many things will change in the years to come, and your list might be very different from this one.

Table 20.3   Leading Clean-Tech Stocks

Company	Ticker/Exchange	Headquarters	Technology	Market Value, 6/27/08 ($ millions)
First Solar	FLSR/NASDAQ	U.S.	Solar	21,230
Gamesa Technologica	GAM.MC/Madrid	Spain	Wind	11,580
Itron	ITRN/NASDAQ	U.S.	Smart grid	3,090
Monsanto	MON/NYSE	U.S.	Biotech	70,430
Ormat	ORA/NYSE	U.S.	Geothermal	2,030
Q-Cells	QCEG.F/Frankfurt	Germany	Solar	7,669
Suez	LYOE.PA/Paris	France	Water services	82,050
SunPower	SPWR/NASDAQ	U.S.	Solar	6,160
Veolia Environment	VE/NYSE	France	Water services	25,750
Vestas Wind Systems	VWS.CO/Copenhagen	Denmark	Wind	24,650

Clean-Tech Conglomerates

You may have noticed a few names like General Electric, United Technologies, and Siemens popping up frequently in this book. That's because they're conglomerates with interests all over the green part of the map. This makes them interesting ways to gain exposure to several areas of clean tech with less risk than buying pure-play stocks. In deciding among these companies, the main things to investigate are how big a role clean tech plays in their overall business and how strong they are in the clean technologies with the best near-term prospects.

- **General Electric,** for instance, has made an explicit, public commitment (even giving the program a cutesy name, "ecomagination") to both develop best-of-breed products in a wide range of clean sectors and minimize its own environmental footprint. It is now a leading maker of solar panels, wind turbines, advanced light bulbs, and desalination membranes, among many other things.
- **United Technologies** is the eighteenth-largest U.S. manufacturer, with divisions that make aircraft engines, elevators, helicopters, and security systems. But it's also a leader in geothermal and fuel cells and has some innovative solar thermal technologies.
- German multinational **Siemens** is a leader in water treatment and related equipment, has its own wind power division, and is big in next-generation transportation and building technologies.

Table 20.4 lists a few clean-tech conglomerates. To find more, pay attention as you research the various clean-tech sectors and note the recurring names. Then check those firms' financial reports for division-by-division breakdowns of revenues and earnings.

Pick and Shovel Makers

On a cold January morning in 1848, a carpenter named James Wilson Marshall ignited one of history's great mass migrations by finding a nugget of gold on a farm owned by John Sutter near San Francisco. Wilson and Sutter, no dummies, tried to keep the discovery to themselves. But they failed, and as word spread, hundreds

Table 20.4 Clean-Tech Conglomerates

Company	Ticker/Exchange	Headquarters	Technology	Market Value, 6/27/08 ($ millions)
3M	MMM/NYSE	U.S.	Green materials, desalination	48,950
General Electric	GE/NYSE	U.S.	Everything	261,740
IBM	IBM/NYSE	U.S.	Smart meters, building controls	164,890
Sanyo Electric	6764/Tokyo	Japan	Solar cells, batteries	4,669
Siemens	SI/NYSE	Germany	Water, wind	99,520
United Technologies	UTX/NYSE	U.S.	Fuel cells, geothermal	59,510

of thousands of would-be mining tycoons poured into the western United States. Most found only mud and rock and moved on when their seed money ran out. But another group—the steadier folks who sold the picks, shovels, and other gear needed to prospect for gold—did better. They got paid up front, and when their customers failed and left, new ones showed up with ready cash. A San Franciscan named Levi Strauss, for instance, sold durable denim pants that became the uniform of choice for prospectors. As an estimated 300,000 prospectors passed through San Francisco in the five years following the gold strike, Strauss sold a whole lot of "Levi's," eventually building a company that still bears his name. The lesson for clean tech? Every hot market follows the gold rush script: "Prospectors" pour in with hopes of hitting it big. Most fail, but all buy the requisite materials and equipment. The suppliers thus have a chance to prosper no matter who ends up winning the race. So for less volatile ways to play booming markets, look further down the supply chain to the miners, processors, and machinery makers that can profitably serve winners and losers alike. Using solar power as an example, consider the following.

Solar Power Supply Chain

To make a solar cell, you need a semiconductor material like silicon or the more exotic compounds that go into next-generation thin films. And you need specialized machines to turn raw materials into intermediate products and then into solar cells. The result is several distinct supply chains, each with its share of public companies.

Silicon Solar-grade silicon is made from silica, a ubiquitous material that makes up nearly 26 percent of the earth's crust. Before it can become a solar cell, its impurities have to be removed in a complicated refining process. Table 20.5 gives a partial list of the public companies that do this.

Purified silicon is processed into ingots, which are then cut and polished into wafers by the companies listed in Table 20.6.

The microchip industry contains a similar supply chain (hence the name "Silicon Valley"). Before the solar boom, silicon was already the main raw material for microprocessors, which have evolved from specialized, expensive brains of large computers to cheap, ubiquitous brains of everything from toasters to wristwatches. Because demand

Table 20.5 Silicon Suppliers

Company	Ticker/Exchange	Headquarters	Market Value, 6/27/08 ($ millions)
Mitsubishi Materials	5711/Tokyo	Japan	5,478
Renewable Energy	REC.OL/Oslo	Norway	12,998
SolarWorld	SWVG/Frankfurt	Germany	5,025
Timminco	TIM.TO/Toronto	Canada	2,939
Wacker Chemie	WCHG.F/Frankfurt	Germany	9,958

Table 20.6 Silicon Wafer Suppliers

Company	Ticker/Exchange	Headquarters	Market Value, 6/27/08 ($ millions)
BP (BP Solar)	BP/NYSE	U.K.	213,250
Evergreen Solar	ESLR/NASDAQ	U.S.	1,180
Kyocera	KYO/NYSE	Japan	17,960
MEMC	WFR/NYSE	U.S.	13,310
Mitsubishi Electric	8058.T/Tokyo	Japan	52,408
Renewable Energy	REC.OL/Oslo	Norway	13,005
RWE	RWEG.F/Frankfurt	Germany	61,680
Sanyo Electric	6764/Tokyo	Japan	4,669
Sharp	6753/Tokyo	Japan	19,050
SolarWorld	SWVG/Frankfurt	Germany	5,025

was soaring, the companies in the microchip supply chain tended to periodically overexpand, causing a pattern of booms and busts in which silicon prices would spike and then plunge, taking the earnings and share prices of the various players along for the ride. In this decade, the solar power boom caused by German and Japanese subsidies amplified the wave, sending silicon demand far beyond suppliers' capacity. The shortage caused solar-grade silicon prices to soar, which sent the profits of the silicon makers through the roof. This in turn caused everyone in the business to add capacity, and now a glut is projected for the final two years of the decade.

If the glut occurs, the silicon makers will see their margins contract as rising supply pushes down prices, while the solar cell makers will respond to falling silicon prices by embarking on a price war of their own. The year 2009, in short, may not be the most auspicious time to buy into the silicon supply chain. But within a couple of years this excess supply will be soaked up by soaring PV demand around the world, and the cycle will begin again. Knowing the players will be very helpful.

Solar Cell Machinery Turning silicon into solar cells is a lot like turning silicon into microchips, so for microchip equipment makers, solar is a natural growth path. California-based Applied Materials, for instance, makes equipment that deposits thin layers of various materials onto microchip wafers and flat-panel display screens. This expertise is easily adapted to solar cells, and when solar took off, Applied Materials became the supplier of choice for rapidly-growing PV companies. And it now operates as a factory integrator, essentially building solar panel factories from scratch by supplying the key gear and acquiring whatever else is needed.

One of the keys to understanding suppliers is assessing the relative importance of the green part of their business. In Applied Materials' case, sales to solar panel makers accounted for only about 10 percent of 2007 revenues, so this is not yet its mainstay. But solar will be its fastest-growing segment for years to come, especially as it introduces new lines capable of working with bigger glass panels that dramatically lower solar cell unit costs. More of a pure play is Germany's Roth & Rau, which makes 10-meter-long, $3 million machines that give about 40 percent of the world's silicon wafers their antireflective surface. Solar panel makers account for about 90 percent of Roth & Rau's sales, which makes it a bit more vulnerable to the coming glut but also more sensitive to the upswing that will follow. Some other possibilities are listed in Table 20.7

Other PV Materials Silicon is no longer the only semiconductor material used to generate solar power, and eventually it might not even be the main one, as new thin-film materials like cadmium telluride (CdTe) and copper indium gallium selenide (CIGS) become more cost-effective. Since these new materials are composites, they create complex new supply chains that present both opportunities and risks.

Table 20.7   Solar Cell Machinery Makers

Company	Ticker/Exchange	Headquarters	Market Value, 6/27/08 ($ millions)
Applied Materials	AMAT/NASDAQ	U.S.	26,150
Centrotherm Photovoltaics	CTNG.F/Frankfurt	Germany	1,928
Cypress Semiconductor	CY/NYSE	U.S.	3,750
Meyer Burger Technology	MBTN.S/Swiss	Switzerland	902
Roth & Rau	R8RG.F/Frankfurt	Germany	740

Tellurium, for instance, is a key part of the CdTe thin film that helped make First Solar the lowest-cost PV producer. One of the rarest elements on earth, it's harder to find than platinum. And it isn't mined directly, instead being produced as a by-product of copper, lead, and gold refining. A smelter has to process 500 tons of copper ore to get a pound of tellurium, which until recently wasn't a problem because it was used only as an additive in the smelting of certain metals and as a catalyst in a few chemical processes. But now it's about to become very popular, thanks to two developments: First, chip makers Intel and Samsung are introducing tellurium-based "phase change" flash memory devices that use less power and hold more data than conventional memory technologies. Their potential market extends from computer hard drives to cell phones to RFID (radio-frequency identification) chips. Meanwhile, CdTe thin-film solar is generating cost and efficiency numbers that imply nearly unlimited demand. Already, before either of these new uses really kicks in, tellurium's price has soared from $6 per pound in 2000 to $36 in 2007 (see Figure 20.2).

Now, there are two ways to use this information. One is to find the miners most likely to benefit. But since there are no pure-play tellurium miners, we're left with copper companies that might decide to emphasize their tellurium production to give themselves a bit of market cachet. The other advantage of understanding a material like tellurium is the clues it offers to the fortunes of the companies that use it. In early 2008, for instance, analysts were discussing the impact on First Solar of a tellurium shortage and wondering whether its aggressive expansion plans would be derailed. This was pure speculation in early 2008, but it's a great example of the kind of potentially useful data that an understanding of an industry's supply chain offers.

Dollars per pound

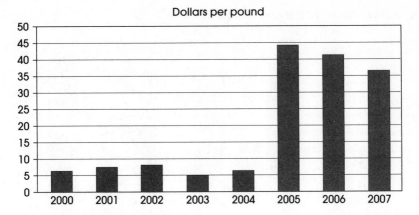

Figure 20.2   Tellurium Price
Source: U.S. Geological Survey

Indium, meanwhile, is a soft, gray metallic element crucial to CIGS, which is made into low-cost PV films that can be sprayed on pretty much any surface and are nearly as efficient as conventional silicon PV. Nanosolar and several other CIGS pioneers are attracting massive venture funding and building factories, and they will soon be out in the marketplace buying large amounts of CIGS.

Like tellurium, indium is a by-product of the mining of other metals. According to the U.S. Geological Survey, the United States produces no domestic indium and relies on imports from China, Canada, Japan, and Russia, with China accounting for about 60 percent of the world's refined indium production. The electronics industry is already consuming increasing amounts of indium for use in video screens. Consumption has about doubled so far in this decade, to about 1,000 tons annually in 2007, which caused the price to soar from $70 a pound in 2003 to over $350 in early 2008 (see Figure 20.3). And that's before thin-film solar ramps up, which some analysts predict will cause demand to double. Indium isn't exactly an intensively studied market, but in the opinion of some researchers there's not enough of it in the ground to satisfy prospective demand at anything like current prices.

Again, the result is potential trouble for the currently hot CIGS thin-film makers and a possible windfall for the miners that produce it. As a by-product, most indium comes from much bigger zinc mines,

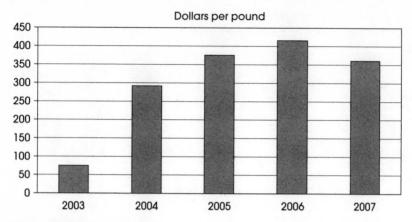

Figure 20.3   Indium Price
Source: U.S. Geological Survey

so it's not a major part of most miners' stories. In the future, though, its higher price might cause some smaller operators to see it as a viable specialty. So be alert for a new generation of "indium plays."

A World of Supply Chains

A complete analysis of clean-tech supply chains would uncover dozens, populated by hundreds of public companies. Chapter 16's discussion of green materials, for instance, is all about companies that supply various end users. The transportation industry has supply chains for everything from platinum (a key part of catalytic converters), to the exotic compounds necessary for next generation Li-ion batteries, to bioplastics for tomorrow's fenders and dashboards. Biofuel supply chains range from genetically engineered enzymes to bioreactor machinery. The water industry requires all manner of equipment, while wind turbine makers buy carbon fiber for blades and power converters for their generators. And the list is growing as each new breakthrough creates a new supply chain. All are fertile ground for investors willing to do some digging.

Systems Integrators

At the opposite end of the supply chain from the pick and shovel companies are the systems integrators that combine clean technologies from various sources into solar farms, green buildings, and smart grids. California-based Akeena Solar, for instance, installs rooftop solar systems on homes and businesses and connects them to the grid. Germany's Phoenix Solar AG constructs and operates large PV power plants like the 6.5-megawatt, 40,320-module facility it recently planned, built, and now runs in Spain. And recall from Chapter 13 that Tallahassee, Florida, recently hired Honeywell to install a smart metering network for electricity, gas, and water.

The appeal of the system integrators is that they're able to buy what they need from a range of technology makers. So they actually benefit from the kinds of cutthroat competition and price wars that might devastate other parts of the supply chain. In both smart meters (which, like most pieces of information technology, tend to decline in price) and solar panels (which may be heading for a temporary glut), both price and demand trends look favorable for system integrators. Table 20.8 presents a few of the larger players in this space.

Snowbelt Real Estate

Here's an offbeat, long-term thought: People have been moving to warm, dry regions for decades, and they are now facing the inevitable conflict between falling water supplies and rising populations. For Americans living in Arizona, Southern California, and several other western states, life is about to become a lot more expensive and complicated as water prices rise to bring supply and demand into balance. And water problems are not confined to the Southwest. Georgia is in the grip of an unprecedented drought, and even Florida is running short of fresh water. The Sun Belt, in short, is no longer the cheap, restful place to retire or raise a family that it once was. Meanwhile, warmer weather is making those nasty northern winters a lot less onerous. How long before the realization begins to dawn that places like Michigan and Ohio offer an intriguing combination of cheap real estate and abundant fresh water? The northern United States has nearly 20 percent of the surface fresh water on earth. No one there worries about washing their car in the driveway or watering their lawns. Simultaneously, cities like Detroit and Cleveland are being hollowed out by people moving to the Sun Belt, leaving homes and land for laughably low prices.

Governors in the South and West are already calling for a "national water policy" in which Washington forces the North "share" its water

Table 20.8 Systems Integrators

Company	Ticker/Exchange	Headquarters	Market	Market Value, 6/27/08 ($ millions)
Akeena Solar	AKNS/NASDAQ	U.S.	Residential solar	166
Honeywell	HON/NYSE	U.S.	Power management	36,510
IBM	IBM/NYSE	U.S.	Building automation	164,890
Johnson Controls	JCI/NYSE	U.S.	Lighting systems	17,010
Phoenix Solar AG	PS4G.F/Frankfurt	Germany	Large-scale solar	622
SunPower	SPWR/NASDAQ	U.S.	Residential solar	6,160
WorldWater & Solar Technologies	WWAT.OB/NASDAQ	U.S.	Water/solar	134

with dryer states. This is a nonstarter politically, but it will serve to draw attention to the growing water wealth disparity between the Rust and Sun belts. Over time, this might translate into a reversal of the post–World War II migration pattern, with people leaving the parched Sun Belt and moving north. The result might be increased demand for Rust Belt real estate. This is neither a clean-tech play (though it is driven by the same forces that make clean tech so interesting) nor actionable right away. In the short run, northern real estate is suffering along with the rest of the national property market. But at some point, it will become a classic value proposition. When that happens, the way to profit from it will be through the shares of the handful of home-builders, developers, and community banks that survive the real estate bust and are healthy enough to start lending and building again.

Divide and Study

As you dig into clean tech, you'll find that it has dozens of subcategories like those listed here, many of which are worth exploring. The "divide and study" approach is a good way to build up the kind of background knowledge that leads to sound judgment. The following chapter will explain how to use that judgment to profit not just from the winners you discover but also the losers.

CHAPTER 21

Short Candidates

WHO LOSES WHEN CLEAN TECH WINS?

If some companies will thrive in a clean-tech world, it follows that others will suffer. You'll want to avoid those stocks, obviously. But you can also profit from their declines by actively betting against them. The generic term for betting on a decline in the price of an asset is "going short," and there are several ways to do this. The traditional method is called short selling, and it works as follows: You identify a stock that you think is overvalued and sell some of the company's shares—without first owning them. Your broker borrows the requisite number of shares from another client's account and sells them, depositing the cash into your account. After the stock goes down, you close out, or cover, your short position by buying back the shares at the lower price and pocket the difference. Recall from Chapter 19 that exchange-traded funds (ETFs) can also be sold short, making them ideal for betting against specific sectors. In some ways they're better than stocks, because they diversify away the risk that you'll be right on the industry but wrong on a given stock.

Shorting is very clean and simple, but it takes a bit of preparation. It can only be done in an account that is authorized for it, which means you'll have to set this up in advance with your broker by signing an extra contract that discloses, among other things, the risks involved in shorting stocks. If the stock you short pays dividends, they're your responsibility, adding a bit to the cost of holding a short position. And the risk–reward calculus of shorting is the opposite

233

of going long: Your maximum upside is the potential downside of the stock, and since a stock can only fall to zero, your profit potential is capped at 100 percent. But your downside is the stock's upside potential, which is theoretically unlimited, so short positions have to be watched very closely. If your positions move against you (that is, if the stocks or ETFs you short go up), your broker might demand more money to cover the potential risk. This is known as a margin call, and if the money isn't quickly forthcoming, the broker will close out your short position or sell other shares in your account to raise the needed cash.

Another popular shorting vehicle is the put option. As the name implies, an option is a contract that gives its owner the right, or option, to buy or sell a specified number of shares at a predetermined price within a set time period. A call option allows a holder to buy (i.e., call away) shares, and a put option enables its owner to sell (or put the shares into someone else's account) at a given price. They're "derivatives," in the sense that their value is derived from that of an underlying security, most frequently the stock of a publicly traded company (though options exist for lots of other things). Stock option contracts control 100 shares of the underlying stock, so a quoted price, or premium of, say, $5 implies a cost of $500 for a contract. Because you're only paying for the right to profit from the change in the stock's price for a limited amount of time, you pay a lot less than if you bought or shorted the shares outright. Yet you gain, if you're right, almost as much as if you traded the shares directly.

Traditional options have one huge drawback: They're short-lived. Most run for nine months or less, so unless you're right on both direction and timing, your puts will expire worthless and you'll lose your entire investment. In response, the exchanges have designed longer-lived options, called long-term equity anticipation securities, or LEAPS, which last for two and a half years, allowing you to be fuzzy on "when" but still make money. You pay more for the extra time, but you'll still get more bang for the speculative buck than with short selling. Most brokers offer online options tutorials that explain the basics in more detail.

A Different Mind-Set

Shorting takes a bit of a mental adjustment because most people are used to thinking only in terms of things that go up. You can watch CNBC all day long and hear only one or two fleeting references to shorting. And if you ask the typical financial advisor for ideas, he'll go on for hours about what's likely to rise but will be stumped by a request for short candidates. This institutional blind spot ignores half the market, sometimes by far the better half. In 2006, for instance, a typical financial planner or stockbroker would have probably recommended a list of long positions that looked something like this:

- Cash: 10 percent of total capital
- High-grade bond fund: 20 percent
- S&P 500 mutual fund: 30 percent
- Commodities fund: 10 percent
- Russell 2000 stock fund: 20 percent
- Global stock fund: 10 percent

But someone who recognized the massive financial imbalances building up in the housing, consumer finance, and foreign exchange markets—and who was comfortable doing something about it—might have constructed a portfolio of the following short positions:

- Merrill Lynch
- Lehman Brothers
- Citigroup
- Countrywide Credit
- Beazer Homes
- KB Homes

Table 21.1 shows how the two portfolios performed.

Clearly, it was better to be short bank and homebuilder stocks than to be long a traditional diversified portfolio. And just in case you suspect that 20/20 hindsight made it possible to cherry-pick the biggest losers, note that our short list excludes Bear Stearns, Ambac, and MBIA, big-name financial stocks that lost an average of about 80 percent between 2006 and 2008—and were obvious short candidates at the height of the housing bubble. Dozens of other homebuilders and banks did nearly as badly, while most subprime mortgage lenders went bankrupt. So the short list presented here is actually conservative, in the sense that it's composed of companies that survived. That may not be true by the time you read this, however, since Lehman Brothers and Merrill Lynch were looking very shaky in mid-2008. The lesson: Just as there's always a bull market somewhere, there's

Table 21.1   Long and Short Portfolios

Long Portfolio	Cumulative Return (percent), 1/1/06–12/31/07*	Short Portfolio	Cumulative Return (percent), 1/1/06–12/31/07**
Cash: 10% of total	6	Beazer Homes (BZH)	90
High-grade bond fund: 20%	24	Citigroup (C)	35
S&P 500 stock fund: 30%	17	Countrywide Credit (CFC)	72
Commodities fund: 10%	41	KB Homes (KBH)	69
Russell 2000 stock fund: 20%	9	Lehman Brothers (LEH)	(5)
Global stock fund: 10%	35	Merrill Lynch (MER)	20
Total Return	**20**	**Total Return**	**47**

*The long portfolio's total return is the weighted average of its components. Returns for individual components are derived from leading funds in those sectors.
**With a short portfolio, return refers to the decline in price of shorted stocks. A negative return (the result of a shorted stock going up) is denoted in parentheses. Dividends are assumed for the sake of simplicity to average 2% per year and are subtracted from the short portfolio's return.

also always a bear market, frequently caused by the same forces driving the bull market. In tomorrow's world, the conditions and trends that will allow clean tech to thrive will devastate other industries, giving you a chance to make money in both directions. Let's consider some likely short candidates.

Water Users

The cushy lifestyle that Americans and Europeans now take for granted requires a lot of increasingly scarce water. Scarcity leads to higher prices, which will, all else being equal, narrow the profit margins of the companies that turn water-intensive raw materials into products for sale. Take McDonald's: The world's biggest burger chain, it buys immense amounts of beef (recall from Chapter 13 that a Quarter Pounder requires more than 200 gallons of water to produce) and wheat flour (which tripled in price in 2007). The soft drinks that provide McDonald's with much of its profit are made mostly of corn syrup (grown with water and natural gas–derived fertilizer) and water. Because the company operates on razor-thin margins, generally earning a few pennies on each item sold, more expensive water has the potential to either vaporize its profit margins or force it to raise prices and risk driving away increasingly cost-conscious customers. The same cold equations apply to the rest of the world's restaurant and coffee chains.

Also likely to suffer in a water-constrained world are the cereal makers. The prices of flours and sweeteners are soaring, but there's a limit to how much the typical family will pay for a box of Frosted Flakes. So a devastating margin squeeze is a real possibility. Ditto for major meat packers and processors that turn beef, pork, and chicken into sausages and steaks. Table 21.2 presents a list of water-dependent short candidates.

Oil-Dependent Companies

Higher oil prices, lower consumer spending, and tighter pollution regulations will make cars a tough business, especially for GM and Ford, which earn most of their profit from trucks, vans, and SUVs (what kind of idiots . . . oh, never mind). I'll go out on a limb and predict that those two will be bankrupt or under new ownership by

Table 21.2 Water-Dependent Companies

Company	Ticker	Market Value, 6/27/08 ($ millions)
Burger King	BKC	3,630
Coca-Cola	KO	120,410
Darden	DRI	4,520
General Mills	GIS	20,060
Kraft Foods	KFT	43,040
McDonald's	MCD	64,040
Smithfield Foods	SFD	2,670
Starbucks	SBUX	11,900
Tim Horton	THI	5,310
YUM Brands	YUM	16,590

2010. The other carmakers also face a rough road, with the transition to plug-in hybrids slow because of battery issues and big, high-margin gas-guzzlers selling badly. On the other hand, Chinese and Indian demand should be robust, so the industry might bifurcate in coming years, with the companies best able to serve those markets doing well and the others suffering.

The outlook is even darker for the major airlines and trucking firms. Fuel costs are rising and consumer spending is falling, resulting in a classic margin squeeze. But with oil prices soaring in early 2008, these stocks may have already taken their tumble by the time you read this. If not, Table 21.3 contains some juicy targets.

Property and Casualty Insurers

We've spent the past few decades building houses, hotels, and shopping malls as close as possible to the sea. But melting polar ice means rising sea levels, while warmer oceans spawn more big storms. This is very bad news for the companies that insure cars and buildings. Insurance, meanwhile, is a strangely cyclical business. When insurers are hit with a large number of claims, as in post-Katrina New Orleans, they typically raise rates for a while to rebuild their reserves, which produces a period of rising earnings. Then they start seeking out new business, cutting rates to attract more customers and causing earnings to fall. That was the situation in early 2008, with the past year's dearth of big claims causing carriers to cut rates

Table 21.3 Oil-Dependent Companies

Company	Ticker	Market Value, 6/27/08 ($ millions)
AMR	AMR	1,333
China Eastern AIR	CEA	1,500
Con-Way	CNW	2,110
Federal Express	FDX	23,950
Ford Motor	F	11,171
General Motors	GM	6,642
JB Hunt	JBHT	4,123
Landstar	LSTR	2,856

and write policies more aggressively. They're setting themselves up, in other words, for the next Katrina (see Table 21.4).

Corn Ethanol Makers

Ethanol from corn is a dead end, for reasons that have been repeated in this book several times. Yet Washington is encouraging increased ethanol production. This flawed strategy is already causing the inevitable problems in early 2008, so it's possible that by the time you read this the major ethanol makers will have had their bear market and shorting them will be pointless. But in case they've managed somehow to hold up, the weakest of them will make great targets (see Table 21.5).

Commercial Real Estate Developers

Office buildings and shopping malls have enjoyed a decade in which their values rose and record numbers of new ones were built. But

Table 21.4 Property and Casualty Insurers

Company	Ticker	Market Value, 6/27/08 ($ millions)
Allstate	ALL	25,620
American International	AIG	69,150
Allianz SE	AZ	102,450
Berkshire Hathaway	BRK-A	186,690
Travelers	TRV	26,790

Table 21.5 Corn Ethanol Makers

Company	Ticker	Market Value, 6/27/08 ($ millions)
Archer Daniels Midland	ADM	21,200
Aventine Renewable Energy	AVR	199
GreenHunter Energy	GRH	254
Pacific Ethanol	PEIX	88
VeraSun	VSE	710

Table 21.6   Commercial Real Estate Companies

Company	Ticker	Market Value, 6/27/08 ($ millions)
Avalon Bay	AVB	6,790
Boston Properties	BXP	10,780
Equity Residential	EQR	10,350
General Growth Properties	GGP	9,390
Host Hotels & Resorts	HST	7,210
iShares Dow Jones Real Estate ETF	IYR	1,410
Kimco Realty	KIM	8,820
Prologis SBI	PLD	14,110
Simon Property	SPG	20,410
Vornado Realty Trust	VNO	13,390

now the cost of heating and air conditioning is up, while consumer spending is being squeezed by high gas and food prices. Combined with lean times in the banking industry (which makes cheap construction loans scarce), this will lower the value of many commercial properties and make the shares of the companies that own and manage them a lot less valuable (see Table 21.6).

Chemical Companies

The makers of plastics, cosmetics, and other consumer products have a lot to worry about. Their main raw material, petroleum, is becoming more costly, while several major product lines are presenting increasingly visible health issues. Europe has banned many widely used industrial chemicals, while the United States still permits them. This presents a legal risk for the chemical companies: If it can be proven that certain industrial chemicals cause harm and that viable products are being sold in Europe without those chemicals, then U.S. chemical companies can't argue that they have no alternative but to use the harmful substances. The possible result is a trial lawyer's dream and a CEO's nightmare (see Table 21.7).

Long/Short Clean-Tech Combinations

By 2010, there will be several kinds of batteries competing for the plug-in hybrid market. Biofuels derived from different feedstocks and produced by different means will be vying for the same flex-fuel

Table 21.7 Chemical Companies

Company	Ticker	Market Value, 6/27/08 ($ millions)
Albemarle	ALB	3,750
Dow Chemical	DOW	32,410
Celanese	CE	6,980
DuPont	DD	38,450
Eastman Chemical	EMN	5,230

vehicle market. Several types of stationary power storage technologies will be available to industrial users. Data will be flowing in from these and other markets that will make it possible to separate winners from losers. Obviously you'll want to buy the most likely winners, but simultaneously shorting the losers will produce even bigger gains. Here are a few possible long/short strategies:

- Buy the most promising next-generation biofuel makers and short the corn ethanol stocks.
- Buy the clean utilities and short those that are slower to adopt renewable energy.
- In the solar power market, the old-line crystalline silicon cell makers are being challenged by an army of exotic thin films, each with extraordinary claims, proprietary production methods, and unique supply chains. If the emerging thin films live up to their billing, then buying them and shorting the silicon solar cell firms might make sense. On the other hand, if raw material supply bottlenecks slow the thin-film makers' sales or raise their costs, the opposite trade might be worth considering.

Like most previous chapters, this one has only scratched the surface of its subject. As you become familiar with clean tech and shorting, you'll find dozens of opportunities for playing both sides of the market. There is one complication, however, that this chapter didn't mention: Many of tomorrow's biggest winners and losers trade on foreign exchanges. The next chapter explains how to get at them.

22

How to Trade Foreign Stocks

Clean tech is global, with more public companies headquartered in Europe and Asia than in the United States. And some of the leaders—like Danish wind turbine maker Vestas Wind Systems and German solar panel giant Q-Cells—don't even list their shares on U.S. exchanges. This complicates things for American investors, but it is not insurmountable. As with most things that involve the exchange of information, trading foreign stocks is getting easier all the time.

Welcome to the Rest of the World

This chapter offers an overview of the currently available ways that U.S. investors can find, research, and trade foreign stocks. The choices are arranged in more or less ascending order, from the simplest to those that require more capital and/or expertise.

ADRs

An American Depository Receipt (ADR) is created when a U.S. bank buys a large block of stock in a foreign company and bundles the shares for reissue on a U.S. stock exchange. The stock will have a normal ticker symbol, with "ADR" appended. For example, the Yahoo! Finance listing for Japanese electronics giant Sony looks like this: SONY ADR (NYSE: SNE). Unfortunately, Sony is one of the exceptions. To qualify for an ADR listing, a foreign company must issue financial reports that conform to U.S. accounting conventions and Securities and Exchange

Commission rules. Since the passage of the Sarbanes-Oxley Act in response to the corporate scandals of the 1990s, this is no simple thing. To make it worth the trouble, a company must be big and sufficiently well-known to attract large numbers of U.S. investors. This limits the potential field to just a few hundred companies—and the number of those willing to list ADRs is falling rather than rising. Since the beginning of 2007, a growing list of global multinationals, including Vivendi, Suez, Groupe Danone, and LaFarge, have either delisted or announced their intent to delist their ADRs. Currently there are only a handful of major European or Asian clean tech companies with ADRs.

Pink Sheets

Foreign stocks that don't have ADRs can still be traded in the United States on an exchange called the Pink Sheets, where non-U.S. stocks are assigned five-letter tickers ending in "F," to denote foreign, and are quoted with a U.S. dollar price. Trading Pink Sheet stocks can be tricky, for a number of reasons. First, the company's home market—which ultimately determines the value of its stock—might be closed when a U.S. investor places an order, which means the last quoted price may no longer be valid. Second, to place an order here and have it executed there requires that the order cross several desks, racking up fees on each pass. Here's how it works in practice:

An investor calls his broker and asks to buy 10,000 shares of XYZ, a Hong Kong-based company that doesn't have a U.S. ADR. The broker calls a "market maker"—a specialized trader who is responsible for executing orders in several stocks. The market maker looks up the price of the stock on her Bloomberg terminal, notes the previous closing price, trading volume, and breaking news, and makes a judgment about how easy it will be to buy the shares when the market opens. Assuming for the sake of simplicity that the stock closed at the Hong Kong equivalent of $1 per share, the market maker quotes a spread of $0.90 to $1.10. That is, she'll buy the stock for $0.90 a share and sell it for $1.10. The U.S. broker agrees to the $1.10 offer price, and when trading resumes in the foreign market, the market maker buys the stock there for $1.00 and sells it to the U.S. broker for $1.10. The stock goes into the customer's account, which is charged the standard trading commission. Notice what has happened: The investor thinks he bought the stock at the market price and paid only a commission, but in reality he also paid the spread, an extra $.10 per share, and is down

10 percent the minute the trade is executed. If he later decides to sell, he'll have to "hit the bid," which might be 10 percent lower than the current market price. The moral: If you're going to buy Pink Sheet shares, never do so "at the market" because you'll end up buying and selling on the wrong side of a very wide spread. Instead, always decide on the price you're willing to pay and enter a "limit" order in which you offer that price and nothing more. But, of course, choosing a limit price isn't easy for a stock that's quoted in a foreign currency on a market that's closed during U.S. business hours.

Discount Broker with Foreign Access

Brokers recognize both the attraction of foreign stocks and the difficulties they present for the average customer, so some are making it easier. Big discount broker Charles Schwab (866-232-9890, www .schwab.com), for instance, has a Global Investing Services Group that helps clients trade foreign stocks. If a client is interested in, say, wind power stocks, a Schwab broker will print out a list of global wind companies and help narrow the search down to a couple of suitable prospects. Then they'll execute the trade, on the Pink Sheets if it's a small order or directly on the relevant foreign exchange if it's large. Limit orders can be placed in U.S. dollars. According to a Schwab spokesman, "The foreign market maker will see the U.S. dollar limit and when they transact the price they'll handle the foreign currency exchange, any markups, clearing costs, or settlement costs. The limit price is all you pay in addition to the Schwab commission." Because of their complexity, foreign stock trades are done over the phone rather than electronically, with the client speaking directly with the trader who's placing the trade. As part of the same conversation, the trader will also explain the tax implications of capital gains and dividends generated in the foreign market. And after the investment is made, Schwab promises to forward financial reports and other information.

Full-Service Foreign Stock Specialist

You might recognize Peter Schiff from his frequent appearances on CNBC and other media. He's made a name for himself as a "bear" on the U.S. financial markets, correctly predicting much of the turmoil that was gripping dollar-denominated investments in early 2008. He also owns a brokerage house, Euro Pacific Capital (800-727-7922, www.europac.net), that specializes in giving U.S. investors access to foreign stocks. Schiff and his brokers trade directly on foreign exchanges for their customers, charging commissions that are higher than the discount brokers but providing all the full-service handholding of a Merrill Lynch. "When I get an order to buy shares in Hong Kong I'll wait until that market opens and I'll buy the shares just the way the market maker would. The customer gets the same price the market maker would have gotten," says Schiff. Another benefit of working with a specialist is the ability to help clients determine the right limit price. "When you trade on the Pink Sheets, there's no one who understands the markets. But we specialize in foreign stocks, so my brokers know exactly what to do, how to find the stock, how to get a price, and how to translate the foreign currency price into a local currency. They'll understand the rules of the exchanges and the hours they trade. They might even be familiar with the stock already and be able to offer an opinion on it."

Euro Pacific charges a minimum commission of $50 per trade, but beyond that, fees vary based on the size of the order and the amount of advice given. A big order entered by a customer who knows exactly what he wants will have a lower per share fee than a small order from a customer who needs extensive advice.

Global Trading Platform

Most people need help with foreign stocks. For those who don't, Interactive Brokers (IB, 877-442-2757, www.interactivebrokers .com) offers a very slick universal account (minimum balance $10,000) from which clients can trade foreign and domestic equities, options, commodities, foreign exchange, futures, and bonds. IB isn't well known among individual investors because it caters to hedge fund managers and other professionals. But it's been around for 31 years and is very big, handling 700,000 trades per day and 14 percent of the world's equity options volume. With foreign stocks, "You're directly connected to more than 70 electronic exchanges around the globe," says IB spokesman Andrew Wilkinson. On the IB workstation, a customer can look up a stock's ticker on its home exchange, convert dollars to the requisite amount of foreign currency (on favorable terms, according to Wilkinson), and enter the trade directly. Or the customer can make the trade and let IB handle the currency translation. Here's a snippet from IB's web site that illustrates the sophistication of its system: "IB SmartRouting is designed to search for the best price available at the time of your order, and unlike other routers, dynamically route and re-route all or parts of your order to achieve optimal execution. According to The Transaction Auditing Group (TAG), a third-party provider of audit services, Interactive Brokers' customer equity options orders were improved 14.85 percent of the time vs. an industry improvement rate of 0.57 percent."

Commissions are very low; the maximum fee for a European stock trade is €29. There are a few downsides, such as an inactivity charge of $10 a month for accounts that generate less than $10 in commissions and interest paid only on cash balances exceeding $10,000. But all things considered, this is a technologically impressive platform with every conceivable capability.

More Choices All the Time

Most U.S. brokers are adding foreign stock trading capabilities, so it's possible that by the end of 2008, the typical brokerage account will offer many of the services described here. Meanwhile, the Securities and Exchange Commission is easing restrictions on foreign brokers opening U.S. accounts, which might soon allow the leading European and Asian brokerage houses to take on U.S. customers.

CHAPTER

23

Breakthroughs

TOMORROW'S GAME CHANGERS

Announcements of potentially disruptive clean-tech breakthroughs are a weekly occurrence, and though most will come to naught, some will have a huge impact. This is both fun to watch and exhilarating, since each announcement brings a world of sustainable abundance that much closer. But for investors, rapid change means heightened risk to incumbent green technologies. If they work, it may be at the expense of that high-priced stock you just bought.

This chapter presents a sampling of the breakthroughs that were announced in late 2007 and early 2008. But just a sampling. For every one listed here, there were many, many more.

High-Temperature Concentrating PV. California start-up Sunrgi claims to have developed a means to concentrate sunlight 1,600 times (far more than current concentrating solar systems) and focus it on high-efficiency geranium solar cells to produce electricity at a coal-competitive $0.07 per kWh.

Genetically-Engineered PV. Scientists at the University of Tel Aviv are using genetically engineered photosynthesizing proteins to make solar cells that they claim are 25 percent efficient and cost around 1 percent of silicon-based solar cells.

Solar Balloons. California start-up Cool Earth Solar has developed helium-filled balloons containing thin mirrors that concentrate sunlight and direct it at internal solar cells. Because the balloons and reflective materials are cheap, Cool Earth claims that by 2010, it will be able to deliver power for $0.29 per installed watt, or less than 10 percent of a typical solar panel.

Prefab Solar Thermal. California start-up eSolar has attracted $130 million of capital (including $10 million from Google) to develop a system for guiding large numbers of cheap, mass-produced mirrors to concentrate sunlight and drive a steam turbine. The cheap mirrors and sophisticated computer controls lower the capital cost of a concentrating solar plant dramatically, theoretically into a range where it can compete with fossil fuels. The company's goal is to offer 33-megawatt prefabricated plants that can quickly be installed wherever there's sufficient space. Early 2008 tests proved the concept works, and by year-end, eSolar intends to build its first working power plant.

High-Efficiency Silicon Thin Film. MIT researchers announced that by texturing the surface of amorphous silicon and using thinner wires, they were able to raise the efficiency of thin film cells to 19.5 percent, comparable to that of conventional crystalline silicon cells. They estimated that cells based on this process would cost about $1.30 per watt.

Inkjet Thin Film. Massachusetts start-up Konarka Technologies announced that it had figured out how to deposit PV materials using cheap off-the-shelf inkjet technology. The result, says the company, will be far lower production costs.

Silicon Nanowires. Stanford University researchers have developed "silicon nanowires" that dramatically improve the performance of lithium-ion batteries. Silicon is superior to the electrode material used in today's batteries but in previous configurations tended to wear out quickly. Stanford's nanowires are more durable and, when incorporated in Li-ion batteries, give them 10 times the power of current versions.

Thermoelectric Nanowires. Researchers at Lawrence Berkeley National Laboratory have fabricated silicon nanowires with "thermoelectric" properties, that is, the ability to convert heat to electricity. Since most of today's power sources lose vast amounts of waste heat—15 trillion watts annually, by some estimates—the ability to turn some of this heat into power would improve power plant economics and lessen the need for new generating capacity.

Safer Li-ion. Daimler has found a way to use vehicle cooling systems to keep lithium-ion batteries from overheating, preventing them from bursting into flames and lengthening their service life. The company claims to have protected the process with 25 patents.

Algae Bioreactor. Texas-based Valcent Products has developed a "bioreactor" that can be attached to a CO_2-producing facility like a coal-burning power plant. It captures the CO_2 and feeds it to algae, which then produce oils that can be turned into biodiesel, among many other related products. Valcent projects far higher yields than for conventional oil-producing crops like palm and soy and expects the process to qualify for emissions reduction credits.

Cellulose Gasoline. Researchers at the University of Massachusetts at Amherst have developed a new method of refining hydrocarbons—the building blocks of gasoline and plastic—from cellulose. The technique involves heating and then cooling cellulose for precise amounts of time, turning about half the cellulose's energy into hydrocarbons. If the yield can be raised to 100 percent, the researchers put the cost of gasoline produced by the process at $1 a gallon.

Bacteria Gasoline. California-based Amyris Biotechnologies has altered *E.coli* bacteria to turn sugar into hydrocarbons which can then be refined into gasoline or diesel.

Bacteria Diesel. California start-up LS9 has altered bacteria to produce biodiesel, and in early 2008, it was building a pilot plant to test the scalability of the process.

Nanoparticle Hydrogen Storage. Dutch chemists demonstrated that hydrogen can be efficiently stored in 30-nanometer particles of the metal hydride sodium alanate. Storing hydrogen in metal hydrides has been pursued for years but has yet to produce a marketable system. Reducing the particle size appears to speed the absorption and release of the gas, bringing this technology closer to viability.

Sunshine to Petrol. Sandia National Laboratory is operating a prototype reactor that turns carbon dioxide into a liquid fuel. Dubbed "sunshine to petrol," or S2P, the process uses concentrated sunlight to convert carbon dioxide to carbon monoxide, which is then used to make hydrogen or syngas. If the process is scalable, the first step would be to capture the CO_2 from power plants and other industrial sources. But eventually, say the researchers, CO_2 could just be drawn from the air.

Shape Memory Alloys. GM has developed alloys and polymers that change their shape, dimensions, strength, transparency, or stiffness in response to stimuli like heat, stress, magnetic field, or electrical voltage. When the stimulus is removed, they return to their original shape. Devices made of such "shape memory alloys" will sense their environment and respond automatically—and they'll weigh a lot less than what they replace, making cars both smarter and more efficient.

Bamboo Bikes. New Jersey start-up Sol Cycles has designed a high-performance bike frame made of bamboo, a rapidly renewable resource. Bamboo grows fast, sequesters carbon, and doesn't die when cut, so the same trees can be harvested multiple times. The bike frames, as a result, have a negative carbon footprint. The company claims its $2,000 bikes outperform $6,000 carbon fiber models, in part because bamboo does a better job of dampening high-frequency vibrations.

Tomorrow's Silicon? Graphene is a flat, single layer of carbon atoms (related to graphite, as the name implies) that can transport electrons at 10 times the speed possible with silicon. Until recently, it was hard to make in quantity. But in early 2008, Rutgers University researchers developed an easy way to make transparent graphene films that, speculate the researchers, might be a cheaper, better replacement for materials now used in solar cells and transistors.

Sewage to Electricity. Synthetic Genomics, founded by genome pioneer J. Craig Venter, has designed a microorganism that turns human wastewater into electricity, and another that produces a type of jet fuel. Work is ongoing on a number of other designer bugs for various renewable energy and pollution control uses.

Sterility Vaccine. Washington-based biotech firm Amplicon has developed a vaccine that effectively sterilizes a wide variety of mammals. As a humane, much cheaper replacement for surgical castration, its potential market ranges from zoo elephants to feral cats and dogs. With government approval, it could also replace castration in the beef industry.

Rice Supergene. Researchers in China have pinpointed a gene that determines a multitude of favorable traits, including the number and size of a plant's grains, its height, and its flowering time. The gene, called Ghd7, can be manipulated to match various climates, theoretically boosting harvests around the world.

Virus-Built Electronics. MIT researchers are using viruses to bind to and organize inorganic materials, such as those used in battery electrodes, transistors, and solar cells. The programmed viruses coat themselves with the materials and then, by aligning with other viruses, assemble into crystalline structures useful for making high-performance devices. One possible result: threadlike batteries and other electronic devices that can be woven directly into clothing.

Wave/Tidal Power. This isn't technically a breakthrough, but it's a niche that deserves mention, if not an entire chapter of its own. Here's the story: Right up there with sun and wind on the list of free energy that the earth is kind enough to provide is moving water. Rivers flow continuously and the ocean tides go in and out regularly. This is clean, abundant energy, just waiting to be tapped. And lots of different methods are being tried: buoys anchored to the ocean floor that generate electricity as they rise and fall with the tides, rotor blades turned by ocean tides and river current, and segmented snake-like devices that generate electricity as ocean waves make them undulate. The list goes on, and all sound at least intriguing. But as of this writing none have managed to generate cost-effective power for long periods of time. This last stipulation (longevity) is the deal breaker, because bodies of water are tough environments for machinery. Waves come at submerged generators from varying angles and speeds, while seawater is corrosive, reducing conventional metals to rust-frozen junk in no time at all. But the lure of all this free power is such that ideas abound, and many are getting a tryout. Among the generators and projects that bear watching:

- **Breakwater Systems** consist of an opening below the water level that is connected to a column of air and water chambers. Breaking waves force water into the opening, altering the air pressure in the column and driving a turbine. British firm RWE Innogy plans to build such a generator off the Scottish coast.
- **Pelamis Device** is a snake-like series of cylindrical, hinged sections that generates power when the waves move the sections. In early 2008, Scotland-based Pelamis Wave Power was installing four such generators as part of a Scottish Power-sponsored trial.
- **PowerBuoy** consists of modular, ocean-going buoys (12 feet in diameter and 52 feet long) that rise and fall with waves, creating mechanical energy which is converted into electricity and transmitted to shore over a submerged transmission line. Canadian firm Finavera Renewables is installing its own version of this technology in projects off the coasts of Portugal and North America.

Like I said, wave power holds promise because there's so much water energy out there. If one or more of the devices now being tested turn out to be cheap and durable, then wind and solar might face some new competition.

Eternal Vigilance

That so many of the breakthroughs listed here (which, remember, are just a fraction of those that actually occurred in 2007 and early 2008) seem to have such dramatic potential means that no clean-tech investment is entirely safe. Let MIT come up with solar power for $0.02 per kWh or Synthetic Genomics design a bug that produces biofuel for $0.50 a gallon, and it's game over for yesterday's favorites. So the final piece of a good clean tech investment program is, like Mad-Eye Moody says, eternal vigilance. Track the developments in the fields where your money resides and assess their potential as both threats to your existing stocks and as future investments themselves. The following chapter presents some sources that will streamline this process.

CHAPTER
24

Creating a Research Program

One of the great things about hot industries is the quality of information that becomes available. In clean tech, there are literally hundreds (soon to be thousands) of people who spend their days analyzing the field's technologies, companies, and trends and making their conclusions available to the rest of us. So here's a list (partial and no doubt pathetically incomplete by the time this book goes on sale) of sources that will help you create an ongoing clean-tech research program.

Background Reading: The Problems

The following books explain the environmental threats facing the global economy.

- *Collapse*, by Jared Diamond. Penguin, December 27, 2005, $17.00. UCLA professor Diamond's best-selling chronicle of past ecological disasters. Some of his conclusions are controversial, but the stories are entertaining and eerily familiar.
- *Twilight in the Desert*, by Matthew Simmons. Wiley, June 5, 2006, $16.95. A detailed dismantling of Saudi Arabia's claims of unlimited oil reserves. If Simmons is right (as he seems to be), the giant Saudi oil fields are aging just like their lesser cousins and will soon enter a rapid production decline. Peak oil, in other words, is here.
- *The Long Emergency*, by James Howard Kunstler. Grove Press, March 2, 2006, $14.00. Kunstler is apocalyptic when it comes

to U.S.-style suburban life. His take is that it's over, along with most of the rest of civilization as we know it. He's too pessimistic about alternative energy, but his work is entertaining and useful for its critique of the modern world.

- *Beyond Oil,* by Kenneth Deffeyes. Hill and Wang, June 13, 2006, $13.00. A readable explanation of how oil comes to be, is extracted, and eventually runs out. And a good introduction to the work of M. King Hubbert, of Hubbert's Peak fame, the legendary petroleum geologist who first came up with the idea that oil wells have finite lives.

- *When the Rivers Run Dry,* by Fred Pearce. Beacon Press, March 7, 2007, $16.00. Subtitled "Water—The Defining Crisis of the Twenty-First Century," this is veteran science writer Fred Pearce's guided tour of the world's water hot spots, where wells are sinking, groundwater is being polluted, and yes, rivers are running dry. What used to be a localized, one-place-at-a-time issue is now global in scope and worsening quickly.

- *Peak Everything,* by Richard Heinberg. New Society Publishers, October 16, 2007, $24.95. Heinberg's previous books focused on peak oil, but here he explains that lots of things besides oil are running out, and doing so rapidly. In his worst-case scenario, the global economy melts down and resource wars become endemic.

Background Reading: The Solutions

The following books and reports define clean tech and, in some cases, explain how to invest in it.

- *Clean Tech Revolution,* by Ron Pernick and Clint Wilder. Collins, June 12, 2007, $26.95. Pernick and Wilder run Clean Edge, the clean-tech research firm whose web site is profiled later. Their book is a clear, readable overview of the various clean technologies, with a wealth of company profiles and predictions.

- *Solar Revolution,* by Travis Bradford. MIT Press, September 1, 2006, $24.95. Travis Bradford is a venture capitalist and founder of the Prometheus Institute for Sustainable Development, a solar energy think tank. Here he gives an in-depth look at why solar's time has come.

- *Green Investing,* by Jack Uldrich. Adams Media, March 1, 2008, $14.95. A nanotech expert's take on clean tech. Organized as a series of two-page profiles of the leading clean-tech companies. Very useful for getting familiar with the big names in the field.
- *Profiting from Clean Energy,* by Richard Asplund. Wiley, March 3, 2008, $60.00. A veteran financial analyst's detailed investigation of clean tech. Lots of background information and statistics with in-depth explanations of how the various technologies work. Highly recommended, especially for sophisticated investors.
- *Clean Energy Trends,* available at http://www.cleanedge.com/reports/reports-trends2008.php. An annual report published by Clean Edge. It's available online in PDF format and is a good introduction to the state of the market for the major clean technologies.

Key Web Sites

Dozens of web sites now follow various parts of clean tech, with more emerging all the time. Here are a few that do an especially good job.

- Alt Energy Investor—www.altenergyinvestor.org: A nice clean site that presents the latest news on solar, wind, and the other emerging alternative energy sources, along with extensive news archives.
- Clean Edge—www.cleanedge.com: The site of a clean-tech consultancy that offers breaking news and a number of free reports on various aspects of this market.
- CleanTech—www.cleantech.com: An investors group that offers access to indexes of clean-tech stocks and private equity deal flow. The same firm also runs the Inside GreenTech web site, a good source of breaking news.
- EV World—www.evworld.com: Electric vehicles and alternative transportation, with everything from guest blogs to photo archives.
- GreenStockInvesting—www.greenstockinvesting.com: My site, designed to present the latest clean-tech news and track the leading clean-tech stocks, sector by sector.

- Greentech Media—www.greentechmedia.com: The CNN of the clean-tech world. Breaking news, blogs, and a big clean-tech investing section. Plus a large selection of research reports and newsletters available for purchase.
- Hydrogen and Fuel Cell Investor—www.h2fc.com: A newsletter that's been covering fuel cells for a long time, through the technology's many ups and downs.
- Smart Grid News—www.smartgridnews.com: Breaking news and research on everything from utility regulation to advances in smart grid technology.
- Prometheus Institute for Sustainable Development—www.prometheus.org: Solar expert Travis Bradford's site. A clearinghouse for news on solar power, plus professional-grade reports for sale in the $1,000 and up price range.
- Reuters Stock Finder—www.reuters.com/finance/stocks: An invaluable tool for figuring out where foreign stocks trade most actively. Type a name into the "symbol look-up" window and it gives a complete list of the exchanges where the company's stock trades.
- XE Universal Currency Converter—www.xe.com/ucc: After you've used Reuters to discover that a company trades most actively on the Paris Exchange, XE converts the euro price to dollars.

These sites and others like them are at the center of the transition to a more rational, sustainable, and ultimately richer world. So they'll be happy places to visit even if you're not an avid clean-tech investor. But if you are (and you really should be), they will be the source of some of the great investment ideas of our lifetimes.

About the Author

John Rubino edits the popular GreenStockInvesting web site. His previous books include *The Collapse of the Dollar,* co-authored with GoldMoney's James Turk (Doubleday, 2004); *How to Profit from the Coming Real Estate Bust* (Rodale, 2003); and *Main Street, Not Wall Street* (Morrow, 1998). After earning an MBA in Finance from New York University, he spent the 1980s on Wall Street, as a currency trader, equity analyst, and bond analyst. During the 1990s he was a tech stock columnist with TheStreet.com and a frequent contributor to *Individual Investor, Online Investor,* and *Consumers Digest,* among many other publications. He currently writes for *CFA Magazine* and edits the DollarCollapse.com web site.

Index